MANCHURIA

Harbin •

Mukden •

Newchwang •

SHANSI

Peking •
Tienstsin •

SHANTUNG

Chefoo •
Weihaiwei •

Tsingtao •

Yangtze Gorges

Chinkiang •

'AN

Ichang •
Shasi •   Hankow •

Nanking •
Wuhu •

Shanghai •

Chungking •

Kiukiang •

CHINA
SEA

gtze
er

FUKIEN

Foochow •

• Kweilin

Amoy •

Swatow •

Canton •

Bias Bay

Hong Kong

The Lion and the Dragon

The Lion and the Dragon

British Voices from the China Coast

Christopher Cook

Elm Tree Books · London

For G.Y., L.H.T. and M.M.

First published in Great Britain 1985
by Elm Tree Books/Hamish Hamilton Ltd
Garden House 57–59 Long Acre London WC2E 9JZ

Copyright © 1985 by Christopher Cook

Book design by Craig Dodd
Maps by Rosemary Turner

British Library Cataloguing in Publication Data

Cook, Christopher
   The lion and the dragon.
   1. British—China—History—20th century
   2. China—Social life and customs—1912–1949
   I. Title
   951'.00421   Ds775.2

   ISBN 0-241-11411-X

Filmset by Servis Filmsetting Ltd, Manchester
Printed in Great Britain by
Fletcher & Sons Ltd, Norwich

Contents

Preface and Acknowledgments

This book owes its existence to an extremely generous act of patronage by the directors of John Swire and Sons Limited. In 1977 I was partly responsible for producing a series of films for BBC Television entitled *Tales of India* in which men and women who had lived and worked in the sub-continent during the twentieth century recalled the British Raj between the two World Wars. The directors of Swires, which has traded in the Far East since the middle of the nineteenth century, appeared to have enjoyed the series and I was asked whether I had ever considered recording the memories of British men and women who found themselves in China in the inter-war years. I knew little about China and less about the Western presence there, but I was curious and my curiosity led me to accept their invitation to interview a number of men and women who had served the company on the China Coast between 1919 and 1939.

My brief was extremely simple. I was free to talk to these retired members of staff about anything they wished to remember, but we were to concentrate on their social rather than their commercial lives. In practice it was often difficult to separate the two as the chapter on sugar travelling makes clear; but generally I saw my task as being to discover how certain things were done, rather than why particular commercial decisions were taken. In any event the frailty of human memory means that even had I been interested in individual commercial transactions my questions would have been unlikely to have provoked detailed responses, for experience teaches most oral historians that with age witnesses tend to forget the cut and thrust of their business careers in favour of more generalised and more personal experience.

The Lion and the Dragon, it must be said, is not a history of the British in China in the second and third decades of the twentieth century. That would be a formidable undertaking, and at the very least would need to include an account of the work of the consular and diplomatic services, the Royal Navy, the Christian missionaries and the other commercial organisations which flourished in the country if it were to lay claim to being comprehensive. What follows are some of the memories of men and women who worked for one company, Butterfield & Swire as it then was, which traded along the China Coast and partly into the Chinese interior. As a company their experience of China was as great as any other concern, and perhaps greater since apart from their insurance and sugar selling activities from those principal Chinese towns and cities open to Westerners, their subsidiary, the China Navigation Company ran shipping along the coast and right up the Yangtze River. But it has to be remembered that B & S were only one of many companies trading in the country, though the life that their one-time employees lived and remember cannot have been significantly different from that enjoyed by other Westerners in China at the same period.

I undertook the interviews which form the substance of this book between 1978 and 1982. Interviewees were selected on the basis of where they had served and what they had done during their time in the East, for it was always our intention that collectively the interviews should give as wide an account of the varieties of work and leisure experienced in China as possible. Each interview was transcribed and has subsequently been edited for publication but only in such a way as to make it easily read. It is a truism that the immediacy of the spoken word seems halting and awkward when transcribed on to paper, so my whole endeavour in preparing selected passages for inclusion in *The Lion and the Dragon* has been to preserve the fluency of an informal conversation while at the same time making it truly accessible to the reader. It is my most earnest hope that I have done no violence to the material substance of what any interviewee allowed me to record, that I have held proper faith with their memories. I should also stress that I alone bear the responsibility for having selected material for this book from the original interviews.

Throughout the text I have chosen to use the transliteration of Chinese proper names that would have been familiar to anyone accustomed to speak or write of China and things Chinese in the 1920s and 1930s. I freely plead guilty to the charge of perpetrating anachronisms, for Peking has long been Beijing under a newer system of transliteration, but this is a book about the past and it has therefore seemed appropriate to me to spell Peking as anyone travelling to or living in China would have done fifty years ago.

To help the reader who is unfamiliar with China to take his bearings there are maps on each endpaper marked with the principal towns and cities mentioned in the text. And a brief glossary at the end offers explanations of unfamiliar terms.

It will be understood that my principal debt is to the directors of John Swire and Sons who invited me to talk to some of their retired staff. And then to Michael and Jacquie Fiennes who never lost faith in the project or the book despite its elephantine gestation. Of course the unsung heroes and heroines of it all are my interviewees whose names can be found at the end of the book. They were generous with their time, generous with their patience, and generous with their hospitality. I hope that they will not feel that this generosity was misplaced.

No one who writes about the British in the East in the inter-war period in the manner of *The Lion and the Dragon* can fail to acknowledge a profound debt to Charles Allen whose *Plain Tales from the Raj* broke the ground and sowed the seeds of a harvest that many of us have since reaped.

The list of other people who have contributed to this book is a long one and one cannot hope to thank them adequately, but Stephen Peet taught me how to interview witnesses with a proper measure of personal humility; Shirley Whitton collected the photographs with enthusiasm and dedication; Lois Wheeler Snow, Mr and Mrs Charles Temlett, Maurice Lister, Winifred Whitaker, Norah Elworthy, Barbara Fowler, Pan Ling, Commander Thomas Marchant, Mr and Mrs Gordon Campbell and William MacQuitty generously allowed me to reproduce their photographs; Elizabeth Cowen read successive drafts of an early chapter and set me off in the right direction; June McMullen typed and retyped the transcripts of the interviews; Madge Coverley gave me houseroom in Portugal to write three chapters; Kyle Cathie and Caroline Taggart at Elm Tree were firm when my resolve to finish the book was wavering; and my colleagues in the Department of Liberal Studies at the Central School of Art and Design, particularly Jane Graves, Charles Taylor and Stuart Evans listened to *my* tales of what life in China had been like with unflinching good humour. None of them share any responsibility for what follows. That is mine alone.

Introduction

The story of the British in China between the two world wars is only one small corner of the vast canvas on which the history of China in the twentieth century is laid out. For the British were rarely involved in a decisive way diplomatically or commercially in the events which followed the overthrow of the Manchu Dynasty in 1912 and which would eventually lead to the establishment of the Chinese People's Republic thirty-six years later. They were bystanders, but like any bystanders their lives were affected by what they saw and what was happening around them, and to that extent it is important to know something of China's own history in the first four decades of this century in order to be able to locate the memories and recollections of some of the British who found themselves in the country in the inter-war years – which are the subject of this book – in a broader historical context. Then perhaps one can properly appreciate the particular qualities of that small British corner of the canvas.

In fact it is valuable to return to the nineteenth century, to the period when the Western powers first took a concerted interest in China. For it was then that the conditions under which the British lived and traded in China had been laid down. It was principally commerce that took the British to China then, not colonial or imperial ambition. China seemed a vast untapped market for Western manufactured goods, but over the years the Imperial dynasty had stubbornly resisted attempts by the West to open trading relations. It was true that at Canton in the south of the country foreign merchants had been permitted to trade since the eighteenth century, but to their Victorian descendants, flushed with the success and profits of the Industrial Revolution, this seemed no more than the smallest of windows into China. They wanted to push open the front door and this they did by force of arms in the 'Opium War' of 1840–2 and fifteen years later when a joint Anglo-French force attacked China. The particular *casus belli* of each of these military incursions is of less importance to this book than the concessions which were wrung from the Chinese at the two treaties which concluded the hostilities: the Treaty of Nanking of 1842 and the Treaty of Tientsin of 1858. Britain's principal gains were the island of Hong Kong and an agreement by the Chinese to permit an expansion of trading relations. The West had indeed forced open China's front door, and more than that they had been granted property rights in the front room. For the Chinese authorities were compelled to cede to the victorious powers land in certain towns and cities which were to become nothing less than small parcels of England and France to be administered in the English and French manner. Worse still, from the Chinese point of view, they were compelled to accept the principle of extra-territoriality whereby foreign nationals who broke the law had the right to be tried in their own national courts under their own system of law. The West could afford to be well pleased with itself, particularly since it had also forced its diplomats upon the Imperial authorities in a specially designated Legation Quarter in Peking. For whoever was in power in China over the next century the overturning of these 'unequal treaties' was to be a major foreign policy objective.

The West busied itself about its trading activities, buttressing its special position in the country by undertaking the administration of the Chinese customs in return for assisting in the suppression of the Tai-ping revolt in the middle years of the nineteenth century. Then in the wake of the Boxer Rebellion of 1900, when the Boxer rebels, fired by xenophobia and tacitly supported by the Imperial throne, murdered Westerners in China and destroyed property, the Western powers insisted that the revenue from these customs be yielded up to them as an indemnity for the loss of lives and properties they had experienced – the so-called 'Boxer Indemnity', which was later to be returned in one form or another to China.

By the first decade of the twentieth century the British were trading along the whole length of the China coast from Tientsin in the north to Amoy, Swatow and Canton in the south. Other nations had followed; America, Russia and Germany. And Japan, which had emerged from over two centuries of isolation from the rest of the world when Commodore Perry had sailed into Yokohama in 1853, had begun to impose its will on China in the wake of the 1894 Sino-Japanese War. The British, along with other nations, had penetrated into central China too, along the Yangtze River on which they were permitted to carry their goods on their own ships protected, as were their interests in the river ports, by a flotilla of British gunboats. It was as if this country had been forced to accept the right of Chinese warships to patrol the Manchester Ship Canal or sail the Thames between Tilbury and Windsor. In the 1900s China did indeed seem the sick man of Asia.

But some Chinese had begun to consider ways of wresting back complete control of their country's destiny and under the leadership of Sun Yat Sen in 1911–12 they caused the overthrow of the last Emperor of the Manchu Dynasty, P'u Yi. In the wake of this revolution they established a republic with Yuan Shi Kai as provisional president on 15 February 1912. Less than two months later China's first republican parliament opened and by the end of that momentous year Yuan Shi Kai had been elected to the republic for a five-year term of office. But hopes for any kind of political stability within the new republic were quickly dashed. The inheritors of the Manchu empire soon fell out amongst themselves. Parliament was dissolved in 1913 and the south of the country, largely under the control of a group of Nationalists called the Kuomintang, rebelled against the northern government. For their part in this uprising Kuomintang members of parliament were deprived of their seats. China was ripe for civil war.

War, in the meantime, was the abiding preoccupation of the Western powers who had secured such a favourable trading position for themselves in China over the past half century. The new, albeit fatally divided, republic was barely caught up in the European hostilities, although in 1917 she had decided to enter the war on the side of the allied powers and as a consequence despatched two hundred thousand or more Chinese labourers to France to work in war industries and assist in the digging of trenches, other construction work and transport. China's principal motive in siding with Britain, France and Russia was the hope that a defeated Germany might be forced to yield up her concessions and trading privileges in China, but the Versailles Peace Conference put paid to any such hope. Japan was given the former German rights in the province of Shantung which she had taken in 1914 after capturing the city of Tsingtao with the aid of a small detachment of British troops.

In China the response to the arrangements made at Versailles was immediate. On 4 May 1919 students were on the streets of Peking carrying banners with nationalistic and anti-Japanese slogans. Some thirty-two of them were arrested and while superficially their anger may seem less than important, their protest was endorsed by many throughout the country who were convinced that the government had once again capitulated to Japanese pressure, just as Yuan Shi Kai had done four years before when his government had accepted the majority of what are known as the 'Twenty-One Demands'. The precise details of these demands need not detain us. It is Japan's crude attempt to assert her hegemony over China that is important and which was so distasteful to concerned Chinese. It is legitimate to link later events surrounding the Japanese attack on Manchuria in 1931 to the ill-conceived 'Twenty-One Demands' and China's humiliation at Versailles.

But this is to anticipate events. In 1920 China's southern provinces proclaimed themselves the Independent Republic of Southern China, though within a year this had deteriorated into a loose federation. Yuan Shi Kai, who in 1916 had ascended the Dragon Throne of the Empire, had died in June of that same year. The era of the war lords had begun, as rival military commanders throughout the country sought to impose their will upon large and small parts of China. Some had armies of tens of thousands of troops and ruled over territories as great as whole countries, others operated with a handful of armed ruffians from a single town or city:

> 'Many, despite the fragmentary nature of their activities, were fiercely nationalist. Some were Christians. There were those who sought the highest offices in China – as president, premier, cabinet ministers, provincial governor – and attained them (though usually fleetingly); others were content with a local base that might furnish revenues from opium smuggling, transport dues, or rural taxes, or else perhaps lived on semi-legalised handouts from other military commanders or local district governments.' (Jonathan D. Spence: *Gate of Heavenly Peace*, Faber 1982)

Few Europeans had first-hand experience of warlordism, though newspaper reports of their lives and their skirmishes seem to have caught the imagination of some young men who were already disposed to consider a career on the China coast. But travelling traders, missionaries in the interior and British troops, who were often required to protect national interests from the potential depredations of a war lord's army on the march did encounter them. Most Westerners, however, were safely ensconced in their 'concessions', those small islands of, say, Britishness or Frenchness which had been ceded to certain Western powers by the Manchu Dynasty.

In the early 1920s warlord squabbling was at its worst in the north of China, for in the south, centred upon Canton, Sun Yat Sen, father of the Chinese Revolution, who in May 1921 formally assumed the post of President of China to which he had himself elected by his southern supporters, retained a more generous vision of China's future, even if the tactics by which they proposed to achieve the eventual reunification of the country were open to question, and would eventually lead to the downfall of his Kuomintang party. Between 1924 and 1927 the Kuomintang Nationalists made common cause with the Chinese Communist Party and under the guidance of the Bolshevik Michael Borodin set about transforming themselves into a more effective instrument of revolution. The first priority was the creation of a revolutionary army and with the aid of forty 'advisers' a military academy was established with Chiang Kai Shek at its head and Chou En Lai as his deputy political commissar. By the summer of 1926 the Nationalist Revolutionary armies were ready to march against the northern war lords and on 9 July the Northern Expedition was at last launched. Changsha was captured on 17 July, and by autumn the whole of the Upper Yangtze Valley was taken. The Lower Yangtze region was a harder prize to win, but Chiang Kai Shek's forces entered Shanghai on 22 March 1927 and two days later Nanking fell to the Nationalists. The taking of Nanking was accompanied by attacks on the foreign community in the city which were only halted by vigorous shelling by American and British gunboats anchored in the Yangtze.

Clearly the British in China were not untouched by this civil war, though it was principally those communities which came into direct contact with the advancing armies who were most affected. But in 1928 in Shanghai there had occurred an event which more than anything else in the inter-war years must have convinced thoughtful Europeans of how tenuous their continuing claim to special privileges in China was. In February of that year a series of strikes against Japanese-owned cotton mills were launched by the Communist-controlled West Shanghai Workers Club. It was widely supported by students and patriotic businessmen. Further strikes followed and then in mid-May a Chinese striker was killed by his Japanese foreman. Communist leaders called for a demonstration of anti-imperialist solidarity on 30 May and on that day in the International Settlement British-led police fired into the crowd, killing eleven marchers and wounding some fifty or so more. In the weeks that followed there were sympathy strikes and rallies. Picket lines were armed with clubs. The Western and Japanese authorities mobilised their military volunteer corps, declared martial law and landed marines from twenty-six gunboats at Shanghai. Altogether some sixty or more demonstrators were killed. Throughout China there were rallies and strikes in support of the Shanghainese, and a boycott on goods from British and Japanese firms. In time the troubles subsided, but 30 May became a potent date in the Chinese calendar, to be remembered with annual demonstrations. The West had been served notice of the strength of Chinese feeling about their continuing privileged position in the country.

The Kuomintang and their Communist allies now commanded all of China south of the Yangtze, but they were preparing to fall out with each other. The end of what had always been an uneasy and unlikely alliance came in June 1927. Michael Borodin and the other Soviet advisers left China and the leaders of the Communist party fled after a wave of executions had begun in Shanghai. They offered some armed resistance, but it came to nothing. Throughout Nationalist China revolutionaries and radicals were outlaws to be hunted down and destroyed.

There was dissension too in the Nationalist camp and it was not until December that Chiang Kai Shek felt strong enough to assume the reins of Kuomintang power once again. Within ten months, as a result of fortunate accidents and

Japanese interference in Shantung the northern war lords were vanquished and Chiang was able to establish the National Government of China with its capital at Nanking on 10 October 1928. But it was military government and its writ effectively ran only in the five provinces of the Lower Yangtze region. Military rulers elsewhere in the country might be of the same party as Chiang, but this in no sense drew the sting of their personal political ambitions and at this time some two and a quarter million men were under arms throughout China. There would have to be negotiations about disbanding the armies that were feeding on China like so many plagues of locusts, and indeed a conference convened in January 1929 to discuss the matter.

The Nanking government was recognised by the Western powers and from the Chinese point of view some progress was made in abrogating the more hateful terms of the 'unequal treaties'. Britain for example gave up her 'concessions' at Chinkiang, Amoy and Wei Hai Wei; Belgium and Denmark's nationals lost their privilege of extra-territoriality. Japan on the other hand was determined to yield up nothing, indeed her army in Manchuria was bent on an expansion not a diminution of its authority.

Japan's relations with her much larger Asian neighbour had been far from equable throughout the twentieth century. The Chinese for their part never forgave the presumption of the 'Twenty-One Demands' or forgot their humiliation at Versailles. The Japanese on the other hand were determined to preserve their trading privileges intact and continued to regard Manchuria as a legitimate sphere of their influence, a logical geographical extension of their colony of Korea. The question for Tokyo was whether their policy aims were to be pursued by diplomatic or military means. However, as the third decade of the twentieth century began, this question to a greater extent became an academic one since Japan was entering that period of her history known as 'the dark valley', a time when her government was dominated by soldiers not civilians.

The first Chinese fruit of this change in national leadership was the Mukden Incident. In June 1931 three Japanese soldiers in civilian clothes were arrested by the Chinese in a restricted military zone in Manchuria. On 1st July they were executed as spies. Less than two months later the Japanese army struck at Mukden and the 'Manchurian Incident' had begun. Within a year the Japanese had almost conquered all of Manchuria, though an attack on Shanghai in January had been rebuffed. Now they set up the puppet state of Manchukuo with P'u Yi, the last Manchu Emperor of China as ruler of what had once been Manchuria.

Meanwhile the League of Nations had been wringing its hands at this act of Japanese aggression. But Tokyo had twice ignored time limits set by the League for the withdrawal of their troops. Sanctions were considered but without the support of the United States, Japan's principal Pacific rival, who had not joined the League, they were unlikely to prove effective. So the Lytton Commission was despatched to the East to report to the League. It was not until early 1933 that the findings of the Commission were debated in Geneva. And in any event Japan decided to withdraw from the world body in March when the League adopted the report it had commissioned. Truth to tell, with the onset of the great depression the Western democracies had too much to worry about in their own back gardens to be overconcerned about a military adventure in the Far East. In any case Japan and China had signed an armistice.

Temporary peace gave the Japanese time to consider how they might accomplish their conquest of the whole of China. A conquest that would be unchecked by world opinion and assisted by an ill-organised enemy. Indeed in 1930 and '31, while Japan was contemplating its conquest of Manchuria, Chiang Kai Shek and his Nationalist energies had been devoted to suppressing resistance to his regime by units of the Red Army in the Middle Yangtze region – 'Red Banditry' as the Nanking government chose to call it. The Mukden Incident should have concentrated the Nationalists' minds marvellously; the more important of their enemies was at the gate and as a result they ought to have been able to turn their attentions away from what was happening within their walls.

However, in April 1933, the Japanese penetrated the Great Wall and entered Hopei province. Chiang's response was swift. He met Japanese demands for a demilitarised zone in Hopei and busied himself again with his civil war with the Communists. It was not until 1936, two years after the twelve-month-long epic 'Long March' over six thousand miles by the Communists into the north west of China that the Communists and the Nationalists joined forces to oppose the invading Japanese.

The second Sino-Japanese war began in July 1937 when fighting broke out near Peking between Chinese and Japanese troops – the so called 'Peking Incident'. In August there was fighting in Shanghai. Peking fell to the Japanese on 8 August and Shanghai was taken on 9 November. It was still an undeclared war, and a war on two fronts, in the north and in the Shanghai region. Now Japanese armies in the south advanced along the Yangtze Valley and on 12/13 December stormed Nanking. The rape of that city and the excesses committed against its citizens appalled all who witnessed it, though Japan did its best to suppress any details of the atrocities. Westerners in China too were made painfully aware of the extent to which their interests were being put at risk by the Japanese invasion when the USS *Panay* was bombed and sunk in the Yangtze and a British gunboat, HMS *Ladybird* fired on by an 'ultra-nationalist Japanese firebrand'.

Chiang Kai Shek had been compelled to move his capital upriver to Chungking, and it was generally assumed he would be compelled to accede to any demands the Japanese might care to make. But he stood his ground and the war continued. In the autumn of 1938 Hankow was taken and after a landing at Bias Bay in southern China Japanese troops rapidly advanced and seized Canton. Once again Chiang refused to accept Japan's offer of peace. It was true that the Japanese never commanded the countryside, that their writ only ran in the cities and along the railways which they had conquered, but there was every reason to suppose that in time they could subdue the country areas as well and that they would indeed establish a 'New Order in East Asia', the political, economic and cultural union of Japan, Manchukuo and China. But across the world in Europe Hitler had overreached himself. His attack on Poland, the expiry of the British government's ultimatum and the beginning of the European war marked the effective end of Japan's ambitions in China though they were not to know it until 1945. It also, though no-one could have foretold it then, heralded the end of Chiang Kai Shek. And it was certainly the beginning of the final chapter of the story of the British living in a China which afforded them special privileges and particular rights. It was almost one hundred years since the Opium War of 1840–2 by which the British had first begun to amass those privileges and rights.

Shanghai-
"The Paris of the East"

It was in the years between the two world wars that Shanghai completed its transformation into one of the great cities of the world. 'The Paris of the East', Shanghai Lily's home, where one presumes it had taken more than one man to change her name, a cosmopolitan community devoted to the making and the increasing of vast personal and company fortunes, a city where a man could go mad and put a bullet through his head while his fellows shrugged their shoulders and congratulated themselves on not having let the East get the better of them. Shanghai was like nowhere else on Earth, free from the Edwardian colonial corset of custom, usage and right form that made Hong Kong so dully respectable. Shanghai had lifted her skirts, bobbed her hair and was looking for a good time.

So it seemed to the casual visitor to Shanghai, Noel Coward perhaps who wrote *Private Lives* while staying in a hotel in the city, and particularly to the armchair traveller whose liveliest fantasies were fed by newspaper reports of skirmishing war lords, and by Hollywood and Marlene Dietrich. But for the men and women who lived and worked in the city, who had perhaps grown up there, it was certainly an international community, but there was plenty of old England to keep homesickness at bay: an Anglican cathedral, English schools, an annual parade on the king's birthday and the sober certainty of daily work with one of the British-owned companies, the Hongkong and Shanghai Bank, Butterfield & Swire, Jardine Matheson, and so on. There were 'messes' for bachelors to live in, houses for married couples, Jessfield Park to stroll in. And afternoon tea at the Majestic before drinks at one of the city's clubs and a dinner party with one's friends. It was a secure and privileged world where a little money went a long way towards buying you a standard of living which would have been unimaginable in the Home Counties.

But this Shanghai was no more the complete Shanghai than the 'Paris of the East' Shanghai, for beyond the thin strip of land where the Europeans and Americans lived and traded lay Chinese Shanghai, waiting for its time for come. And between the wars it only occasionally seems to have bothered the Europeans and the Americans in their settlement and concession.

Western Shanghai was built on land that ran along the Whangpu or Shanghai River some thirty miles from the sea. The land had been reclaimed from the river and a Western style skyline put up to create the celebrated Shanghai Bund. Originally as in every other city in the nineteenth century where the Chinese had

The back of the
Bund: Chinese in
Shanghai; in the
background
buildings on the
Bund.

been compelled to grant trading concessions and accept the principle of extra-
territoriality, each foreign nation which wished to do business with the Chinese
had built its own little piece of England or America or France by the river. These
bits of land were governed by their own laws, policed by their own officers and
their citizens sentenced in their own courts, but by the end of the First World War
these concessions had amalgamated to produce just two contiguous European
areas in Shanghai: the International Settlement and the French Concession. The
ever-insular French ran their concession as if it were in France, the Shanghai
municipal council ran the International Settlement.

'It was a wonderful city for people who only saw the cream, and there was an awful lot of cream in Shanghai. The International Settlement, which was the British, American and Japanese settlements combined, was run by the business men at the top on a municipal council, and then the professionals, the police, the secretariat, and so on and so forth below. And that was the way all the concessions were run too. The local business people ran the municipal councils and so on, but there was a big dividing line between the amateurs at the top and the professionals at the bottom.'

'The French concession was different, in so far as it was a concession and was run very much as a French town would be, but the corruption was very high because they were free of the Chinese authorities, and therefore you got a lot of doubtful people making use of the town. I have known times when we arrived with passengers on board the ship and they've just walked ashore. Admittedly the customs searched baggage but even then Europeans could leave their country and come over to Shanghai and start a real gambling hell, and who was going to stop you? There was no restraint.'[17]

'It did have its lurid side – it was a sea port. Shanghai had everything. It was a city that could give you everything you wanted, from the highest to the lowest. There were no morals of any sort. It was an absolutely amoral sort of place.'[5]

From the moral and the amoral alike Shanghai offered one climate, a cycle of seasons which, with the possible exception of the hottest parts of the summer, was very much to the British taste. In the hot months some of the British women like their sisters on the central plains of India were able to head for the hills, for a resort called Kuling up the Yangtze or to the north, but fewer women it seems availed themselves of such an escape between the wars than had done so before. They preferred to stay in the heat of Shanghai.

'The really hot weather would be about June, July, August. It would be very hot, terribly sticky, the temperature would go up to and above a hundred, about a hundred and two, hundred and three, with this very heavy humid atmosphere. You would go to bed wet and you would wake up wet. It was terribly sticky, particularly at night. And then you'd get a wonderful autumn which would be about September, October, November. And then you'd go through a winter which was very much the same as in London. Quite a lot of rain, and cold, not really quite so cold as we get here but similar. You had to wear winter clothes, overcoat, and all that sort of stuff. That was November, December, January, February.'[8]

Western Shanghai was pre-eminently a city of bachelors, young unmarried men who had come East to work for one of the British or European or American companies that ran their China business from that city. Thus most young Britons embarking upon a career on the China coast began their working life in Shanghai. Many of the companies, and certainly Butterfield & Swire, provided accommodation above the office for some of their juniors. But the usual thing was to begin life in the YMCA or a hotel and then make friends with fellow juniors from your own or from other companies and hope to be invited to 'mess' with them. These messes were generally the homes of senior married staff who had gone on long leave. The young bachelors took over the house, its contents and the servants until leave was over. Then they looked for another family off to Europe for ten months. Daily routine for a junior in the Butterfield & Swire office or the Shanghai Bund was a great deal different from the way it might have been had they stayed in London.

'We used to get up fairly early, except for the very hot days in the summer, because many of us were riding before breakfast or visiting the Company's ships in the harbour. In the really hot weather we laid the ponies off, partially for them and partially for us, so we hadn't got to get up so early. Anyway we would get up about six o'clock. We had breakfast at about half past eight, and then we'd go to the office. To get to the office I had a small car, a small Morris Cowley. Of course there weren't so very many cars in those days so if we hadn't got one it's quite likely we got a taxi in. If we were in a Mess we'd all go down together.

'And then for lunch, or tiffin as it used to be, we had a canteen I suppose it would be called now, up on the top floor where we had lunch. And then we'd go back for the afternoon, to office work and we'd probably finish about five o'clock. Supposedly five o'clock, but it's not like here where people have more or less got their hat or coat on at five o'clock. As you probably know, out East time doesn't make any odds, you worked overtime when you had to and didn't get paid for it. And then you'd take work home as well, still not paid for, and there was always quite a bit to do to keep up with things. There was none of this business of, "Well tomorrow will be all right." You just had to do it. And anyway when you were finished in the evening you might play tennis or if one of you was a member of a club you might go along there just to have the odd drink. Then you'd go out a bit in the evening.

'On the whole you'd eat at home but we did go out quite a bit. You'd be invited out and there was a certain amount of dancing in the evening. I must admit I wasn't a member of the French Club, which was in the French Concession. They had dances and the Majestic Hotel had dancing and very probably we'd make up a party and go to the Majestic. At the weekend, probably on the Saturday night, we'd do something or other anyway.

'And you could be in bed any time between one and three or four, depending how you felt. I think a lot of people have gone through a whole night without going to bed. And were still starting their day again at 6.30 a.m. How did we keep going?

'I don't know. Somehow we did. We were much younger in those days.'[8]

One of the first social tasks awaiting the newly arrived junior was the 'dropping' of cards. These cards were his ticket into Shanghai society and as important as calling at the Consulate and signing his name in the book there. Both rituals had a practical basis to them: they were a simple if somewhat formal way of announcing your arrival.

'I used to take a rickshaw or walk up right through Shanghai to the residential sections of the town and at a B & S married man's home I would drop two cards. I'd certainly drop a card on the husband, and if one didn't

**Flying the flag:
Social life at the
Shanghai Aero Club.**

do that one was not invited. I really forget whether I dropped one on the wife. The important thing was that one called on the taipan and the sub-managers, and all the married people. It wasn't terribly formal and I don't think everybody did it, but I'd been brought up to do so and so I continued.'[2]

'Up to a point it could be got round, because if you happened to make a friend of one of the wives and she happened to be calling anywhere where you hadn't and ought to call, she would say, "Look, give me a couple of your cards and I'll drop them in for you."

'After you'd called and left your card they usually said come and have tea with us, or come to a tea dance, or come and dine with us. It was a rather formal way of getting into circulation and it seems to have completely come to an end now.

'As a young bachelor just out you weren't expected to return hospitality, though I think if you made real friends with married couples apart from the formal social round, then, of course you probably would. In my Mess there were two other people in B & S and the third man was an outsider, but we tended all to have the same friends and we did our share of entertaining our friends.'[3]

'I had been born in Shanghai and been to the girls' school there. My parents did entertain on a small scale, and one of our favourite ways of entertaining was to have Sukiyaki. It was easy because you could ring up the Japanese place and tell them how many people you were having and they would do the whole thing for you. They would turn up in a taxi with two or three girls – depending on how many guests there were – all beautifully dressed in their kimonos. They would bring everything with them including a round table and cushions and the charcoal chatties (they didn't have electrical ones then). And all the food was beautifully prepared, and then they would cook it for you, and all you had to do was to make yourself comfortable on the cushions – if that's possible – and eat it. It was a lovely way of entertaining. Not exactly unique because a lot of people did it, but very easy. Otherwise one would just have a normal sort of dinner party.

'Dinner parties could be very formal. We didn't entertain on that scale, but they could be formal. People liked to do the thing properly, and have a nice beautifully laid table with wine and everything like that.

'If you were invited to a formal dinner party you would probably turn up about seven. Quite often ladies wore long dresses (black tie was only for special occasions). And you'd have drinks and sit down to dinner and have probably a four course meal if it was a really big party. And sometimes people did follow the tradition of the ladies leaving the room first, but not usually. The parties were generally on a smaller scale and you would leave the table and have coffee, and chat, and more drinks afterwards. And you'd probably go home some time towards midnight. Late hours usually were only if you went to night clubs or dances, because everybody had to get up pretty early.'[16]

It was its night clubs and its life after midnight as much as anything else which furnished Shanghai with a reputation as the Land of Cockayne. But if pleasure did rule supreme then much of it was thoroughly respectable. Young women certainly did not venture out on the town on Saturday night on their own.

Night Clubs

'You had to wait for your escort to pick you up. He might have his own car, otherwise you'd get a taxi. They had dances in most of the clubs on a Saturday night. Let's say you were going to the French Club, which I belonged to. He might have a drink in your home first and then you would go straight to the club. In the case of the French Club, if it was summer they had dancing out on the terrace and you would go out there and have a drink. More often than not there would be more than just the two of you in the party and you would meet up there. You would have your dinner, and the band would play during the course of the dinner, and you would dance as you would here at the Savoy, for instance, in between courses, and just carry on until everything packed up and he would bring you home and that was that. And Mummy would make sure that he did, and that you were in at a reasonable time. In those days, parents were strict and you had to be home and no nonsense.'[16]

太
古

'One of the most popular night clubs was the Little Club, and it was very small, and you had to go upstairs to it. They used to have a string band. I can always remember the sound of domp domp domp domp rhythm, going on as you went upstairs.

'It was all rather dim, and there were curtains all over the windows. In fact somebody once leant against the curtains and didn't realise the window was open behind and fell into the street, but his fall was broken by some telegraph wires, and so he wasn't hurt. But it was all rather dim, I can't exactly remember quite what the decor was, except that it was very romantic and very exciting.

'The floor was quite small, and we used to sit round little tables, the lights would dim. They usually had a floorshow. One could stay on there till two, three, four in the morning, but I always had to be home by half-past two, my mother said that was my deadline. I thought it was terribly early, because in those days, we didn't suddenly get one steady boyfriend, like you do here, because luckily for us girls we were outnumbered by men, so we had lots of boyfriends and we usually went out in a foursome or a sixsome. And as not all of the young men had cars, we would probably hire a taxi and drop the girls home. I'm afraid that I used to break up lots of parties. "You've got to go home? We don't want to go home yet." Anyhow, there was the Little Club, and then there was the Canidrome where they had a dance floor and greyhound racing. So you could watch a race and dance, but that wasn't so much a night club. There was a place called Del Monte, and for some unknown reason I was there once at three in the morning and I had six fried eggs – they were tiny pullets' eggs then. In Shanghai people could dance practically all night long.'[21]

'I remember going to Del Monte, which was a huge place across a little creek. There was a little bridge to it, and you would go in there at three in the morning and nobody would be sober. It was just like that. They wouldn't have come there otherwise. There'd be all sorts of splendid uniforms of the various nationalities who had drifted over there. It was the only place open and there you had to buy champagne. I was arriving there one morning and I saw a man being thrown out by the big Russian chucker-outs. And as this chap came out, pushed out through the door, these two seized him and threw him down the four or five steps. I'd often heard about people being thrown out, and on the cinema people are always thrown out and they don't get hurt. They flung this chap down the steps and he just got up and walked away. And I thought, "Fancy. It's the first time I've ever seen a man thrown out." Literally picked up and thrown out.

'And another time when I was waiting to join a ship, there was another well-known cabaret. It was called Ladow's Tavern. I had to go up river and the ship that I was going on as a passenger was full up, and so the Captain said that he would take me on his settee. It was Christmas Eve; it would be Christmas Day when he sailed early in the morning, and I thought rather than disturb him (he was sailing at dawn) I'd go up to the cabarets and sit there and have a drink until it was time to board the ship, and then I could always sleep when we were sailing. It was a very respectable place, and I went there, and I remember I had a cold, and naturally I would have liked to have been elsewhere but I was leaving and so that was the end of it. I sat quietly by myself until it was time to leave. (I was rather smart in those days, and I was wearing a sort of check tweed thing with single buttons.) A fight started, and if you've ever seen a fight with people with paper hats on, it's the funniest thing. Somebody got my coat and ripped most of the buttons off, and the fight carried on to the bottom of the stairs. The doors were shut the wrong way so that you couldn't get out. You could not open them. And this fighting mob of people had jammed the doors. There was a chucker-out, the doorman, and he had his hands above his head and he was saying, "Gentlemen, gentlemen, Christmas Day, everybody happy, everybody happy." But there wasn't a happy man within a square mile of the place, and to this day I don't know what was the cause of the fight, but it was a fight and everybody joined in except me with my torn coat.'[17]

The night out, with or without trouble, eventually became the morning after. Young bachelors in Shanghai had their own way of squaring that particular circle.

'I must admit sometimes the following day it was difficult to keep awake. We used to rely a bit on benzedrine, which was not a certifiable drug in those days, and that used to wake you up if you had to be awake.'[5]

'It could be a very hectic life but I remember before I became properly engaged I was very keen on riding and I used to beat it up with the boys and get back at some ghastly hour in the morning, three or four probably, very full of drink and then get on to my pony and ride for a couple of hours out into Hungjao, which was on the outskirts of the settlement and that shook up the old liver and got rid of a lot of the alcoholic fumes.

'One time when I was out riding I wasn't looking and wasn't gripping with my knees and I came off in Jungshan Road and landed on my bottom. In fact I cracked my coccyx and was completely paralysed when I got home. I was paralysed for about three weeks; it did not hurt in the slightest but I could not feel anything down below. So I lay in bed and all my friends came to see me and we drank an incredible amount of gin and when I could arise again I think I was fifteen and a half stone or something ghastly. So that really did not meet with my fiancée's approval.'[10]

The Little Club and Del Monte were only the respectable tip of the after-dark iceberg. Shanghai was a great sea port and its red light areas offered sailors, travellers and others all the traditional opportunities to be parted from their money. In back streets and alleys, and more particularly in the notorious Blood Alley, there were small clubs and dance halls, cabarets as they were called. At the back there would be a bar, around the walls a few tables and chairs; a trio of musicians, perhaps just a man at a piano played as the girls sat around waiting for custom. These were 'taxi girls' who you paid to dance with you and in the wake of the 1917 Soviet Revolution, many of them were White Russian refugees.

'A "taxi girl" was to be found in the dancing places especially nearer the sea port, where you went in for a drink or a meal. You got a lot of girls

Hunting and eating:
Menu covers for the
1935 and 1936
Shanghai Paper
Hunt's Annual Ball.

sitting around, most of whom came from families of Russian refugees. (Many of them came out through Harbin.) And you merely paid your dollar for a dance with one of them.'[5]

'They sat at their tables at these cabarets and the male clients would go in and they would have a look around and would say, "I fancy her." They'd go across, and as soon as one of the girls saw a man heading in her direction, she was so keen, especially if business was a bit slow, that she would be on her feet meeting him halfway. And off they would go and dance. Then perhaps she might persuade him to buy her a drink and they would sit down and have a drink. Then they would dance a bit more and if they wanted to go and do other things perhaps that was on the cards as well.'[18]

'In Didi's bar there were about five young girls the other side of the bar and they would shake dice with you for drinks. I think they were all quite respectable, but it put ideas into people's heads. Nowadays it's quite a popular thing to say how wonderful everything was but I saw a certain amount of the underneath side, being on board a ship, and lying at the wharves, which were down near Blood Alley. Even in those days I had no

'Blood Alley'

23

The pleasure of her company: A Chinese prostitute (bottom right) walks the Shanghai streets with her amah.

great desire to spend every evening in the cabarets dancing about. Mostly men went there for a dance.

'Blood Alley was a name that came to it afterwards. It was just a street of cabarets. It had a certain notoriety because the single men went there quite a lot and for most of them it was purely a place where you got a drink and if you could afford it you got a girl at your table. There was very little going off together. They'd know who was "on the game", but there was a respectability even in their poverty. I never saw any bloodshed, though there was one time a man was shot with a revolver and the notoriety of that shot rang around the place for years. It was probably the reason for it getting called "Blood Alley".'[17]

'It was very close to the French Bund where B & S ships tied up. The mate and engineers would go there, and if you wanted to meet someone it would invariably be in Blood Alley. They called it Blood Alley, not because of the seamen, but because that was where the British troops used to go along and have a scrap maybe with other national troops, generally French or Italian.

'I saw one time a chucker-out beating up an old fellow. I think he was a Frenchman or some other nationality, and I did not like it and I said to this fellow, "Ease up, don't hurt him." I never saw any soldiers and sailors fighting, I only saw this chucker-out; he was an American, I think, a bouncer, beating up this old fellow. I don't know what he did. I just happened to be passing by when it happened and when I said this to him he seemed to be glad to stop.'[19]

'The different nationalities always had their naval vessels in Shanghai, and their crews were quite famous in the city. There was always rivalry between the British sailors and the American sailors. I remember one particular evening going into a small bar and the American sailors were all sitting on one side of the room and the British sailors along the other side. We sat down at a table in between. The boy brought our beer along and as he was taking the bottle away a matelot from the British side came up and told us, "You don't want to let your boy take away your ammunition." So it was time to get out.'[20]

The White Russian community in Shanghai, some of whose women were forced to work in the seamier cabarets while their men folk were paid to guard the doors, were perhaps the unhappiest national group in the city. For they were quite literally 'stateless', washed up in Shanghai on the full tide of their own country's revolution, without a passport and thus with little chance of ever being able to 'move on'. It was difficult to cling to any kind of respectability in such circumstances, and while undoubtedly many did, others fell into poverty and prostitution. In this last respect they were not alone, for there were Chinese and Eurasian and indeed European prostitutes in the city, on its streets and in its brothels, but for respectable Europeans the White Russian fall from grace seemed all the greater.

'They were beautiful most of them, and the Russian men too. Fine looking men and it was a shame. I was writing a letter to a chief engineer not long ago and I said that when I looked back on these Russians that were in Shanghai – men and women – I looked back in shame. They could not get jobs. They were in that position where people would not employ them. They were white people and yet they were paid little more than coolies. The Russian men, a lot of decent men, were willing to work but people did not want them. You would not see foreign firms using them in their offices for instance. And I told this chief engineer that I realised all those nice Russian ladies in the dance halls were victims of circumstance. There was one lady there who I was told was an admiral's daughter. Of course we all heard about the "Russian princesses", but there is no doubt that a lot of them were officer-type families when they were chucked out after 1917. Lots of them ended up in Paris, Constantinople, Shanghai, Harbin and all around. They were victims of circumstance and when I look back I look back with shame that I was not in some organisation that could have helped them.

'The club owners most certainly exploited the girls. They would say certain nights had to be swimming costume nights and the girls had to put swimming costumes on. I don't think they liked it. I am sure they did not like it. I do not know who owned these clubs, maybe it was the Chinese or maybe the Russians, but it was a shame to see the men and the women exploited. Russian men, for instance, were watchmen and they were very very poorly paid.'[19]

'Most of the Russian girls had one aim in life and that was to get a passport. British passports were the most popular. The girl would find a

The pleasure of their company: A Shanghai chorus line in the 1930s.

British male and say to him. "Look, you don't turn me on or anything like that, but I want a British passport, can you do anything about it?" And if he was the unscrupulous type and if he knew anything about the racket, he might say. "Yes, I think I can work something out." And they would agree on a figure which she would pay him and he would go to the registry office and marry her quite legally. She became Mrs Smith with her British passport, which meant she could wander all over the world, whereas before she could not go out of Shanghai; she did not have a passport of any kind. They were known as stateless persons, but if they married a British man then they became British subjects. So it was worth a lot of money to them and I remember one particular man who was alleged to have married a Russian for five hundred dollars. But I would not say it was the general practice.

'There's one particular story which is rather touching. A young ship's officer had a Russian girlfriend, with whom he lived in a flat, and I think she must have been quite an honourable type, because she always waited for Billy to come home. He paid her sufficient to run the flat and to keep herself without her having to go and work in cabarets. So that went on for two or three years. She spoke with a slight "pidgin" accent. And they agreed to get married, I will not say she persuaded him to get married, he was maybe as keen as she was, anyhow after living together for a year or two they decided to get married, and her first remark after the ceremony was, "Belong proper marry now Billy." This "proper" word meant that it was real. Bank of England, you know, security.

'I am afraid that bad girls did share their favours around. The

26

unscrupulous ones did, I am quite sure, but I think there were quite honourable ones who stuck to the same man all the time. However, when some found their husband was not there, but a thousand miles away the other side of China, and there was no possibility of being seen by any of his friends, they probably made a little bit on the side.'[18]

'If a young fellow was obviously losing his head over a Russian woman it was known that he would be discreetly shifted to a ship that would not be coming to that port until he cooled down a bit. I remember one chap who was madly in love with a Russian girl. (Mind you they were not all cabaret girls. There were some nice family girls as well.) Anyway this fellow was a bit of a hot head and nothing could divert him to change his mind, so he got a "shifting chit" and then he went to see the superintendent. "Captain Johnson, I don't want this ship, I have got my young lady here." "That's all right," he said. "We are shifting you this time; you can go down south." "But I don't want to go to Bangkok," he said. "You go to Bangkok," he said, "you'll get a bit of black velvet down there." Of course he had to take his shift but by and by he came back again and in due course he married the Russian girl and was very happy with her, I believe.'[19]

'A chap of ours, very much against the firm's will, married on the night of Pearl Harbour, a Russian usherette from one of the cinemas, terribly nice. She proved it too because he had a bad accident some years later. He was run over by a tram in Hong Kong, and she was so marvellous that anybody who had objected to his marrying her was proved wrong. Nonetheless I think in the big Hongs they had this idea that Russians were not acceptable. There were exceptions; some men did marry Russians and it didn't make too much difference to their careers.'[16]

Like any great city Shanghai offered its young men an opportunity to taste all manner of forbidden fruits. As well as above board betting on the city's race course, there was illegal gambling. Illicit roulette wheels were set up inside the International Settlement and moved on from club to club, often just one turn of the wheel ahead of the police. Prostitutes chaperoned by their 'amahs' walked the streets and if arrested let their amahs pay the fine and were back at work within hours.

For the young English bachelor it was the arrival of his fiancée, or the new wife he had acquired on his first leave home, that could put such temptations out of mind had he ever been prey to them. And certainly the Shanghai these fiancées and brides met for the first time was quite free from any taint of moral corruption.

'I was extremely untravelled. I'd been all over the continent but I'd never been further than that. I was surprised at such majestic buildings on the Bund. The Hongkong and Shanghai Bank for example was almost like a National Gallery. If it had been a collection of little mud shanties I might not have been so surprised. It was a similar reaction to that of the women whom

A Bride's Arrival in Shanghai

I lived amongst in a club in London. When I told them I was going to China they said, "You won't have a decent bathroom there." They thought of people as living in a very primitive way instead of in the height of luxury.

'When we first got to Shanghai after we were married, I forget where we lived. I think my brother was there, so we must have stayed with him for a week or so. And then somebody told us about a place called Cathay Mansions, it was a block of service flats and, remember this was in the '30s during the worldwide recession and as a consequence a lot of these flats were empty. They couldn't get the price they wanted and I went along and just bargained with a charming Chinese who ran them. And as he came down by $100 a time I said, "No, no, no, no." And finally he came down to $400 a month, which would really be a peppercorn rent now, though it wasn't to us on our salary at that time. So I agreed to $400 Shanghai dollars and the Shanghai dollar was then worth ten pence. And for that we had a very nice sitting room and a bedroom and a bathroom and a little hall with a telephone in it.

'They provided all the servants. You rang a bell and a boy came and you said you wanted tea or breakfast or anything. There was a restaurant on the top floor and you could go up there or you could have anything from there brought down for an extra dollar. We had lots of meals brought down for our extra ten pence. We had a wonderful life with no responsibilities at all. It was a prolonged honeymoon, really.

'It might have been difficult to make ends meet but nobody ever said so; my husband never cried poverty. I knew that we hadn't got a lot of money, though I wasn't used to a lot of money. I'd got plenty of clothes. We went out a lot. The married people, as in England today, didn't expect young married people, even if they came to dinner two or three times, to do more than perhaps make a gesture and ask them in for a drink some time. I remember saying to my husband over our wedding presents, "This is embarrassing. We shall never live long enough to repay all this kindness." And he said, "Don't you worry, before we die you'll have given far more wedding presents than ever you receive", and how right he was. It's life. It's as it should be.

'I soon found social life less formal in Shanghai. And we seemed to have much more to do with the Chinese then I'd expected. The top Chinese used to ask us to Chinese parties and things. Never shall I forget an old man I was sitting next to with absolutely black teeth; he put his chopsticks into a bowl and got out a pigeon's egg with them. My brother used to say that the acid test when it came to using chopsticks was if you could get a pigeon's egg out of a bowl of soup and into your mouth without dropping it. Anyway this old man put it in *my* mouth with his own chopsticks and I swallowed it whole, I didn't think I could cope otherwise. But they were meaning to be kind.'[12]

For young married couples, and indeed for young bachelors, Shanghai offered quite another club from that to be found in Blood Alley in the early hours of the morning, the social club, a small island of Englishness or Frenchness or Americanness away from home. Some such clubs were often devoted to the pursuit of a particular sport, for in China as in India or Africa or the most distant outposts of Empire games mattered. For the China hand, just as much as the Indian Sahib, *mens sana in corpore sano* was a rule to live by.

'The Bath Club was one I joined as a junior, and that consisted of a very good swimming pool and it had a lot of members. There was a Cricket Club which everybody belonged to, even if you didn't play cricket. There was the Rugger Club which used the premises of the Cricket Club or the Bath Club at times, and there was the Shanghai Club which more senior members belonged to. It wasn't expected that the junior members would belong to that. There was also a Country Club which also the junior members were not expected to belong to, it too was more for the senior people. There was an American Club. There was a French Club, though quite a few people who were not French belonged to the French Club. It was a very well-appointed club with an excellent swimming pool.'[7]

'The French Club had lovely facilities. It had an Olympic size swimming pool, and you could sit round and there was a lot of space to have snacks; there were lovely diving boards; a lot of super tennis courts, both hard and grass; bridge; a ballroom with a sprung floor; and then the terrace which they used in summer. There was a dining room with marvellous food; and rooms where you could just sit. You could be on the grass if you wished, or on the terrace; just about anything, anything you could ask for was there. It was a lovely club.

'I couldn't join the Shanghai Club because that was a men's club. The Country Club I was also not allowed to join. I probably could have joined when I was working myself, but they wouldn't take anyone who was in a Trade, as my father was. You had to be in a profession or an office; that was just one of their rules, and my father couldn't join so I didn't become a member as his daughter. There was the Columbia Country Club. That was a nice club. American, smaller scale than the French Club, but it was a little bit far out, not quite so easy to get to.'[16]

'The Country Club was used far more in the evenings as a social club, and the same applies to the French Club. The Shanghai Club being on the Bund was very largely for luncheon I would say. I don't think it was very much used in the evenings.

'The Shanghai Club had what was supposed to be the longest bar in the world and there were certain rules about where you could stand at that bar. The senior people, I remember, were on the left as you go in. That was a tradition that the more senior people in the town were expected to stay at that side and the more junior people the middle and right.'[7]

'The Chinese were not eligible to be members of the Shanghai Club in those days. The French Club, yes, anybody could go there. They had a quota for each nationality.'[16]

'The Chinese had their own clubs. I can remember once I was a member of one club, an American club, the Columbia Country Club outside Shanghai and a great friend of mine, a Chinese, who I was going to dine with, said he would come and pick me up. And he came to the club door and I said, "I'm sorry I can't ask you in." He said, "That's all right, I can't ask you into my club either."'5

For the European or the American in Shanghai there were other reminders than those they might find in their clubs of what life was like at home.

Cafés and Shops

'There were some lovely cafés for all nationalities. There was Marcel, the French one which was on the corner of Avenue Joffre and Yates Road – beautiful cakes. We would go in there and have tea. Then there was Bianchi, which was Italian in Nanking Road. They had equally nice cakes, lovely little finger rolls with foie gras – absolutely delicious. I remember those more than anything about Bianchis. Then there was Café Fédéral, that was German, in Bubbling Well Road, again German type patisserie. I don't think you could have tea in there but you could buy anything you wanted. Then there was the Chocolate Shop which was American, in Nanking Road. There was quite a large restaurant there and you could get all the lovely things like cakes and ice creams, beautiful sundaes American style, hamburgers, club sandwiches there – I've never had a club sandwich as good I had there. There was a Scottish bakery. That's what all the ship's masters liked because generally they were Scots. That was all right but a bit mundane compared to those other places which were quite exotic.'16

'They made everything that you would find in a Scottish baker's shop, like scones and pancakes and even haggis at the right season. It was a favourite place with not only the Scottish ladies but other European women. They used to go there for morning coffee.'18

Signing Chits

'Curiously you never carried money. I think largely because of bag snatching or hold ups. You signed a chit for everything, except for your rickshaws. You paid your ten cents for rickshaw fares. But for taxis, for cinemas, you signed chits; with your tailor you signed chits; even I remember in church, the salver came round with a little chit pad on it and you signed. Then at the end of the month or the next month a Chinese man called a "shroff", which is an Indian term for a cashier, would come round with your chits. Each restaurant or church had its own shroff and he would produce the chits, come up to you and say, "Master you pay something?" And you would look at them and look at the state of your bank account and say, "I'll pay those." And he would take the rest away and bring them next month.'5

Shanghai was a small Western enclave surrounded by a Chinese city which in turn was surrounded by a country which in the 1920s and 1930s was in political turmoil. The collapse of the Manchu dynasty in 1912 and the fragmenting over the next decade of the young republic into what were in effect so many private kingdoms each ruled by one time provincial governors, popularly known as war lords, caused Western Shanghai to be on its military mettle. Then in the late 1920s and early 1930s Chiang Kai Shek's march north from Canton in an attempt to reunify the country under the Kuomintang and his civil war with the communists posed a further threat to the city's stability; as did the Japanese invasion of Manchuria in 1931 and their seizing of Shanghai itself in 1937. The precarious nature of the political dispensation under which the West lived and traded with China and in Shanghai in particular was laid bare. In the city itself there was often considerable anti-foreign feeling. As a result of such civil disturbance and the wider political picture the British, American and the Japanese kept warships in the river off the Shanghai Bund, and to augment regular troops posted to the city when necessary there was the Shanghai Volunteer Corps which every able-bodied Briton was expected to join.

The Shanghai Volunteer Corps

'In the early days of the Shanghai settlement which was then mud flats, there was opposition and unpleasantness, shall I say, from Chinese and so it was necessary to form some organisation for protection. The Shanghai Volunteer Corps grew from this. I suppose in the old days it was more policing, but in the more recent time organised policing. We were armed and we were prepared to use our arms in case of need and during the troubles in 1924 when the Generals of Kiangsu province, in which Shanghai is situated, and Chekiang province next door to it, were each fighting for the possession of Shanghai we were mobilised to guard the settlement. The police also helped but we were required to guard the settlement and stop stragglers and looters from getting into the International Settlement. That took place partly on the boundaries of our own International Settlement.'[2]

Keeping the peace: A mounted detachment of the Shanghai Volunteers in the early 1930s. The Shanghai Light Horse were commonly called the Tight Horse.

Covering the
waterfront: Part of
the Bund at
Shanghai.

'We turned out on one evening a week and then on occasions we had
weekends when we went down to the range for firing. We had a camp down
at the range. And we had machine guns mounted in the cars, rifles and
revolvers, so we had quite a bit of firing, and we could get all the
ammunition we wanted.'

'The evening we turned out was really just a question of practising driving.
We'd go round the streets. The volunteers were very useful because we had a
lot of trouble. When I first got there there were Chinese generals and their
wars up north and also down south too, I've forgotten which general it was
but there were all these civil wars going on, and there was one lot who were
beaten and we were guarding the boundary and there was a bridge and we
had to open up the bridge for them to surrender, to let them come in.

'They came through and they laid down their arms, then we let them go
where they wanted. The area was called Chapei which was the Chinese kind
of city, and they obviously made straight for there.

'Then the next thing was May 1925 in Shanghai. I can't exactly remember
what happened but a whole lot of students started it all off, and all the
various units were mobilised. We were mobilised for about six weeks keeping
the peace, stopping the rioting, all that sort of stuff. And it was a bit of a job
because we had our own work to do for the office as well, so very often we
didn't get any sleep at all, what with doing our night duty and then going
straight to the office.

'We used to patrol round in the streets and I think that kept them quiet.
There was the Light Horse, known as the Tight Horse, which was the
mounted group. And then there were the ordinary rifle people – A Company
or B Company or whatever it was, and goodness knows what would have
happened if we hadn't been out in the streets.'[8]

Until the end of the 1930s, British life in Shanghai went on its annual round as it always had done. Horse racing and paper chases, dancing at the Majestic Hotel and the Little Club, lunch at the Shanghai Club and shopping in Bubbling Well Road, the king's birthday parade and, of course, the great annual balls.

On course: A China pony is led out at the Shanghai Race Club.

Almost off: The race course at Shanghai in the 1930s.

The Annual Balls

'The British and Irish communities of course had all their balls, the St Andrew's, St George's, St David's and St Patrick's balls. St Andrew's was the most popular because it was at the beginning of the winter season and we all did reels. They used to have three practice meetings at the old town before St Andrew's ball, so that we could all polish up our eightsomes and foursomes, and on the night of the ball they would have the chieftain and all the debs, the girls who were coming out into society were introduced. They used to have the pipers and before the dinner came they would march all round the floor, and the haggis would be paraded round. And St George's ball was the same sort of procedure, except that it was the roast beef of Old England, and the Beefeaters came round. On one occasion the Beefeater carrying the roast beef had to step on to the dance floor from the surrounding part and the roast beef which was made of rubber fell off and it went plomp, plomp, plomp, plomp all over the floor, and so he seriously walked all the way round with this empty platter and then somebody picked it up on the return journey and put it back. And there we used to do the Sir Roger de Coverley and all those sorts of dances, it was great fun.

'Shanghai *was* terribly romantic. Mind you we did good things as well, we weren't all play, the men worked like Trojans, but the night life was quite fantastic, and I think there must have been something about the air in Shanghai that meant we didn't need a lot of sleep.'[21]

Another China- Sugar Travelling in the Chinese Interior

With the notable exception of the Christian missionaries, few of the Europeans who lived and worked in China between the two world wars ever had a first hand opportunity to sample life in the villages and small towns in the interior of China. The 'Treaty Port System' and the supposed xenophobia of the Chinese – not to mention the language difficulties – tended to confine Europeans to the coastal cities and the string of ports along the Yangtze River, where the principle of extra-territoriality was at least observed, if not always honoured, by the Chinese. And then China's inherent political instability during this period did not encourage any but the most intrepid of travellers to journey out from the small citadels of Western civilisation into a countryside overrun, as it was generally believed, by the armies of rival 'war lords' locked in combat for the control of this or that province, and later the Civil War between the Nationalists and the Communists.

To be fair there were enormous difficulties with transport. Travel was far from easy apart from in Manchuria and the north of the country where, thanks to the Russians and latterly the Japanese after they had begun their conquest of that part of China in the 1930s, there was an adequate, if not altogether reliable, railway system.

However, one group of European men did travel extensively in the interior. They were the representatives of the major companies based in the Treaty Ports with business interests throughout China. And in the case of Butterfield & Swire it was the sugar trade that took them out of cities like Shanghai, Hankow and Tientsin into the countryside.

Butterfield & Swire had been refining sugar from Java and other sugar producing areas in the Far East since 1884 in their own refinery in Hong Kong. This sugar was then sold in China through a series of local agencies.

'We had Chinese agents throughout the country who were usually business men, or shopkeepers, in the various towns and the company had agreements with them and provided them with stocks of sugar to sell.'[3]

The Sugar Agents

These agents, who were often no more than the village grocer, were sent their stocks of sugar on consignment and only paid the company after they had sold it to their local customers. So the company employed a number of their juniors to travel round these agencies to protect their interests. Books had to be checked to ensure that the amounts of sugar sold corresponded with the sums of money that had been remitted to the company's nearest distribution point; stocks must be inspected, since until it was sold the sugar legally belonged to B & S; and prospects for increased sales investigated. It was a laborious business, but it did entitle these juniors to membership of that elite band of Westerners who were fortunate enough to see another China beyond the bright lights of Shanghai or the comfortable familiar routine of life in a small Yangtze river port.

These 'sugar travellers' as they were called, set out on their inspection journeys from either Tientsin in the north of the country, Hankow on the Yangtze River, or Shanghai. They took with them a cookboy to prepare their meals, and an interpreter.

Above. Summer sailing: The sugar traveller and his party of two shared this sampan in the summer months with a Chinese crew and five Chinese passengers in the waterways outside Shanghai.

Above right. Peking businessman: The B&S agent for Peking (centre).

'The only person who could converse in English was my interpreter. It was one of the finest and quickest ways of learning working colloquial Chinese that you could imagine because you learnt your Chinese with rhythm and in phrases and that is the only way to learn it quickly. It's useless trying to build your own sentences, you have to know *how* a thing is said. For example "It doesn't matter" sounds like "Bu yao gin". Well, I have no idea to this day what that particular word "gin" means, but I know "It doesn't matter" is "Bu yao gin" and I know that after months of questions and answers I quite quickly reached the stage where I could triangulate, and that I did not need to have an answer translated to me, but of course I could not ask the question or elaborate on the question. (It was really like being pitchforked into a French family who could not speak English. You had to learn from your own efforts.) You wanted to be sure that the interpreter had understood your question and was giving you a truthful answer. At any rate the sooner you reached the stage where he dared not do anything else the better.'[1]

Most sugar travellers elected to take their own European food with them on their journeys, and most certainly packed bottled drinking water.

Food on the Journey

'I took a lot of tinned food, pork and beans. And I think we even tried stewed lamb on one occasion in tins, but mainly it was soup, pork and beans, and bottles of water – not the aerated type but plain drinking water bottled. Watson's in Tientsin sold it under the name of Aquarius Water. My boy, the servant used to call it "querous". "Do you want some 'querous', master?" I eventually discovered that he meant this bottled water!

'On my travels I also carried bottles of iodine, aspirin and whisky for use in case of need. We had to take our own bread, or at least I took my own bread. Of course they don't eat our sort of bread in China, but in the north where they grow wheat they have a form of bread which they call mantoes, which is very stodgy stuff. My bread would be all right for the first few days, but as time went by it got harder and greener until we got back to the main port again. I didn't eat much Chinese food, but I did occasionally eat with Chinese though I wasn't very fond of it. I was always very doubtful of what I was getting.

'I remember once I'd been up on the Great Wall and then eventually on to Tangsham where I was in a Chinese inn for a night. And this servant of mine produced a steak, which was quite an unusual event, but it seemed edible. I ate it anyway and afterwards he said, "Did you like that steak?" And I said, "Yes, thank you very much, it was very nice, thank you." "Oh," he said, "it was very fresh; I got it from a cow that died only yesterday." He was very pleased with that but it was too late for me to be worried about it. It was just one of the things that happened in China.'[2]

The climate was less than kind to those travelling in the north of China; blazing hot summers gave way to achingly cold winters, which necessitated two completely different wardrobes.

Clothes

'I used to do a lot of walking so I had my riding breeches, canvas gaiters and boots, and warm woollies. And shirts and ties of course. And a jacket and a leather overcoat and leather gloves and a fur hat for the winter time. The kind of fur hat that comes down over your ears. In the summer time I wore shorts and a shirt, but I put on trousers and a jacket and tie when I called at the agencies. Otherwise one wasn't at all dressy.'[2]

The way in which the sugar traveller reached his agencies depended entirely on which part of China he was based in. If he was based in Shanghai or one of the river ports then more often than not he would travel in comparative luxury on one of the company's houseboats. It would have been a leisurely, even stately journey with abundant time to observe and enjoy the countryside. But there were days when it was necessary to leave the houseboat and travel overland to another craft on a different river, creek or lake. Then it was a case of hiring a type of sedan chair and literally being carried across country.

Sedan Chairs

'They were two-man chairs of light bamboo and the two bearers who carried one padded along at about three miles an hour. One of my interpreters was not a believer in athleticism and he just sat. I remember one day we did thirty-two miles. He rode all the way and I walked all the way, first of all to the great amusement and then to the gratification of my chair coolies because they were being paid to walk thirty-two miles instead of carrying one hundred and fifty pounds that distance, but that was how we moved – a cavalcade of three chairs, my interpreter, the boy and me. And of course in my chair was my camp bed.'[1]

'The length of each day's journey varied. The distances were rated in the Chinese linear measurement known as the li, and theoretically there were three li to one mile. A normal day's journey would vary from sixty li to one hundred and twenty. Actually the li varied in length according to the terrain, in other words it was really a unit of coolie power. A mile over very rocky terrain would be far more li than a mile on flat country.'[4]

The total length of time the sugar traveller was away from home depended upon whether he was based in Shanghai, or on the River Yangtze or in the north of China in Tientsin or Harbin.

Travelling by Rail

'The longest journey that I ever made lasted six weeks; the shortest about three. After my two trips in Shanghai I went up to Tientsin, and travelled for a year from there and the distances then were very considerable. Of course in that part of China you had railways to break the back of the mileage. You would get off at a railway town, and from there you would radiate out to various agents and depositories. I calculated the mileage I had covered during the two years, from Shanghai and in a small way from Tientsin for a year, and from Harbin for another year, as being something over thirty thousand miles.'[1]

The railways in the north of China certainly helped the sugar traveller to cover greater distances than were possible elsewhere in the country. They were, for the most part, a legacy from China's drive to modernise itself at the end of the nineteenth and beginning of the twentieth centuries, when huge sums of money had been raised to finance the laying of track and the acquisition of rolling stock

and engines. In the case of the Chinese Eastern Railway, which ran through
Harbin, the Russians had not only financed it as an extension of their Trans-
Siberian route, but actually provided the personnel to run it in the hope of
extending their political influence over the Chinese. Little had really changed since
the revolution of 1917, and although Soviet Russia had returned the railway to the
Chinese, Harbin in the 1920s was in all but name a Russian town, made up of
Russian exiles.

However, by the 1920s the efficiency of the whole railway system was being
threatened by the political instability in that part of China. The collapse of the
Manchu dynasty, the failure of the Republic to establish its authority and the
fragmentation of power amongst various war lords, who were quick to see the
strategic significance of the railways, made train travel a chancy business for the
sugar traveller.

'The railways in China were quite good but they had been allowed to run
down in the anarchy that prevailed in the '20s, and they were mostly under
military control so that travelling was quite difficult.

'Essentially there was very good rolling stock, but most of the trains and
all of the carriages were crammed full of soldiers, and the roofs of carriages
were crammed too. So it was quite impossible to get into them, and the
alternative, which I usually adopted, was to get into a freight truck and sit on
top of bags of beans, which was at least in the fresh air, but could be damn
cold in the winter, bitterly cold in fact. Of course there was no kind of
schedule. If one wanted to get from A to B in Hunan in 1925, you could not
find out when the train was due. You just went to the station and joined the
general bivouac, which might be for one hour, half a day or a whole day.
You had to be there when the train came. (There was usually a train at least

once in twenty-four hours.) Then there was a scramble for the best places on the roofs of the carriages because there was no room inside.'[4]

As one B & S traveller recalls, journeys from Tientsin to Shansi Province were long and involved frequent changes of train.

'I used to take the train and travel first class up to Peking where we'd always spend a night. I had to travel under what they called a Hu Chao, in other words a passport, which was a piece of paper written in Chinese and stamped, or chopped, by the local magistrate or whoever it was, saying who I was, where I was going, and why. I would spend, say, a night in Peking at the Grand Hôtel des Wagon-Lits, which was a first class hotel and then next morning my interpreter and a boy and I would meet at the railway station in Peking and go down the line to, say, Shihkiachuang. I had a first class carriage and sleeper and the interpreter and the boy were together in the second class. Shihkiachuang was the junction for Shansi Province and as I was going up to Taiyuan in this case, we had to spend a night in Shihkiachuang and get the early morning narrow gauge line train from there up to Taiyuan. That took a whole day.

'This was one of my better trips and it was interesting going through Shansi to watch the people working on the hills and digging out coal alongside the railway line – good-looking coal too – among the growing crops. On arriving in Taiyuan I stayed in a European type hotel, which I was very pleased to find as I'd done a lot of trips without that sort of thing at the end of them. But it didn't have any European food, the flushes didn't work, nor did the wash basins!

'I would do my inspection there at the agency, make other visits and then get ready for the return journey. I remember on one return journey to Peking we had difficulties at Shihkiachuang because of Chiang Kai Shek and his troops, who were working their way up from Hankow on the Yangtze. We got to Shihkiachuang to get a train on a Monday evening back to Peking, but there wasn't any train. We'd have to wait. By Friday, I think it was, the great news came that there might be a train coming in that evening, so we got packed up and it did come that evening. We got down to the situation, a cloud of steam approached and it was an engine with some coaches behind it, but they were all third class, with hard seats and no glass in the windows. Remember this was late November or early December so it was getting very cold indeed. Now normally a train would have got back to Peking overnight or at least within twenty-four hours, but our train could only just struggle along and the poor engine was absolutely worked out. We stopped at every station, and as we had no food left, no tinned stuff that is, we bought ground nuts and what they called 'varnished ducks' from hawkers who were selling the stuff on the station platforms. (Varnished ducks are squashed ducks which had been cooked and varnished to preserve them. They were quite tasty.) So we all sat together in these trains, getting colder and colder and colder until finally we got to Peking.'[2]

Not all the towns and villages where the company had their sugar agencies could be reached by train. In that case the traveller took the railway to the nearest station and made his way into the country as best he could, often running the risk of unfortunate encounters with the local banditry. The most common form of transport in the northern part of China was a vehicle called a Peking cart.

Stately progress: A Peking cart.

'A Peking cart was a two-wheeled unsprung cart with a canopy covering of blue cloth and it was drawn by a mule that had seen a pretty long and hard life. It hurt me to see them with sores on their backs and I used to remonstrate with the wretched muleteers, but, of course, they're very callous about animals and they just laughed it off. So I used to walk most of the way rather than ride, although occasionally I did ride on the shafts of these Peking carts. Our baggage was in the carts.

'Peking Carts'

'We visited a number of agencies along the route and I remember that on one occasion it had begun to snow. We came to a village where we were to do an inspection and it had snowed all day, which was very unpleasant. We got into the agency and they were very surprised to see us; they had heard we were en route but they didn't think we'd come. But we said, "It's only snow so we've come!" The agent then said, "It's not only the snow, but there are bandits around just outside the town and nobody's travelling now!"

'Anyway the next day we did our normal inspection but we didn't go round the town too much. And all day we thought about our position. Clearly we couldn't stay there so we said, "Though it's very bad weather and the country is absolutely snow covered, we think we might escape the bandits because they have moved close by the hills. They know that any movement on their part in the snow might give them away." And the Chinese agent agreed with us. He'd seen them there and he said "Yes, there's nothing else to do." So off we went next morning with our Peking cart and our luggage and trudged through this snow. We carried on and we did a number of inspections on the way and finally got back to Tientsin where they were quite glad to see us.'[2]

Peking carts were just one of the ways that the sugar traveller made his way round the parts of China that the railway did not reach. There was also a kind of passenger-carrying wheelbarrow.

'They were rather like an Irish jaunting car but with seats suspended over one wheel. You could sit on either side. Your baggage would be on one side and you would sit on the other side of the wheel, which would be about three feet in diameter. And no wheelbarrow in China was any good unless it had a built-in squeak; and so when you travelled on the wheelbarrow, you were accompanied by this horrible scraping and screeching of the wooden wheel on its axle! It was propelled by a man who held the two shafts in his hands with a strap attached to the shafts round his neck over his shoulders, and he waddled along the narrow footpath and he'd probably been eating garlic, because they all eat garlic these rickshaw pullers and wheelbarrow pushers. And by Jove they reeked of garlic – oh it was dreadful!

'I also had to take a mule litter, with one mule in front of your litter and another behind. The shafts of course rested on the harness on either side of the two mules. It was quite comfortable in a way, but the mule in front was always lifting its tail and polluting the atmosphere and the one behind had nothing to do but nibble your hair or your hat!'[2]

Only on the rarest occasions was the sugar traveller fortunate enough to be able to hire a motor car. Suitable paved roads scarcely existed in the interior of China at this time, and what few cars there were had generally been commandeered by the military.

'On one trip I really hadn't the time to go off by cart or by foot and I wanted a car. Well there were about seven or eight Model T Fords to be had in Taiyuan and we could get one provided it was released by the military governor of that rather splendid walled city. His name was Kao, and I well remember him. So I went to ask if I could be permitted to hire a car for the day. He was a grave and dignified youngish man with the insignia of a lieutenant general. I was satisfied that my young interpreter's presentation of my careful phraseology and the respect in my manner gave us a fair chance of success, but, after a long interchange, Kao turned me down, and he was courteous enough to explain why, in Chinese that I could follow. As I walked away from the Yamen, to my amazement I met a foreigner (all Europeans were so called). I told this Dr Livingstone, who belonged to a mission just outside the town, about my fruitless visit to the Yamen. "Didn't you find Kao Fu Kwan charming?" he asked. I said I supposed so but for me there was the language barrier. "Heavens," Dr Livingstone said, "Kao speaks English as well as you do. He wasn't three years at Cambridge for nothing." I have often thought about that incident. I suppose really that Kao's thought was "I'm a Chinese in a position of authority and I am going to behave like one. And if, though off his guard, this man behaves like an Englishman asking for a favour from a senior Chinese official, I will speak him fair, but it is beneath my dignity to speak his language and it is not proper that he should expect me to."'[1]

Generally the sugar traveller had little or no direct contact with China's provincial military governors. But the evidence of these war lords struggles for power was there for all to see.

'I really only came across warlordism in central and northern China. There the armies were really regarded as locusts. If Chang Tso Lin, for example, was making a move into Wu Pei Fu's territory, his soldiers commandeered the carts and the rolling stock, fed off the country and passed on, and life resumed its normal pattern. The people themselves did not care a hoot who won what; it did not make the slightest difference to the average peasant; it was simply that these raggedy-ass armies were straggling about in meaningless bloodless manoeuvres.

'There were no real fights, or if there were they were conducted in a very civilised manner. If it was known that the other side had twenty thousand men marching to a place where you had five thousand men, you just moved off. Your movement was an awful nuisance to the locality though, and it was hoped that when the next wave broke through it would not break on the same shore, but would roll on to somebody else's. It was the presence of hordes of people living off the land that affected the life of the peasant, and if they were not there, his life was unaffected.'[1]

'I only really began to take an interest in China's politics when I felt the effects of her warlordism. Its effects had a real impact on my affairs, because when one travelled and planned one's journey up-country one had to make quite sure that it was not into bandit country. You see a military provincial governor, the war lord, the tuchun, would control reasonably well a fairly wide area, but between his sphere and the next chap's there would be a no-man's land which was bandit country and you could be kidnapped. My predecessor as sugar traveller at Hankow was in fact kidnapped on one of his trips up the Han river, but he got away all right. But it became necessary to know what to do, to keep one's ear to the ground to learn how military politics were working, who was in charge where and whether there was a war brewing and so on.'[4]

'I remember getting mixed up with Chinese soldiers in southern Shantung at a place called Tsining. I arrived there one afternoon and I noticed all these mounted troops. They were dismounted then with their ponies tied up in the street, as they were cooking or resting. They looked nice sort of chaps, so I walked up the street after I'd got settled down and had a chat with them and they were all quite cheerful. I patted a pony and said it was a nice looking animal and asked this soldier if he liked horses. "Yes," he said. And he went on, "And do you ride?" "Oh yes, yes," I said. And he gave me a leg up on to the bare back of a chubby little pony. And as it was unsaddled and had no bridle (just a rope off the pony), I thought I'd simply sit on it and see what it was like. But then this chap, who had a belt in his hand, give it a whack across the backside and off we went down the street. And when we got to the other end, I got the animal turned round and somebody else gave it a belting and we got back again. They were tickled to death, and fortunately I was still in one piece on the pony. And they all shouted "Ting hao – ting hao" which means "Very good – very good."'[2]

Once the traveller had arrived at his destination he made his way to the B & S agent's shop to begin his inspection.

'It was well known that you were coming, the bamboo wireless would have taken care of that. So the agent would be ready for you, and you would walk along to his shop, which was usually one of the principal shops in the village (we would call it a grocer's shop) where they sold sugar, tea, medicaments, cigarettes, general stores, kerosene and so on. The agent would be waiting for you and you would then go through the motions of checking the stocks in his godown (warehouse), checking his returns and remittances, seeing that he was up to date, if necessary urging him to do better in the way of keeping his remittances up to date. You might have some suggestion to make as to how he could improve the storage of his sugar, which was still your property until he had sold it, and then you would probably go back to his little room behind his shop and with his assistant, usually another member of the family, you would discuss the past and present and the future; decide on whether he was getting enough or too much in the way of stocks of sugar; whether it was lying there too long for the volume of sales he was doing; and talk about the competition that was provided mostly by big Chinese importers in the main ports.

'You were there to check up, to see that they were honestly administering the stocks the company had put there. Often you encountered delay in reporting the sale of goods until the inspection was due, and there would then be some remarkable sales in the last week or so before you arrived, all of which would be accounted for and due remittances made. I am quite certain that no Chinese would consider this in the least dishonest. They delayed recording and remitting until there was occasion to force them to do so. Just as practically all debts in China are settled at the Chinese New Year and you are not really supposed to badger anybody very much until then, so the agent's books were cleared when the next inspection was due.'[1]

'One trick that one had to be on the look out for was what we called "hollow stacking". A man might have a consignment of say a thousand bags of sugar (they were straw mat bags of about eight pounds each) which he'd stacked neatly and as you were looking at a stack you'd see all the bags very nicely stacked all the way round and easy to count. But you couldn't take the stack at face value, you had to climb up to the top of it to see that the middle was full of bags of sugar and it wasn't hollow, because we'd been caught once like that quite seriously.'[2]

'Then you would always be invited to a feast in the evening. You would go along to that, and they varied enormously. One I remember had seventeen courses all of water-originating food – water chestnuts, fish of various kinds, duck and so forth (this was in the north of China). And I remember it was my first experience of eating not with ordinary chopsticks, but with ebony chopsticks with pointed silver tips and that did test my skill very considerably. That feast lasted I think for three hours, and it was an experience which I was glad to have had but was never again anxious to repeat.

'However at the other end of the scale it might be a simple four-course meal with rice, vegetables, pickles, a little dried fish perhaps, and the local wine, with which you were plied very vigorously. It behoved one to have some appreciation of its relative strength compared with the other districts or villages you had known, because the fatal thing to do was to have too much. You fell in their esteem if you did, because the Chinese are not a drinking race; the ordinary person never drinks at all except at a feast.

'One curious thing was that they would sometimes hire professional drinkers for these feasts when Westerners were entertained. The agents were prepared for harder drinkers than they themselves had any intention of being so they'd get a "professional entertainer and drinker"! And really they were quite astonishing some of them. There was one I knew who was reputed to be able to drink three bottles of raw brandy without being incapacitated! But one learned very quickly who was the person deputed to ply you and you treated his advances with appropriate caution.

'One of my interpreters was rather clever. He arranged that his heavy drinking of a pale yellow coloured "wine" should consist in fact of tea. This was considered rather a dirty trick but I did not give him away. I often wished that instead of repeated refusals I could have had some similar substance or subterfuge, but on the whole anyone who gives you a picture of a Chinese feast as a drunken orgy is quite wrong. It was, above all, social and conversational and there were long pauses between the courses. They brought one on at a time, you would eat it to destruction, or semi-destruction, or until it got cold, then there would be a pause and shift around. There'd be chat and then another course would be brought on and you would apply your chopsticks to it. It would go on for two hours or more. They were not set pieces in the way that our feasts are. The population of the table was always changing (the ideal number was nine) and people could move about, particularly if they were connected in any way to the host.'[1]

And once the feast was over, if he had been lucky enough to be entertained by the agent, the sugar traveller would retire to the village inn for a night's rest before resuming his journey the next day.

'The inn would consist of a courtyard, a number of rooms, kitchen, a frightful lavatory and a tremendous hubbub of people coming and going. I imagine it was rather like an inn in Dickens' day in England as far as the constant turmoil was concerned: the uproar when people are loading up, everybody shouting at once. It amazed me that anything got done, but it did. There was always a lot of noise and it could be very cold and very primitive, but quite genial. The thing that struck one in China as a whole was the amiability of the Chinese and the way they would always be smiling and joking.'[4]

'The inns that I lived in were very close to nature, and the sanitation was always a nasty problem to be dealt with. As far as possible one used the fields, as the sanitation in the village inns and in the agencies was nil; or if there was anything, it was horrible even to think about. If it was a good class of Chinese inn, it would have quite a pleasant appearance on the outside. The windows didn't have glass, they had frames which were covered with paper. You went inside into a big room and there would probably be a table and a few chairs and not much in the way of drink or food displayed. The rooms were mainly for sleeping. The food was cooked away outside somewhere. It was just sleeping accommodation, either on the floor or on a "kang". (A kang is a raised platform made of mud and supported with bricks.) Sometimes there'd be a musty bed. It wasn't that the room was unpleasant, just the outsides. I mentioned the paper windows: now when a foreigner came in to live in a place and stay the night then the village children would all come round and poke holes in the paper windows to have a look at the foreigner, at the "Yang Kweitze", the foreign devil. They expected you to have red hair and a bright nose. Of course the broken paper windows would also let the draught in and in the cold weather I can remember staying in some of these places with sleep impossible it was so cold.'[2]

Five stars: A comparatively luxurious Chinese inn.

Two stars: The courtyard of a simple country inn.

'I remember on a trip that I made once between the Yangtze and the Tsientang River that in the inn I stayed at I was told that I was the second foreigner they had seen in two years. So you didn't expect anything elaborate and didn't get it. But the nice thing was the friendliness that you met. Provided you showed that you were appreciative of the fact that you were among a superior people, and behaved with reasonably decent manners and willingness to learn, you got a very friendly reception.

'The coolies who had brought my baggage over the hills and my chair (though I didn't use it; being young and active I walked) invited me to join them for a cup of tea, when they gathered in the centre of the yard round the kettle, which I did. It was delightful to encounter a friendly egalitarianism; their attitude seemed to be, "Here's a young chap who's obviously trying to get what advantage he can from living and moving in a civilised country, and he's even trying to learn the language and is therefore deserving of encouragement." They corrected in a villainous dialect my efforts to communicate with them and we had a splendid time.

'When I went to bed that night and was having my supper, noses kept on being pressed against the paper window until finally I went outside and said, "Have a good look in here once and for all." There were about six people, including, I gathered, the village schoolmaster. And he said, "We've never seen a foreigner before, do you mind if we do?" I said, "Certainly not." So the schoolmaster came in, looked at my socks and shoes and asked me what they were made off. I was able to tell him and we had other simple exchanges, until he ended up by saying, "Thank you very much indeed; that's been the most interesting experience for me." And they all faded away into the night.

'I remember one inn up near the Black River in Manchuria. Here I was put into a room – I usually took a camp bed with me by the way – with seventeen cart drivers. And I, having been charged the highest fee, was put nearest to the cast-iron stove, and therefore it was extremely hot and of my seventeen colleagues in the room no less that sixteen (I counted carefully) had several good-night pipes of opium, so the atmosphere was fairly thick. But one was grateful for it because the temperature outside that night was minus forty, which almost meant that if you spat out of a first floor window, it splintered.

'That was the real China and I am extremely lucky to have had an opportunity to have seen what it was like inside. The attitude of the people depended largely on one's own attitude. If you had not acquired a respect for the atmosphere and character of the people you would not get very far with them, but if they felt that you were not looking down on them because of your material circumstances or your Western background, they met you more than halfway. You learnt a great deal more from them and you found that your respect was justified. They were simple people but their character was admirable in many respects – very human. There was no hostility.

'The comfortable thing about moving about in the real deep China, whether it was the centre, the north, the west (I did not know much about the south), was that you were moving among people who had from top to bottom a superiority complex as far as you were concerned; and that is an extremely restful thing to experience if you can respond to it. The horrible thing is when you are living in an inferiority complex atmosphere, for that breeds aggression and touchiness, which is difficult.'[1]

But before returning to his destination the sugar traveller had an unrivalled opportunity to take a close look at Chinese village life, a life that can scarcely have changed in any significant respect over the centuries.

Village Life

'If I had to make a point of reference as to what a Chinese village was like, I think the thirteenth century in England would be a fair comparison. Those towns with their open drains and ramshackle buildings of wood and mud. I think you would find in a poor medieval village, say in the north of England, the same clannishness, intermarriage and community spirit as I saw in China. And the standard of life would be very similar. Everything required – leather goods, cloth, carts and things of that sort – would be locally made. It was really thirteenth century Europe as regards standards of living and way of life transplanted into the twentieth century.

'What one really noticed was the closeness of the community: they were clans almost, and transport was so difficult and rare that there was a great deal of intermarriage. In a village of five hundred people few if any would have travelled further than ten or twenty miles away; there was an enormous sense of family and locality. There were of course terrible quarrels within it, and nothing can be worse than a family dispute, but they were all like with like. And by the way do not let anyone talk about the inscrutable Chinese. If they were to see an ordinary village discussion over a short weight in cabbage, or encroachment on another person's field, they would get an exhibition of hysterical histrionics that could not be rivalled in melodrama in any age. They are quite an emotional and theatrical race, in fact, and I suppose their reputation for inscrutability is because of their determination not to let themselves down in public. They will bear pain if necessary. They will bear almost anything without making a fuss because they are not going to show that you have succeeded in making them lose their balance. I think that is really the most important thing about their much talked of "face"; it is really their manifestation of self-respect.

'One noticed the most utter poverty, but on the other hand there was contentment, with little sense of peasantry revolting against the hardness of their lot and the wickedness of the landowners. A philosophical pragmatism seemed to be pervasive, but laughter was common. Again this inscrutable story is quite false: they laughed easily at very much the same sort of things we would laugh at. I believe that elsewhere in the Orient most laughter is provoked by sort of slapstick incidents. In China many more of what we regard as genuinely humorous incidents were met with appreciative laughter and cheerfulness; their sense of fun and sense of laughter was very much more in sympathy with ours, compared with other races of totally different character.

The Travelling Theatre

'One particular diversion I noticed was the travelling theatre. The Chinese villagers loved intimate rural theatre. It rather corresponded to the English fete. Once a year, or whenever the occasion offered and funds seemed to be available, they would hire an itinerant company of players. They were very crude and always played classical operas. Most of the people knew the action by heart and the language was unintelligible to them. But it really was the occasion for focusing on your village all your neighbours from villages nearby. Generally, people did not travel great distances, but they did make a point of turning up for these shows and the performance almost ruined the villagers who'd sponsored it. They needed a rest of at least a year or two, because they were supposed to entertain everybody, all their friends and relatives who could crowd into the village, and they had to pay heavily for the theatre, but it was their big annual, or bi-annual event. In fact it was quite a common penalty to impose on somebody who had incurred a debt to society somehow: his fine would consist of reconciling the parties whom he had wronged, and he would be penalised by having to bring and pay for a theatrical performance. But as I say, the analogy really is a rural fete or horticultural show: it was a temporary blazing into glory of a small star pulling in the satellites.'[1]

Making a
Home from Home

Generally, British women found themselves in China between the two world wars because their parents or their husbands were in the East. As, say, in India or Malaya women were supporters, consorts and were denied a significant voice in British rule or British business. True, in Shanghai a great many earned a living for themselves, but it was in occupations traditionally reserved for women. They could be secretaries or teachers or nurses, not taipans, consuls or customs officials. How could it be otherwise when even at home in Britain so few women had broken into the charmed circle of jobs that were preserved exclusively for men? The one exception to this general rule were, of course, the missionaries. In this field women did work alongside men almost as equals, but then the Christian missions to China were in the interior far removed from the treaty ports along the Yangtze River.

Yet the women who did come to China possible enjoyed a greater degree of personal freedom than their fellow wives and daughters elsewhere in the British Empire proper. The absence of formal imperial rule with its civil and military administration made for a more flexible way of life. The window on to the modern age may not have been thrown open wide, but at least for women in China the curtains had been drawn to one side. Protocol of the 'who should sit next to whom at dinner' kind was a great deal less onerous in Shanghai than in Calcutta or Singapore. There were no Burra Memsahibs to instil a fear of God and duty to Empire in the wife fresh out from England. And since neither the Americans nor the European trading powers sought to rule China, there was no automatic obligation on men or women to set a good example to the ruled.

In fact the cosmopolitan nature of even the smallest of communities in a treaty port where Britons rubbed shoulders with Germans, Italians, Scandinavians, Americans and Frenchmen made for a much freer way of life. If India in the 1920s and early 1930s was aggressively Edwardian, then the International Settlement in Shanghai and the foreign concessions in Hankow or Chungking had at least shaken hands with the twentieth century.

Nonetheless, in common with other British communities abroad in this period, whether under the Imperial dispensation or not, there were subtle distinctions of rank and class. For example there were the 'Shanghai girls', a closely knit group of women whose shared childhood and adolescence in Shanghai, often including an education on the China coast, marked them out as different from the young women who came out East in search of adventure or husbands.

And there were plenty of potential husbands. Every one of the large British companies in China – hongs – trading companies such as B & S or Jardine Matheson, or the Hong Kong and Shanghai Banking Corporation or the Asiatic Petroleum Company or British American Tobacco – had a staff of young and not-so-young bachelors who it was assumed when well on their way to acquiring a good fortune would be ready to embark on matrimony.

But bachelors and their prospective brides were compelled to wait, for every British company had its 'marriage rules' which were written into a young man's contract of employment.

'To begin with a B & S man had to do three years out East before he was allowed to marry, then he had to be up to a certain standard in salary, and there were cases, I believe, where the girls were even interviewed to see if they were going to be suitable.

'My husband did his five years and then he came home on leave in 1929, but unfortunately there'd been a great slump in trade at that time in the twenties and he was still not up to the "marriage salary", so he mentioned it to the London office who said, "You're not up to the salary at the moment." And my husband-to-be said, "I hope to be shortly." And they said, "If she's a good girl and if she's waited for you for five years she'll wait for you a bit longer!"'[11]

'I think in principle it was probably quite wise. I think that there are certain things that have slackened nowadays and attitudes are entirely different. For instance then, if a young man went out to Shanghai or Hankow or any of these outports and proposed marrying a Chinese, it would have been very much frowned upon. In fact, I would say that unless he was a very outstanding man that would be it, he would have to resign, although today such a marriage would be quite acceptable.

'That was one of the reasons I would imagine for the "marriage rules". The other thing, of course, was that they didn't want young men to marry unless they could afford to, and basically you couldn't afford to keep a wife until after your first five year spell. So in a way it was quite sensible. However in those days there were certain companies who were very unfair in my view. Their staff were not allowed to marry until they had served ten years out there. These companies made young men do three to five years in the London office first and then they went abroad and they were not allowed to marry for ten years. Quite absurd.'[15]

A great many girls went East at the invitation of their brothers. The trip may have been called a holiday, but most people at home or indeed on the China coast knew that far more could be at stake than a long sea voyage on say a Blue Funnel or a P & O liner and six months relaxation in Hong Kong or Shanghai.

'Young girls going East were referred to as the "fishing fleet". Any girl who went out East was in the fishing fleet because it was said she was hoping to catch a husband. Before I went East I was living at a women's club in

London and when I told them I was going out to Hong Kong to stay with my brother they said, "Oh good luck. You're going out there because you can't catch anybody here."

'I just said to them, "Yes absolutely right; don't you wish you had the chance?" And it's extraordinary, they all fell silent. Nobody went on after that.

'On the ship on the way out there were some young men going back from leave and I hadn't been spoilt in London. I hadn't been taken out night after night. If I was taken to dinner and dances it was quite an event. But on this ship I was told, "You just stay as you are. My God don't you change." When they said to me, "Come and have a drink before dinner," I said, "That'll be lovely, thank you." And I had a drink and said thank you. They said, "You're going to be a sensation." I couldn't believe it. I said, "Don't be ridiculous, what do you mean?" "In Hong Kong if we ring up a girl and say, 'Will you come to dinner next week?' she says, 'I'll get my book, I haven't got a free evening for six weeks.'" And that was apparently absolutely true. If you just said that you'd love to come tomorrow, in no time at all you'd be booked up for six weeks.'[12]

And when the holiday was over, or when it was time for a brother to come home, it was time for a sister too to pack her cabin trunk. In the late 1920s young women were carefully chaperoned; they were not to be left on their own.

'My brother said I'd got to go home with him, but the older married women said, "She's only just come and she's having the time of her life. You can't take her home." And he said, "She can stay for three months but she'll have to get a job. There's no place in Hong Kong for an unmarried woman on her own." That wasn't so easy because I was really untrained. I had a job in London but that wasn't a good job. Anyway before my brother left I went on with my life of tennis parties and so on and any time I went out the older married women were charming. Every time they took me to a dance, in a party, or I went to dinner or something, I always left that party with another invitation in my pocket. So it was like a rolling barrel. At one particular tennis party I went to, some woman said, "What are you doing here?" And I said, "I came to stay a year with my brother but he's going home on leave and I've got to go home." She said, "You can't do that." I said, "I shall have to unless I get a job, and I don't think I can get a job." And she said, "Oh Dennis," or some other name and sort of waved her hand at her husband who was headmaster of a mission school. "Meet Miss Mitchell," she said, "George Mitchell's sister. He's got her out here and now he's going home, the dirty dog. You want someone to teach English don't you?" And he said, 'Yes I do, but I'm going to play this set." And he just looked at me and said, "Come and see me tomorrow, ten o'clock." So I went back to my hotel because by this time George had gone and I was living in the Peak Hotel and there were one or two very nice women there, who were older than I was. I said to one of them, "I'm going to teach English; I don't know, I'm not a teacher, and I don't know anything about teaching English, what do I do?" One of them said, "That'll be all right, you just ask him if they use the Montessori or the Fröbel system." I said, "What's the Montessori or Fröbel?" "It's a sort of system and they use the same books all round the world. But you don't need to bother about the systems, you'll be all right if you ask the question." So I did exactly what I was told. And the headmaster said, "If you know about Montessori and Fröbel you start tomorrow morning." I said, "What do you want me to do?" "I want you to teach them how to recite *How Horatius Kept the Bridge*." "Oh my goodness, I learnt that at school, I know all about that. '*Lars Porsena of Clusium, by the nine gods he swore . . . .*' but where was Clusium and who was Lars Porsena?" "I didn't expect you to know that. You come tomorrow and I'll put all the questions they're likely to ask you on a bit of paper." And I taught them very good English. I taught them to speak properly and behave properly, and when they opened their desks to look at pictures of naked ladies I said, "You can take that book outside but you're not going to stay in my class." And they said, "I'm very sorry, Miss Mitchell, I do not want to waste my father's money, I will pay attention."[12]

Of course not all the young women who made the journey East were in pursuit of a husband. Some had already acquired a fiancé when a young man had come back to Britain on his first leave. If they were fortunate it was a short engagement and then they were sent for. But for the waiting young man his fiancée's journey to China was not without its dangers. Shipboard romances blossomed and a number of girls never reached their final destinations, having succumbed to the promise of married bliss nearer home than Hong Kong or the China coast. If your fiancée did arrive there was every reason to marry her as soon as possible.

Brides

'In those days the bride arrived today and was married tomorrow; it was an unwritten law. I found out when I was much older why it was. It was because her husband had paid her fare out and didn't want her pinched. Any man who sent a fare to a girl to come out married her as soon as she set foot on the shore.'[12]

Shanghai brides if they were Anglican would be married in the Anglican Cathedral. If they had come out from England it was unlikely that their father or a

Wedding belles: A Shanghai wedding in the 1930s.

member or a close friend of the family would be at hand to give them away, so that honour fell to one of the groom's friends or possibly a senior member of his company. In marrying a man on the China coast, the bride acquired not just a husband but a ready made circle of friends, none of whom she would have known when she set sail from England. The bride who had grown up in Shanghai as a 'Shanghai girl' was perhaps more fortunate: on the wedding day, like any other bride, she would be surrounded by her friends and some of her family.

Once they were married the young couple set about making a home of their own. But of course it was not really their own. In Shanghai they might have rented a furnished flat, elsewhere in China they could take over a house from a couple who were about to return to Britain for a long leave, or if the husband was relatively senior in B & S and was posted as the company's agent to a port along the River Yangtze or up the coast they would be moving into a company house. And the furnished flat, temporary house or company property came with a full complement of domestic servants.

'They were always inherited I would say; whenever you arrived there, they were there. But you weren't obliged to keep them, but I would say, thinking back on it, and remembering all the various places that we stayed in, that I think we only once ever sacked anyone. They were always a good type of servant and in a sense loyal to the company they were working for and therefore they fitted in with your life. They accepted the fact that you might do things slightly differently to the people before you. I think it was a very happy arrangement.

'If you had to find a replacement you would always try to get one of the servants in the house to suggest and recommend someone. Because otherwise if you brought a complete outsider in it might upset the rest of your staff.'[15]

The head servant was called a 'boy' even though he might be twice the age of his employer. After him the most important servant would be the 'amah', who when you had children acted as nanny to them.

'It depended how wealthy you were, but normally you had a number one boy, a cook and a coolie, and an amah. If you had no children, she was the wash amah, or if you had children she looked after children as well.'[21]

'The number one boy was very much the tops, he really organised the whole thing. He ran the house, and you gave instructions to the other servants through him. If there were new servants to be engaged he engaged them – they were quite often relatives or friends of his because that is part of the Chinese life. Nepotism was very strong, but on the other hand he had to see that they did their work because it reflected back on him if they didn't. Nevertheless, you often had, in a large staff, two sections. You had the amah ruling one section and the boy the other, and this was understood and they didn't encroach.

'The amah in charge of the nursery would be the head amah; the wash amah would be under her, although they didn't do each other's work, but quite often she would engage another amah if need be, rather than the boy.'[13]

Serving: Chinese
servants. The boy
wears a white coat.
Amah stands to his
right.

Waiting: A Chinese
boy and coolie.

The boy – 'number one boy' if there was more than one boy – opened the door
to guests, waited on table and was responsible for overseeing all the other servants.

'The boy would be in charge of seeing that you had a good cook. The
cook was a man on his own but instructions about meals and menus went
through the boy. Occasionally if the cook wanted to talk about the difficulties
of certain menus or food he would come in with the boy, and the boy would
probably have to translate. Sometimes the cook could speak very good
English, but not often.'[13]

It was unlikely that any of the servants would speak fluent English; and few women had the opportunity of learning any Chinese. For one thing there were a huge number of Chinese dialects and the wife who had just mastered enough of the local language to make herself understood to the servants in Swatow might, in the case of B & S, find that her husband was suddenly transferred to Canton where the dialect was Cantonese and nobody could understand her Swatonese. It was to deal with this particular difficulty that 'pidgin English' had come into being, 'pidgin' being a corruption of the way in which the Chinese pronounced the English word 'business'. 'Pidgin English' was the lingua franca of the British in China.

'It's an awfully difficult thing to explain. You seem to add double E on to all the words. If I questioned something that the amah said that I didn't think was quite right she would say, "I talkee true, missee, I talkee true."'[13]

'Pidgin English'

Chinese cooks cooked European food for the Western missy, and if they were unfamiliar with a particular dish then the housewife would teach them to make it. They were masters of improvisation.

Giving Parties

'The cook and the other servants were very good at doing things on the spur of the moment. To give one example, snipe was to be one of the courses at a dinner party given by friends of mine, and suprise surprise an unexpected guest arrived and there was one snipe too few. So the missy went out to the kitchen and had a little conversation with the cook, and he said, "Never mind, missee, I can fix." And what he did was, to get a potato and model a snipe out of it and then make it all brown. Then when he was serving it, he saw that the hostess had the potato which wasn't a real snipe, but nobody else knew anything about it.

'They didn't let you down, and they loved giving parties, because it gave them scope. For instance, when they did the table napkins up they would fold them into a lovely water lily shape, or a fan, or a boat. And they dressed up the food. If you had pheasant, they'd get some tissue paper and make it into a little napkin ring, snip it around the edge and slip it on the end of the legs, so it looked nice. Or if you had brandy butter for the Christmas pudding it was usually moulded into the most beautiful flower or a goddess or something. The presentation was always absolutely super. They took great pride in it.

'There was a particular cook who was very good at icing cakes and a very good cake maker. A friend of mine had a lunch party and a beautiful gateau came on, beautifully decorated, and all the guests said "Do tell the cook to come in so we can tell him how lovely this is and ask how he made it." I might say that previously our hostess had gone into Whiteways (in Shanghai) and bought a whole set of icing shapes, and a bag, because the cook was so good at icing cakes. So when he came in she said, "Cook, all missees think your cake very good, can you tell them how you made it?" And he was very flattered and he said, "Yes." And then she said, "And I suppose when you iced it you used that thing I got you from Whiteways." "Oh," he said, "no missee, I not use that, I used one old tooth brush." And when he saw the look of horror on their faces he went on, "Oh missee, not master's tooth brush, one old tooth brush of mine."'[21]

'If you said, "Come back for 'pot luck' with us," it meant that your servants had to have a little warning and they made another course. They were aces at turning something out. If you'd got two fillets of fish and you brought another person in to eat, they didn't complain at all. They'd say, "Oh yes, five minutes. Can do." And they got a very sharp knife and they took a sliver off the tail of one fillet and a sliver off the head of another and stuck them together with white of egg and then you'd got three fillets. It was the same if you'd got two thick chops. If you took a little bit off each, and stuck them together with white of egg, when they were under the grill they stuck together.'[12]

At table: Eating. The boy waits table.

'We were in Changsha up on the Yangtze River and it being St Andrew's day we were going to have a haggis but it was a problem to get it there. So we decided that we would make our own and it amounted to making six or was it eight haggises? We had to explain to the cook what we wanted and in Scotland one packs the mixture into the lining of a sheep's stomach. However we couldn't get sheep's stomachs, so we used a goat's. We said to the cook, "You get eight stomach of goats and all the hearts and livers and bring them and we will make the haggises, you don't need to worry about it." So we got the other ingredients and when the day came the cook produced his bucket full of stomachs and livers and hearts and so forth. And in the Market Book the next day he just entered "Goats' Things". So for a long time after that we called haggis either "sheep" or "goats" things.'[15]

Shopping

'When I was running a house I used to discuss menus every day with the boy. In those days we had a cook-boy, and he was both cook and boy. He did all the shopping and the cooking, though I think some of his family did some of the cooking. We discussed menus each day and he gave me a rough idea of what the menu would cost. And I would give him the money and then he would do the shopping in the morning, and probably in the late afternoon he would come and say what he had spent. He'd nearly always spent more but you questioned this expense account at the end of the month, and if it got higher and higher you suggested that it was getting a bit beyond things, but he was very fair. If there was anything that was extraordinarily expensive, then I would say, "I had better ask master about it."[13]

'To some extent they couldn't help cheating. It's in their bones. They must cheat. It's no good saying, "You're not to say you used ten dozen eggs last week when you didn't. I'll give you another fifty cents pay if you'll be honest." They cannot do it. They call it "squeeze". And they must "squeeze". I think it's a matter of honour with them. However our last boy never "squeezed". He was a northerner and a most charming person, everybody who came out from Swires used to say, "My goodness where did you get this one?" He was absolutely marvellous, a dignified gentleman. And he opened the door and bowed and said, "Good evening sir; good evening madam." Whereas the other boys said, "Hallo missee; hello master." He was absolutely fantastic and he didn't seem to know how to squeeze.

'Usually I think the cook and the boy were in liaison. If the boy told you he had ten dozen eggs and you gave him the price of ten dozen eggs even though you'd only had about six dozen, the cook would probably get about half the profit.'[12]

'Most people were "done", as there wasn't any way, except by talking to other women, that you could check prices. You took it that they were going to get a small cumshaw out of it and it was only if prices rose exceptionally high and you began to smell a rat that you would have to say something about it and then things would normalise.

'When we were up in the north I always thought it was rather odd that prices were always in round numbers, ten cents or fifteen, or twenty cents. So I once said to the cook, "How is it that this fish comes to just twenty cents, cook?" And he said, "You see, missee, the fishman he asks me twenty-three cents, but I always bring it down to twenty cents, to an even number." Of course I knew what had happened, the fish was seventeen cents and he'd put it up to twenty. But still, if they knew you were reasonably cute about that sort of thing they wouldn't take it too far.'[11]

'They got very low salaries there, and they used to feed themselves too, so when you realised that perhaps a little bit extra had been used by them that *you* hadn't actually used, you shut up, you turned a blind eye to it, because it wasn't very much and it made them happy. But if suddenly you found they'd had a dozen bottles of tomato sauce, you'd say, "Look, I think we used rather a lot of tomato sauce last month." But if you nagged your servants too much or you wouldn't allow them to have any squeeze you couldn't keep them. There was one woman in particular who could not keep a servant because she didn't realise how one turned a blind eye to things and so she found that they'd stay a few days and then they'd leave. Eventually she was told that this was was not on and that she ought to be a bit more lenient, and so she had another lot of servants come and before she'd had time to say, "You can't do this or you can't do that, it is too much," they left. And she thought, "That's funny; I haven't done anything wrong." So she happened to go up into the servants quarters, and in the boys' bedroom there were a whole lot of Chinese characters on the wall, and so she got somebody to come in and translate, and of course they gave her a bad name. As soon as new servants had come, they'd looked up and said, "Oh my god, I'm not going to stay here, she's awful." And off they'd go. Then she had the characters scrubbed and the wall white-washed, and surprise surprise when the next lot of servants came they stayed. She had accepted the fact that you had to shut your eyes to a bit of this and that.'[21]

Gardening

The rich British missy might have had outdoor servants too. There could have been a chauffeur and a groom, or mafu and perhaps one or two gardeners, and in the spring or early summer the 'weedy women' might be brought in to clear the lawns of weeds by hand and on their knees while the gardener gave himself over to more important pursuits.

'The gardener we had was always very interested and pleased that my mother got seeds and things from Australia. And we had these beautiful plants. Of course his image went up a lot because of this, and that was a feather in his cap. Also he could produce these plants and sell them on the market. That was a bit of his "squeeze" or whatever you like to call it.'[13]

The indoor servants lived in specially built quarters alongside the European house.

The Servants' Quarters

'In a way they felt that after work was over they could more or less do what they liked. They weren't in the house. If they wanted to have their friends in within reason they could, and not disturb us. Houses were always built like this as a rule, the servants' quarters were a little away. They weren't very far, there was a connecting passage. They didn't have to go out into the storms or typhoons to get to their quarters.

'I learnt to keep an eye on these quarters from my mother who had been in China before me. Round the compound there were always deep drains, deep gullies, coming from the house, the kitchen and the servants' quarters and these were washed out once a week with a hose with Jeyes Fluid which is one of my earliest smell recollections. I always remember this. And they were thoroughly cleaned out, partly for mosquitoes, to see that there was no static water anywhere.

The Relationship with Servants

'I know with my mother and certainly later on when I was running a house, one was interested in one's servants and their families, and if their families were ill or the servants were ill they were always looked after. I can remember my mother often going into the servants' room and giving them anti-malarial medicines, and attending to cuts and bruises and all those kind of things. And I do know that many of my parents' friends used to say (you'd listen to them talking), "My boy or my amah was waiting on the wharf when I came back from leave because she wanted to be in our household again." They knew they were looked after, they were interested in the family, and they were utterly loyal, and we did look after them.

'They were interested in us, and later on in Amoy after the war I unfortunately had a miscarriage and the whole of the servants' quarters were terribly worried about this, and very interested in it. And my amah couldn't have been more helpful because there was no medical assistance in China after the war. There was a missionary doctor but he was naturally very busy with his own missionaries. There was only a Chinese doctor and they were really fussed and worried about my welfare.'13

Chinese servants lived a parallel but separate existence from their European employers; and one household's servants would be as friendly with another's as perhaps were their employers. Certainly if there was to be a big party and one home did not possess sufficient china, glass and cutlery the servants would borrow what was needed from the neighbouring house.

'If we had a big party, they used to do it quite wholeheartedly. Most of our stuff was in dozens so if you had a dinner party or a buffet party where you had more than that you'd borrow from the next door missy. That always happened and you'd borrow their boy too; he'd come along and help. Oh yes it was very communal.

Catering for Dinner Parties

'Shocked? No not at all. I mean you might do it in England if you had a big party. You probably wouldn't have enough knives and forks and so you'd borrow from your neighbour. So one wasn't shocked. I mean you got them all back again. And you see if the boy from next door came to wait at table for you he'd keep his eye on his own master's odds and ends. It was the done thing always.

'The boy would nearly always mention it to me first and I would say, "Yes – you give him what you want but count what you give."'11

'I know things were borrowed but I was very fierce and I forbade them ever to borrow or lend. Whether they did or not I'm not sure but what you've been told is quite right. You could go out to dinner and have your grandmother's dessert plate put in front of you but I wasn't going to allow any of that because we had a lot of our own things with us.

'I absolutely forbade them to do that. If we had a huge party and wanted more things than we'd got, we could always go to the store and borrow things off a ship. The company always had supplies.'12

With so much done for her by her servants and with her husband away at his office all day it might be expected that time would hang heavily on the European wife's hands. After all it was extremely unlikely, except possibly in the large cities, that she might have made friends with the Chinese, and she was expressly forbidden by virtually every company that her husband worked for from taking a job.

'Do you know there wasn't ever a problem filling one's time. I suppose really there ought to have been but there wasn't. There always seemed a lot to do looking after the house and I was very keen on gardening. We always had a gardener and I used to send to America for seeds because California used to grow seeds which were rather suitable for China. For instance the sweet peas I used to get from Bupees in California.

'We were very convivial in the outport. I used to play bridge; I had a piano and we used to have musical evenings. I had two dogs I had to exercise each day. In fact there wasn't anything in the way of social work one could really do in these parts of China because you would not be welcomed by the Chinese in doing it. I mean we were friendly with the mission and if we could do anything at any time that would help them we always did, but apart from that I don't think one could do very much.'[12]

An island of Englishness: Relaxing on the verandah at the Club.

Physical exercise had traditionally been the sine qua non of life abroad for the British, imperial or otherwise. And in this respect China was no different from India or Africa. Men and women played tennis or walked or rode. To ride in China was inexpensive too for there was an abundant supply of what were called 'China ponies' from the north.

Riding

'They came from Mongolia, and they were from twelve to thirteen hands. Thirteen was the biggest, but most of them were twelve something or other. They had short sturdy little necks, and they were very sure footed. They were quite fast, too. But if they made up their mind they were going to take hold, they took hold. They were called "Y" class ponies. For some of the heavyweights they were perhaps a little bit small, and so there was a different type of pony called the "Z" class, which was a cross between the China pony and one from over the border in Russia.

Hunting

'We used to hunt over arable land and so the first hunt of the season was never until after the harvest, which was in the autumn, and the stewards were very careful that we didn't do harm to the crops. We didn't have foxes in Shanghai, and so it was a paper chase. They used to have coloured paper laid in the morning. The ground was very flat, but there were a lot of water jumps because Shanghai's full of creeks and if the creek were too big to jump we had what you called platform jumps. You'd get a mud platform on either side of the creek and you jumped over the middle. Some of them were wadeable, and sometimes when the paper layers went through in the morning it was pretty shallow, but when the hunt went through in the afternoon the water was a bit higher. Once I can remember my pony swimming, but mostly you could get through. They used to dig a lot of jumps as well to make it more exciting, and they had names: one very big water jump was called Clear Water, and then there was another one called Craddock's Crash, because somebody called Craddock crashed there. There was Sparky's something or other and Jim's Joy.

'The finish was always very spectacular because a lot of people who used to go out and watch and the Chinese just loved to see somebody fall off. They'd have a rope along either side of the finish, and there might be three, four, five jumps, and the first person to get through the last red flag would be awarded a pink coat. The first in on a "Y" class and the first in on a "Z" class would get their pink coats. Then came six people who were "on the card", and it was quite an honour to be on the card.

'They used to have lunches before paper hunts. Before the first one of the season, Judge Alman, who had a lovely house out at Hungjao, built rather on the lines of the White House in Washington, used to give a barbecue lunch. But not one of the barbecues you have now. It was just a pit dug in the garden with chicken wire over it and a sucking pig, and the weather was wonderful and we'd all stand around having drinks. The sucking pig would have been cooking since the early hours of the morning. Then after lunch we'd go off to the hunt.

'Because the hunts were all over arable land they were very careful to see the crops weren't damaged in any way, but sometimes they were and so a day or two after the hunt a party used to go out to pay compensation. I went out once or twice just for the ride. We would pay x many dollars for damage to the farmers, who were jolly pleased because it was at least twice what they could have got if they had sold their crops, and these crops all used to come up in the end anyhow. One occasion when I went out was when the Japanese occupied a lot of the area outside Shanghai and there were people in a sort of no-man's land who were thugs, and we were about to pay x many dollars to this little group of farmers, when suddenly up popped five Chinese, very smartly dressed with trilby hats on. They had yellow cords round their necks, with mauser pistols hanging on them and tassles hanging down. And they were demanding a thousand dollars. It was ridiculous. We didn't have a thousand dollars. The head paper hunt boy did a lot of the translation and he said, they want this thousand dollars, and they want to have a meeting arranged so that they can meet the master of the hunt." Eventually they let us go. Then about a week later I was out hunting and I had a spill, and suddenly up popped these five Chinese again, and they made my husband dismount as well. I think they recognised me because they said, "What thing? No money?" Next somebody else came up who was also made to dismount, and then a fourth person came, and I shall always remember the broad grin on his face, seeing us standing there, and suddenly it was wiped off when he saw a pistol poking at him and he was made to get off. There was a lot of argument and my husband, who was a steward at the paper hunt club, had a little card on him, and I think it said in Chinese he was allowed to throw paper around the country. So they decided as he was a steward he must ride to the finish and I should go with him, to bring back the master and the money, and they would keep the others as hostages. So off we went. When we got to the finish, apart from our mafus, our grooms, everybody'd gone home, and it took us some time to locate someone. Everybody rather thought it was a hoax. In the meantime, a Frenchman joined the group of hostages, and he had a dollar in his pocket, so he took out the dollar, and the Chinese snatched it and they were very angry, so each of them fired a shot, five shots up in the air, and they went away. Perhaps they had had second thoughts about us coming back because we might have brought the police or reinforcements.'[21]

In time most families' thoughts turned to families, to having children.

Children and Schooling

'It certainly wasn't ideal having a family in China. The point was that if your husband wanted to work out East and you wanted a family it was a thing you had to do and get on with. You had to make the best of many situations which certainly were not ideal.

'After a time children were sent home to school, but not when they were little. On the whole without any question children came home from prep school age onwards. Climatically I think babies and young children grew very well in China, but they became awfully leggy if they stayed out. Also that sort of life was not ideal living, waited on by servants, so as a rule I would say without question they came home.

'It was a painful thing to say goodbye to one's children, but people still do it today, don't they? I think it's one of the things that you have to weigh up when you are deciding whether you feel life is worth living abroad.

'Once when I was pregnant I lost a child because of an earthquake. We experienced this terrifying thing, quite a big earthquake. I don't mean to suggest that buildings fell down or anything like that, but there was a roar of bricks falling down the chimneys. It was really very frightening and I picked up our eldest girl and ran in great terror from the house and that night I had this miscarriage. And the doctor there, who was a missionary doctor, was highly inefficient in my opinion. He used to give both my husband and me the impression that he kept going back to refer to his books and that he was not quite sure what to do about it. It is quite easy to laugh now but at the time it was very harrowing.'[15]

B & S husbands, particularly if they were senior in the company, could spend time away from home travelling, either along the China coast or up the Yangtze River as far as Chungking at the head of the fabled Gorges. And some wives accompanied their husbands on these trips.

Wives Travelling with Husbands

'There were two bachelors in Chungking and there was a smell in the house. I couldn't understand where it came from. Finally it was traced to all the cigarette ends of weeks and months that had been swept by the coolie under the large fireplace. Having got rid of the smell of cigarettes and things,

I noticed the curtains were black – they were old fashioned lace curtains. They didn't need them to stop anybody seeing in because there was nobody to see. They were so filthy and they smelt, so I sent for the number one boy and said, "I want you to take down all those curtains and wash them, they're

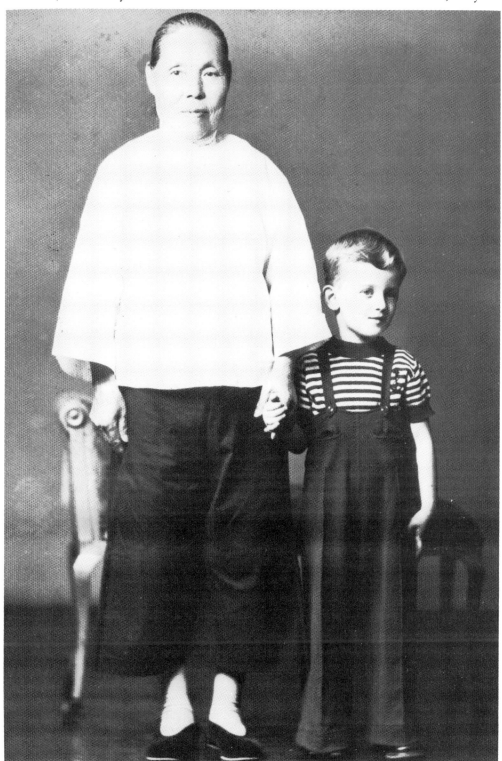

very dirty." And he said, "No can, no can." I said, "Sure can, why no can?" "In this house seven year, missee. No take down seven years, suppose take down, all fall down; all finishee." So I said, "Well just you take down and finishee, then you can makee burn." And it's true he did it and they fell to pieces, dirt and all.

'And then they had a lamp that was one of these old fashioned things that went up to the ceiling. When you wanted to read or see what you were eating, you pulled and a weight went up and the lamp came down. It was a really old fashioned fitting. It had a little pink frill round it that had got burnt – it had been left on the bulb or something, so I went out and bought a yard of silk and made them a new lampshade to make up for their not having curtains any more.

'And then I decided I didn't think much of the water. But my husband said, "It's perfectly all right, they filter it." So I had a look at the filter and it was green with slime, so we got it cleaned. But I still didn't think much of the water.

'And one day I went for a little walk. The house was high above the river on a sort of rock – and I saw the two house coolies, who were supposed to go all the way down that path to get water out of the Yangtze and then bring it up and filter it and boil it, which was bad enough because the Yangtze was just a sewer in all the river ports, but they couldn't be bothered to go down to the river and they were bailing the water off the paddy fields. It had been brought up the river sometimes and now it was full of frogs and mosquitoes and everything. And they were taking it from there to save themselves the trouble of going all the way down to the river. I didn't enjoy that visit much.'[12]

Life in a Yangtze outport could be both primitive and lonely. At Wuhu, 300 miles up the river from Shanghai, a young bride found that the accommodation provided by the company consisted of a 'hulk' moored by the river.

Accommodation on the River

'The "hulk" was a one time steamer that had been altered to accommodate the agent. It had a super-structure on board on top, and a very nice through sitting room, which was for'ard, so that we had a view of the river, which was over a mile wide there, from one lot of windows. And on the other side were the wharves, the "Bund" as it's called in China. Then we had a dining room behind and a pantry and two bedrooms and two bathrooms. In the middle were the servants' quarters and the kitchen and right at the stern was the agent's office. It was moored and it had a narrow deck round the edge so that you could go out of the sort of French windows from the living rooms on to the deck and walk right round. And at the for'ard end there was quite a bit of deck. There was a pier and a bridge which we crossed to go on shore. When we went the river was very narrow because it was early in the spring and you could only just see above the banks. Then as the river rose, with all the torrential water coming down central west China the anchors had to be let out and we rose with it.

'Things were very unsettled at this time. Chiang Kai Shek had not really established himself and unfortunately the Chinese were not very friendly and life was rather uncertain. There were a few warring generals still around and they had had shots through the windows a few months earlier when a retreating general was being subdued. But the part of the harbour where we were on the river was some distance from the Chinese city and we could go ashore and walk about. It wasn't like it would have been had we been right in the centre of the Chinese city.

Once glorious: *SS Pekin* in her heyday. Her later fate was to be the Wuhu hulk.

Middle. Shoreline: The hulk, a retired steamer which provided accommodation for the agent and his wife, was connected to the shore by a pontoon bridge. To the right of the hulk is a sampan for visiting ships on the river: Repairing the pontoon bridge.

Bottom. Maiden voyage: MV *Wuhu*, a new river steamer, moored up at Wuhu on her first river trip. The hulk.

'When I wrote home to my parents they were rather horrified, because of course they thought we were going to Hong Kong, where we would be settled in a nice English colony. But they didn't know where Wuhu was. In fact they had to find out. It was in Anhwei province. Then when they heard that we were going to live in a hulk that was a dreadful thought. But after a while I sent home photographs and wrote and explained things weren't really as bad as all that, and they were somewhat resigned I think and got very interested in what was happening.

'First of all, you had to pay your calls. People called on you first and then you had to return their calls, which was always quite exciting because there were no roads, except paths between paddy fields. Quite a few people lived close to the Bund. But some lived further back across the paddy fields. The missionaries lived quite a distance away and it was a business returning the calls because I hadn't got a clue where to go, but I'd tell the boy I wanted to call on such and such a missy. In China all the firms had Chinese names (Butterfield & Swire was Taikoo, Jardine Matheson Ewo), so if I wanted to return a call on the Jardine missy I'd ask him to get the rickshaw coolie and announce I wanted to go and call on the Ewo missy. He would get the rickshaw and I would be taken down and put in it and off we'd go along these high paths between the paddy fields.

'If it was wet we were covered up to the eyes with a piece of mackintosh fixed across the front of the rickshaw like a baby's pram and you couldn't see out and just hoped you were going to the right place.

'The thing was to be sure that you returned the call on the right person. On one occasion, when we lived in north China, there were two very elderly ladies who were residents. One was a little bit Chinese, but she was very pleasant and everybody knew her and wished her well. But apparently one of these two called on me and I returned the call on the wrong person and the one that I should have called on never forgave me. I had said I wanted to go to the old missy and my boy misunderstood which old missy I wanted to go to.

'In such a small community you had to watch out for who talked to whom and when and you had to be very careful. It wasn't quite as bad as India where you walked about with an army list all the time, but you had to be careful where you sat people at dinner. There wasn't a consul in Wuhu so the Commissioner of Customs, who was in the Chinese government service, was the senior citizen as it were, and you gave him the courtesy of the country. He always got senior seat, but you did have to watch out, as one or two of the firms were a bit you know, "I've been here longer than you", sort of business.

'We didn't meet the Chinese very much as it was very difficult to deal with people you couldn't talk to, and who are extremely unwesternised. We were invited out on two occasions that I remember to dinners. I think my husband was asked out to two or three dinners by some of the Chinese chamber of commerce when we first went, so he was initiated into that, but it wasn't usual really to ask a wife out as well. So it was rather a special occasion when we were asked out by the chairman of the Electric Light Works. We got the invitation, I think, through the German who was the Siemens representative.

He was trying to get his money back, I think, because Siemens had built the Chinese Electric Light Plant and my husband was trying to get the insurance for it. At any rate we were asked there for lunch very soon after we arrived in Wuhu. It was a most extraordinary occurrence because we all sat at one long table in the house and the women of the house brought in the food. My husband and I and the two Germans were the only other Europeans. They were all Chinese and the Chairman of the Light Works didn't speak any English at all and I sat next to him and he kept putting nasty bits of food, which he thought were lovely bits of food, on my plate. At any rate the dishes came along about every ten minutes from about two o'clock to five o'clock and everybody else seemed to be having a good time. I wasn't very happy because I was having rather a dull time and I was rather glad when it was over.

'Then one Chinese who could speak English got up and said that Mr Deng, who was the chief of police, would be very pleased if we'd go and have lunch with him next Sunday and I thought, "Oh dear do we do this sort of thing every Sunday?" In fact I didn't particularly want to go, but Gordon said he was trying to arrange with the chief of police for some supervision against the smuggling of opium on our ships so he thought he'd better go. So we went off and that was when we went to one of these dreadful houses in the main street which were very smelly. The dining room was upstairs and we passed the kitchen on the way, which was simply dreadful, and any rate we had a meal there. Half way through we noticed men were going out occasionally and the old chief of police was ushering them out and later they came back and the next lot went off. Eventually they asked Gordon if he'd go out and he discovered they were all going out to have a pipe of opium on the sly as it were. So he gave up all thoughts of trying to get much protection against the opium on the ships. It wasn't anything I particularly wish to repeat as an afternoon's entertainment.'[11]

From Wuhu in the middle of the Yangtze River, this wife was posted with her husband to the port of Chefoo on the coast of northern China.

'That was entirely different, it was way up in northern Shantung, and it was a delightful part of China. North China is really very pleasant I think. One of the sad things is that since the Sino-Japanese war and the taking over of China by the communists Chefoo has never been opened again to foreigners. Not even as much as Shanghai, which, after all, isn't much. Nobody ever went back there; they did just allow the consul to go back and get his records but no European has ever gone back there to live and it's one of the most delightful parts. The climate is continental; intensely cold in winter, in fact so much so that the harbour freezes and the spray from the waves froze too. And it's hot in the summer. All in all I found it a very pleasant place partly because of the good food we used to get there. Shantung beef is famous and so is the lamb that comes down from Mongolia, Manchuria. We used to grow all European fruit and vegetables: asparagus and strawberries and grapes and apples and pears. Everything was simply delicious. I've never had such good food. Chefoo was a real Chinese town but not so sordid in many ways as those on the Yangtze. We used to ride a

Life in Northern China

Food

Leisure

lot there and we had two ponies, and we were very fortunate because we had a large garden with stables and we used to ride on our bit of beach for early morning rides. But if you wanted to go for a really long ride you had to go to the other side of the Chinese city, so we had bicycles there and the mafu used to take the ponies out to the other beach further out and we would trot along on our bicycles later on and meet them there. Then we'd go for our rides. Sometimes we'd go for a picnic. We could ride through the country quite safely and nobody ever seemed to bother much about you.

'I suppose there were about a hundred Europeans in Chefoo. There was quite a big American mission and then there were a lot of permanent residents who ran silk firms and embroidery. It was a great place for embroidery work and peanut oil but it was a very bad time for them. Trade was very bad and they were all just about limping along. There were quite a lot of Germans in that part of north China, because before the First World War Tsingtao was a German treaty port; it was taken by the Japanese during that war, so quite a number of Germans came and stayed. There were a number of Russians who'd come through from Siberia after the revolution, quite a few though I wouldn't say a lot.

'There was a very big club in Chefoo, rather too big for the needs of the community. In the winter, half of it was closed up and we used to dance and have our meetings in one of the smaller rooms. It was a very very fine club with terraces looking out over the sea. We used to go for sea picnics to the islands. We had oysters there too and the most lovely prawns, great big ones rather like crayfish. You couldn't eat more than two in one meal. I almost drool at the thought of the food I had out there. I don't think I've ever lived anywhere that had such wonderful food.

'In the winter club life wasn't very much. We used to try and have a meeting there once a month. One lady would be a hostess and be at home and we'd have tea. Then all the men would come in on their way home from the offices and have tea and so on and a chat, and perhaps a little bit of bridge afterwards. But it was nearly all Saturday night entertainment. You'd have a dinner party first and then you'd go down and dance a bit, but it wasn't very spry in the winter; anyway it was so frightfully cold to go out in rickshaws.

'The Chinese used to dig down underneath the garden. And they'd put cauliflowers and brussels sprouts and cabbages and potatoes and other vegetables under ground and then cover them over. And they'd dig them out, I suppose, through the terribly cold winter and they seemed to keep marvellously. They used to cut the grape vines down and bend them right over and then cover them with mud. It was intensely cold. The sort of cold that you lost the use of your feet when you were walking along facing the wind.'[11]

'Sometimes when I look back at night at our life in China, I think, God it couldn't have been real. We never had any money to spend, but we lived every moment of it.'[21]

The China Coasters

They were called 'China Coasters', the men who sailed the ships up and down the China coast from Manchuria in the north to Hong Kong in the south. And even in the second twenty years of this century there was something of the spirit of Joseph Conrad's sailors about them, for they were a close-knit fellowship who were faintly contemptuous of their fellow Westerners in the coastal outports or Shanghai, and with that sense of serious matters which must come from long days alone at sea. Not that they were romantics; far from it. They were practical men with tight sailing schedules to maintain along a coast with more than its fair share of nautical problems, who consequently knew their worth.

Many of the 'Coasters' who joined Butterfield & Swire's fleet – The China Navigation Company – were Scots. But whether they were Scots or not any new recruit into a CNCo ship would have already served for a good while at sea as a junior officer before going east, on a steamer, perhaps, around the English coast. And they would have had to have been awarded their master's ticket if they were a deck officer or their engineering ticket if they were to officer the ship's engines.

Traditionally most British merchant marine officers had regarded a career on the China coast as a career of the last resort, but for young men in the late twenties and early thirties it offered an opportunity for breaking through the block on promotion that had resulted from the slump in world trade and consequent decline in merchant shipping activity. Of course, in time the China coast would feel the full effect of the depression, but that prospect hardly seems to have troubled young officers bound for China. As they embarked on a Blue Funnel liner for Hong Kong or Shanghai, adventure was uppermost in their minds; an adventure that began with the Suez Canal, continued through the Indian Ocean, Bombay, Singapore and the South China Sea until they arrived at Hong Kong or Shanghai. They had committed themselves to CNCo for upwards of three years and already they were being better looked after at sea than they had ever been before.

'They gave us ten pounds to spend on the voyage and ten pounds on arrival. There was a bit of a poem about that called *The China Coaster*. "They say you'll find them most obliging kind of people. They will pack you off to China in a trice. Ten pounds to spend upon the voyage; ten pounds on arrival. Ain't they nice."

'You signed on for three years and then if you wanted to stay on with the company you stayed for another three, but if the company found you were

Conditions of Service

not suitable they had the option of saying to you, "We see your contract has expired on such and such a date and we are arranging your passage home on such and such a date." But very few people got that from B & S. They had a good method of choosing in the first place. Very very few people were told they had had their contracts terminated. And they were very polite, they would not fire you.'[19]

'The conditions of service compared very favourably with conditions in home shipping and shipping sailing out of the UK. We got much better service because we had Chinese stewards, who were more plentiful on board; more stewards per man than on any European ship, and we had personal stewards, "boys" as we called them, who attended to us very well, who did our laundry, saw that we had clean clothing every day in the tropics. Clean underclothing and white tropical clothing in summer and in the winter time, again clean underclothing and our navy blue uniforms brushed and kept immaculate – that was something we never got with European stewards. The food depended on the ship, in fact on the cook. There was no refrigeration in those days, just ice boxes, loaded with blocks of ice and then the fresh meat put on top of it, which meant that we probably ate a bit more tinned food and salted food, but we always had plenty of vegetables and fruit.

'So I think compared with the British tramp steamer we were much better off, and we compared quite favourably with some of the passenger ships coming out of the U.K.'[18]

The ships the 'China Coasters' sailed were not particularly large: between two and three thousand tons and perhaps three hundred feet in length and many of The China Navigation Company's fleet had been built in Scotland on the Clyde and sailed round to China. They were officered by a captain, chief officer and second officer and below decks there would have been a chief engineer and a second and third engineer. These six were British and they commanded a completely Chinese crew.

The Chinese Crew

'The Chinese crew would have been about eighty, sometimes eighty-five. A very large crew for the size of the ship because apart from the sailors and the firemen there were what we called the compradore's staff. They were the "tallymen" and they tallied the cargo in and out. Then there were the stevedores and they put the hatches on and took them off and put the awnings up and separated the various cargo consignments. The sailors put the awnings up but the stevedores helped out. The crew were fantastic but they were worked hard because they were in and out of ports fast and sometimes we finished landing cargo at maybe five or six o'clock in the afternoon. Then the hatches and tarpaulins were put on, the screens up, and awnings up and away. We usually arrived at these ports at dawn and sailed at dusk.

'We would generally spend just one day in port. Very often we would go in first thing in the morning maybe at daylight, or at seven or eight o'clock, and maybe sail that night at six or seven and then maybe the next day or in two days' time we would be in another port. In and out all the time.'[19]

'The Chinese made very good sailors. Perhaps I should not say this, but I would be happier I think with a good Chinese crew than a British crew; and definitely they are much better than Indian crews. I shall have to watch what I am saying otherwise I will be having Sheik so and so coming after me with a cutlass or something, but I would go anywhere with a Chinese crew.

'I think it's because of their junk life they're such good sailors. I mean the China coast is seething with junks and they were the bane of our lives at sea because half of them did not show light and you would suddenly find yourself in amongst anything from fifty to a hundred fishing boats, and being very economical they would not light their little oil lamps until you were right on top of them, and suddenly everything in front of you would light up like a Christmas tree, and you would try and find your way out of this maze without hitting them and sinking them or knocking them over. But the Chinese are excellent seamen, and they have pride in their work; more so than most nationalities. I was going to say more so than the British!

'From looking down on the Chinese, to almost despising them when I went out to China first, it did not take me long to appreciate their qualities and before I left I could say that there were quite a few Chinese I looked up to, could consider as friends.

'I had a brush with a Chinese quartermaster once. Now sometimes they looked on us junior officers as men who did not know very much (and probably a lot of us did not) but we were trained to believe that we were officers and above any ordinary ratings and that sort of thing, although some of the Chinese could probably teach us quite a few things. But I felt this particular quartermaster had to be punished. I think he fell asleep on duty as a matter of fact. He had found a quiet little cubby hole which was sheltered from the wind no doubt, and fallen asleep. And when I found him asleep when he should have been awake I sent him up to the "Monkey Island" which was very exposed right on top of the wheelhouse, and I made him stay there. He was very resentful of this because I was very junior and he was a middle-aged man, with lots of experience. And it so happened that he was a favourite of the captain's, so he went down to the captain's cabin (in the middle of the night this was) and reported me for doing this to him. So, the captain came to see me and see what it was all about, and I explained. He was very noncommittal about it and he spoke to the quartermaster and more or less told him, I expect, "Don't take much notice of him, just do as he tells you just the same; you know everything will work out all right", which it did. But that made me realise that, you know, they were human just like ourselves.

'There was a kind of innocence about the Chinese. The Pilots Association offices were on the Bund in Shanghai, the Bund being the river bank where most of the big offices were, and there was always a British naval ship and an

The Relationship between Officers and Crew

Italian and a French ship there. (As you know Shanghai was an international port.) And the manager of the Pilots Association was being driven down to his office by this Chinese chauffeur and when they got down to the Bund on this particular morning they saw this strange-looking ship with a flat deck on it, and the chauffeur was amazed at this and said to his master, "Master, what fashion ship this?" And the manager of the Pilots Association said, "Oh this belong aeroplane ship, boy." And the Chinese said, "Can fly?"

'How did we communicate with the Chinese ratings? The quartermasters, who were sort of petty officers, could speak "pidgin English" and the bo'suns, the heads of the deck departments, and the number one fireman, who was head of the engine department, could all speak "pidgin English" and we got on very well.

'But not the ordinary sailor. Say an ordinary sailor was doing something on the deck, and you wanted him to do something else, unless he was one of the English-speaking ones, you would speak to him and he would just look blankly at you. He would not have a clue what you were speaking about. But he was probably quite a good sailor, and when he had been told by the bo'sun or someone who understood what you wanted, he was very willing. There was never much difficulty in that respect because there was always one of the Chinese who could understand what you wanted and would explain to the non-English speaking one what he had to do, and he would do it quite willingly. It would have been impossible for us to have learnt Chinese because it would have meant mastering five different languages to talk to all the men who crewed our ships.'[18]

'They were generous, kind and very, very clean. And in B & S ships the Chinese boys, waiters, had long white gowns on right down to their shoes. It looked smart and elegant. But they are very clean in themselves, the Chinese, very, very clean. The company standard was that we had to inspect the ship every day. The chief engineer and the chief officer and the chief steward would go along with the captain and open the doors of lockers, drawers, the galleys and the sluice. They all had to be opened up and inspected but the Chinese in no way resented the inspections. In fact they seemed pleased to show their attention to cleanliness.

'The Chinese sailors fed themselves and were not fed by the chief steward. The fireman had his own cook; the sailors had their own cook. And they used to carry their own chickens in a basket maybe on the poop. And on this particular occasion the chief engineer said to his number one fireman, "What is this chicken, all the time, early morning cock-a-doodle-doo all the time, every morning waking me up?" "Oh," the number one fireman said, "That's my chickens, to feed the men." Then the chief engineer continued, "This cock-a-doodle-doo every morning, early morning." The number one fireman said, "Very sorry master, I did not know that." And he said by and by the cockerel would get a new suit and just before he got his new suit he would not sing then. What he meant was that he would be moulting. So the chief said, "All right as long as he doesn't keep on singing too much."

But they were good the Chinese, very good. There was a fellow came in during the war to see me in Calcutta and he said, "Hello do you remember me?". He was Chinese. And to be polite I said, "I can't remember you but I seem to know your face." There might have been a little element of truth in that but there might not but anyway I did not want to hurt his feelings. And he said, "I was your boy on the river between Shanghai and Hankow." "Oh yes," I said, "I remember you now; your wife made me some nice slippers; I do remember you very well. What are you doing in Calcutta?" He said, "Now I own the Lighthouse Chinese Restaurant." 'It was a big one in Chowringhi. "You own it?" "Yes, it is mine." And he was very modest about it and he said, "You come any time, you come to my restaurant any time and you can bring some friends with you anytime. There would be no charge for you." I said, "No thank you if I come I must pay, you are a businessman." '19

'The Chinese crew were usually recruited by the bo'sun who was the head of the deck department, the sailors, and the number one fireman, that was his official category. He chose his own crew. They mostly chose either members of their own family or relations or at least people from their own village, because there were quite a few different dialects in China and they were like a family unit. And the bo'suns who were the head of the sailors department, were very often accused, and possibly rightly so, of being approached by so and so's cousin or brother. They would say "Do you think you could get my Johnny a job on your ship?" and the bo'sun would say, "It's very difficult" and he was making signs at the same time. So the brother who wanted maybe Johnny out of the way, or really wanted to make him a sailor would pay the bo'sun a little cumshaw to take him. And that sailor would be taken away, looked after by the bo'sun. But every pay day he had to give the bo'sun just a little bit of his pay back.

Recruiting the Crew

'The captain went to the bank at one time and latterly the office when it came to paying the crew. He would go to the office with his portage bill which is really an account of the wages for the crew. And in the office he would be given a cheque equal to that amount. He would go to the bank and tell them he wanted so much in five dollar pieces or dollar pieces or whatever and then go back to the ship and send for the head of the department (the bo'sun in the case of the sailors) and say, "This is your pay for this month." And then he would take it and divide it out amongst the crew as he thought fit, deducting the little bits of cumshaw from the ones who were under apprenticeship to him. So the bo'sun was always better off than what it said on paper on the portage bill. The firemen were the same, it was just a Chinese custom.'18

China coast cargoes were principally manufactured goods from the rest of the world, some industrial equipment from Europe and America and China's own natural products – rice from the south, grain from the north, eggs and hogs' bristles, pork and ducks from the Yangtze Valley, tea from Fukien, ginger from Swatow and in the early 1920s beancakes from Newchwang in the north to

Beancaker: The SS
Yunnan which
carried beancake
from Newchwang to
Swatow.

Loading up: Cargo
being put aboard at
Shanghai.

Swatow in the south. These beancakes were made from the dry residue left after the oil had been extracted from soya beans which was then compressed and moulded into large cartwheel shapes and used as a fertiliser.

'They called the ships which carried them "beancakers". They were very smart little ships, with long tapering masts. The funnels weren't as grand as they later became, of course. The great thing was that, as Mr Warren Swire has said, they had a funnel of noble proportions, you built the ship around it. But they were all of one class. They varied slightly but they were all cargo ships eventually, and they all went on the beancake trade from Newchwang to Swatow, and so they followed each other round while the port was open. Then the winter came and Newchwang port closed. And then they went "tramping" God knows where, wherever they could get a charter. That was the sort of thing I liked.'[17]

'Beancakers'

The beancake trade, once so busy and so profitable gradually came to an end in the late 1920s as farmers in the south of China turned to other fertilisers. But for some of the men who sailed the 'beancakers', the specially built ships which travelled between Newchwang and Swatow have always held a special place in their affections.

'When beancakers were in their prime there was no pride in being a beancaker man. If sailors were in the general hospital in Shanghai it was always said that they were sick as sick could be while there was a beancaker in port, and then they all got better as soon as she left. But afterwards it got to be nostalgic, although if you were "a beancaker man" it actually meant that you'd done something wrong or else you were very young or a first promotion. People would say later on they knew all about beancakers but they weren't real beancakers because they'd gone, but some of the old cargo-passenger ships were reverted to cargo ships and they used incorrectly to call them beancakers. I remember listening to an old captain on retiring and having got his watch or whatever it was, at the presentation cocktail party, he went on reminiscing about beancakers. Well I knew he'd joined in 1930 – that was three years after the beancakers had gone. What he was talking about was the old "Chow" class or something similar. But he had to be nostalgic about beancakers to join the club. So there was a certain something about it.

'Beancaker' Lore

'Newchwang was a small town up in the north. I think it had a British concession, a tiny little concession, there was certainly a consul there, but the ships lay off at anchor. There was a wharf, but mainly they laid off, maybe two or three in line loading beancake. Then it was off to Swatow, laid in line there, the beancake discharged, and back to Shanghai to load bunker coal. One night was about the most you would get there, and then back north to Newchwang. So Swires established a club in Swatow. In Newchwang there was a bit of a cabaret started with Russian hostesses. I remember chaps in cold weather used to go up there with the leather boots one used to wear in those days to keep warm, sort of top boots, and you had to lift your feet up to get over the planks as it was certainly no dance floor. There was a similar place in Swatow. I was very young then and didn't patronise these joints. But anyhow the company felt that there was call for a place where people could get some papers to read and buy some drinks without paying the earth and so

Newchwang and Swatow

they established this little club. It was newly built in a sort of compound area, and it was only of value to the beancakers because the other ships came in the morning and left in the afternoon. So there again the beancakers fraternised a bit because there were so many of them that they would have somebody to talk to from the other ships. At least they could have a game of billiards, and there were newspapers and things like that, and so it filled quite a want. It was, I suppose, what you would call the sort of work the Mission to Seamen do.'[17]

The ships which sailed up and down the China coast ran to a strict schedule and with the exception of the beancakers it was extremely rare for any vessel to spend more than a day in port. But on the China coast even the best laid schedule could be brought to grief by the weather.

'In the north east monsoon it blew continuously for months on end from the north to the south, or from the north east to the south west taking the line of the China coast. The wind blew all the time. When you were coming down, you had the wind behind you and you came down at the rate of knots. But going back up again in the beancake days, you might only have half cargo, or practically no cargo at all, which meant you were right up on the surface with the effect of the wind against you. And you would perhaps be reduced from a normal ten knots to even being stopped. I have seen ships actually going backwards, steaming full speed ahead but the wind was so strong and there was too much of the ship above water and not enough underneath, that you would actually find yourself drifting back. So the thing to do then was to look for a nice island where you could go and shelter, and you would drop anchor there waiting for the wind to subside. Then as soon as you saw any sign of the wind weakening you would go out and have another look, and as long as you were making progress you would carry on. Of course, this was in the days of coal when you had to think about the amount of fuel you were burning, because you could not go on burning coal and go backwards or you would find yourself out of coal and back where you started.

'There were not too many lights on the coast although it was not badly lit really, but when you became a "Coaster", when you had been there long enough to be considered a "Coaster" and you had gone up and down so often that you could do it with your eyes shut almost, you seemed to get an instinct about it. You could feel your way and you would go closer up to rocks than a normal seafaring man, who had not had that experience: he would be shunning them by five miles, scared to go near them. But with experience, knowing that you could go right up to them and almost touch them, you could dodge in behind these rocks and make headway, whereas ships five miles off the coast would be dead stopped.

'So being a "China Coaster" meant that you knew the coast, and you could dodge from island to island and get into the lee of an island, where you are sheltered from the wind and you would make a few miles and then dodge out and then behind another island. Coming down from Shanghai to Hong Kong you might come down in four days but against the monsoon you might take fourteen days to go back.

'There were also rocks and reefs on the coast too, but ships went aground only in fog as a rule. We did not have radar in those days and you could not always rely on the currents. Sometimes they would be a bit stronger than you anticipated, sometimes weaker and perhaps there was not a current when you were expecting one. And in fog you could not see very far. I think a lot of people got along on instinct and a fair amount of good luck. I think that every captain on the China coast, if he were honest, would have to admit that he had had a pretty near escape at some time or another. You know, the fog just lifted in time and there was a damned big island in front of him that he did not expect.'[18]

But it was the typhoon season which posed the most serious threats to plain sailing on the China coast.

'They used to say about typhoons, "June too soon, July stand by." They used to say, "September you must remember . . . ." or something like that. There was some poetry about it. But you were very well informed where the typhoon was. The French Jesuit fathers had a meteorological station in Shanghai and various places and B & S co-operated with all these people. We used to take weather reports regularly on a special form distributed by the French fathers and at the end of each voyage we used to send them to them for their records. B & S expected us to keep out of the typhoon. Everybody would be scared of the typhoon, really frightened of it.'[19]

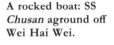

Rocks and Reefs

Typhoons

A rocked boat: SS *Chusan* aground off Wei Hai Wei.

'Typhoons were quite a problem. Different latitudes had different starting dates. You could expect the first typhoon about May, and then you had them perhaps one a week, one a fortnight or maybe two in one week, and they had tracks. They would start a long way south east of Hong Kong almost down towards the equator, and come in a curve towards the coast and very often they would strike the coast and then be deflected and run up the coast. You could "feel" them, you would know that there was a typhoon in the offing anything from 250 to 400 miles away. You could tell by the weather. They originated to the south and east of the Philippines and moved towards the China coast taking varying tracks according to the time of the year; striking Vietnam about January to April and moving northwards towards the China coast proper. They struck the vicinity of Hong Kong and north to Shanghai any time between June and August and then curved towards Japan.

'If there was a typhoon and if you were not going to get too close to it you just carried on. But if you were getting so close that you would have adverse weather and it would be against you and hold back or even make you turn and go back, you would try and get out of its way. And in the early days, of course, you had to be guided by the meteorology you had learned as a young man primarily at navigation school and just through sailing with experienced masters. The formation of the clouds and the way the wind was blowing and so on. And then there were the Americans stationed in the Philippines; the Air Force there was very good and when a typhoon was in the offing they were able to get up above the typhoons, up above the cloud formation, something like the satellite pictures you see now. They could see the swirling clouds with the centre of a typhoon, and they could pinpoint it and then broadcast to their headquarters, who would broadcast to shipping where the centre of the typhoon was. And by doing that at intervals they could tell which way it was moving, which meant that if you were going one way and the typhoon was coming the same way and you did not want to meet it deliberately you would veer off or slow down and let it go ahead of you, but keep out of its way. I experienced lots of bad weather near typhoons, and perhaps a little bit of structural damage done, but I was never in danger of being wrecked or any man lost overboard or anything like that. The China Coasters had a pretty good idea how these typhoons were moving and you would make a safe shelter; sometimes you would have to move out because the typhoon would change its course and just go in the direction you did not expect it to go, and you would have to revise your plans and perhaps shoot off in the other direction. But you did not deliberately get in the way of a typhoon if you could avoid it.'[18]

'I was never caught in one and to the great credit of the company if a master held back, if there was an element of risk that his ship would be caught in a typhoon, for maybe twelve hours at sea to let the typhoon go ahead, there was never a word of criticism. Never the quiet urge to, "Carry on captain." Never like that. They were all for safety, B & S. You see some of the tough companies would be urging captains on. "Why did you do that, why didn't you get on?" But not with B & S; safety first – not only the safety of the ship but of the passengers as well.'[19]

'I did sail through a typhoon once and it was very scary. The one thing you do is to avoid getting in the centre as much as possible. If you are unfortunate enough to be caught it is very scary because in the centre of the typhoon there is no wind but the sea comes at you from every direction. It is just a hole, just a vacuum, and you find birds in that hole flying around in the centre. And just outside, the wind is roaring hard. The centre can be anything from a mile to ten miles, but you would be very unfortunate if you got caught in the centre.'[20]

'There were recognised typhoon anchorages along the coast, bays where there was a depth of water and good holding ground. But very often you got there and found a couple of other ships there before you so you could not get in. But the main policy was to keep out of a typhoon's path.'[19]

The climate on the China coast embraces every extremity from near tropical heat in the south to the most frozen of winters in the north. And winters added to the China Navigation Company officer's sailing burden.

'In the north of China in the winter the weather could be very severe. Not mountainous seas or anything, because if there had been mountainous seas the sea would not have frozen, but the sea was frozen. I should think the ice was up to a foot in depth, and that covered the whole of the Gulf of Pechili. Our ships which were regular traders up there had ice-breaking bows – an extra plate of steel more than the normal ship with the bows sloping. The idea was that the sloping bow was inclined to climb on to the ice and the weight of the ship would crack it and make headway along the crack. This had to be done at frequent intervals when the ice was particularly thick.

'If it was only a matter of the ice being six inches thick or so you could steam through. It would just crack and you'd push it aside, but if it was very thick, and sometimes it could pile up into heaps, and you would get two or three layers of ice piled up either by the sea or by other ships pushing it together, then you could not get through. You could be absolutely stuck dead in your tracks. Then the tactics were to back out and get up full speed and have a good go at it and hope that you could break it and make a little bit of progress. Then if you saw a crack in the ice in the distance, running in the direction you wanted to go, you would make for it. And if you got into that crack, even though you had to zig zag a little bit, you were getting nearer your destination. When you did arrive in port under those circumstances, and went to the wharf and had a look at your ship's side, you would find the bows just like stainless steel, because paint, rust and everything had been taken off by the ice.'[18]

'I remember one night when I was going to Tientsin and making for Taku – that is the bar about forty miles out – there was a "wrff" "wrff" "wrff" noise. I was reading in my cabin down below, it was nine o'clock at night. "Hello, hello," I thought. "We can't be ashore." And there we were in the ice, forty miles out. So I went on the bridge, backed a bit and shot ahead again but we could not make anything of it and so we had to wait until daylight. Then you could see where the broken ice was. To make progress you may have to go south while all the time you want to go east. You would have to go south to get through the broken ice. It was a job – back, say the full length of the ship, and then full ahead again and you knew all the time you might be damaging the bow shell plating and rivets. It was a nasty business. And the temperature was one degree or maybe minus one which was not so bad if you were used to running between Shanghai and Tientsin but if, say, you had just come up from Java, where it is hot, then you knew the difference. The ships were always warm, warm as toast. But the bridge was cold. The only thing was to wrap up in leather coats.'[19]

Iced in: Frozen into the ice in the Tientsin River.

But arriving at one's destination did not necessarily mean an end to navigational problems, for China has very few natural harbours. And nearly every port required the exercise of particular skills before the ship could be brought alongside safely.

Entering the Port

'Going into Tientsin in the north of China, the approach was narrow and the only depth of water sufficient for the ship to be afloat in was right in the middle of the river. (From the banks of the river it sloped down into a "V" shape, and the deepest part was right in the middle.) So if there was another ship coming the other way, both ships wanted that middle part, but they could not both have it, so the tactics were that you came head on at a reasonable speed, because when a ship is travelling too slowly the rudders do not have the turning power; you have got to have speed for the rudder to be effective in turning the ship. So you had to come at a fair speed absolutely head on and just through experience, when you got to a certain distance perhaps a hundred yards off, both at the same instant you would turn to starboard and you could throw a biscuit from one ship to another as you passed. You would get like that and then as soon as you were abreast straighten up again. But you could literally almost touch one ship from the other.

'You did not actually do any signalling, because each pilot knew from experience when to change to starboard. You never changed to port, always to starboard. And then you just glided along each other's sides almost without touching and then as soon as you cleared each other you straightened out again and carried on your way.'[18]

Most of the China Navigation Company's ships carried a few passengers as well as cargo along the China coast. The better off travellers shared a cabin and possibly enjoyed the luxury of a saloon; others went out in the open as deck passengers. But in Swatow in south China passengers took precedence over cargo, for it was the port at the centre of the emigrant trade. In the years between the wars huge numbers of Chinese were imported as indentured labour into Thailand and Malaya and the Philippines where they were contracted to work for a specified number of years – in Malaya for example on the rubber plantations. CNCo carried their full share of human cargo to Bangkok and Singapore and back again.

'The whole shoreside operation was organised by our brokers. They were in touch with all the boarding houses who collected these emigrants from all the country around. The boarding houses arranged for their tickets and transport to the ship like a regular travel agency, the brokers supervising the arrangements and collection of fares for payment to us. There was always a movement of passengers both down and up; they'd go down to Singapore and Malaya, for a few years and then they'd come back again for a holiday. So there was a regular movement back and forth.'[2]

'The procurement of passages was in the hands of brokers tied to our company, Taikoo Nam Kee, in Swatow and in Singapore too, for the Swatow people who were coming back. The ships were certified, of course, to carry so many passengers. The ships in the Bangkok trade could carry about five hundred passengers, deck passengers, and the ships that served the Singapore trade about a thousand deck passengers plus about thirty cabin class passengers. The brokers had the full use of that space, they would procure the passengers at rates which they agreed with us. No doubt there was a bit of manoeuvring by them, that it to say if there was a great demand for space they would no doubt overcharge the passengers, but in my time that hardly ever applied, there was usually space to spare so probably from time to time if there was a Dutch ship on the berth as well they had to dip into their own commissions to get passengers.'[9]

'If the emigrants were pleased with the ship, they used to make a collection amongst themselves and they used to buy a silk flag and present it to the ship and this was called a "Joss Ship Flag". If you flew that flag they were very happy. I always used to think that it was arranged among the people who were booking their passages – they fixed it up so that the passengers would be happy. But they were supposed to come direct from the passengers.'[20]

Conditions for Passengers

'There were rules about the conditions under which passengers should be carried, British rules actually, based on the Simla Rules, an Asian version of the Safety of Life at Sea Convention. And these rules were applied by the British consul and he inspected every emigrant ship before she sailed, and counted the passengers to make sure we weren't overloaded. The Chinese didn't come into it, this was part of the extra-territorial rights really. The Chinese should have come into it in any normal way, but they didn't until we compromised in the end and they were allowed on board as observers; in other words Chinese health officials were allowed on board, but they weren't allowed to issue certificates or take any part in the official inspection.'[9]

A new life: Chinese emigrants, possibly to the Philippines, on deck.

'They were all very clean and the accommodation was inspected every day, of course. They were inspected by the doctor before leaving port and anybody with any suspicion of disease was put ashore again. I might also say we had five interpreters on those ships, who were able to talk with the passengers from Foochow who couldn't talk to the Amoy people. The Amoy people couldn't talk to the Swatow people and from behind Swatow were the old Hakka people and they couldn't talk to any of them or the Cantonese, though they might be able to talk a little bit of Swatow. But the Swatow dialect and these coastal dialects were all quite different, so we had five interpreters to cope with the five different dialects. What a business it was!

'There was a fire on one ship I remember, the *Kweiyang*. She'd taken on her passengers and was due to sail that evening and the instrument on the bridge that denotes smoke in the hold, if there is any, started to blow its bubbles up. Part of the cargo was discharged but we couldn't find the seat of the fire so we had to get all the passengers off again; get them ashore and put back into their boarding houses. The ship was brought alongside the lower property pontoon and the sea cocks opened so that she went down and rested on the sea bed alongside this pontoon which finally dealt with the fire.'[2]

'The ship had to be searched for stowaways each time we sailed and it was a very difficult job. The ship's personnel did a search during the voyage and there was a search before the ship left, but with a Chinese crew and only three really effective officers, British officers that is, searching a ship of four thousand tons with about three decks which could carry passengers, and with storerooms all over the place it was not easy. Because, of course, the Chinese staff were friends with the stowaways. You could be a stowaway if you had enough money to pay for it. And I think the stowaways we caught were probably those who were not willing to pay enough to the Chinese. It didn't happen very often but it happened more often than it came to light.

'If we found a stowaway he was just locked up in a storeroom until we got to our destination, Singapore usually, and kept under lock and key and we were responsible for him. We had to take him back.

'The company supplied the emigrants' food and it was mainly rice boiled in huge cauldrons, like the old-fashioned washing boiler that housewives used for boiling clothes before washing machines came into fashion. And the rice was boiled in that and they ate a lot of vegetables. The Chinese eat a lot of green stuff. And there seemed to be fish. I cannot remember seeing much in the way of beef; it was usually pork and fish, vegetables, rice. They were all provided with their little Chinese bowl and probably had their own chopsticks, and they just queued up and got their rice bowl filled up, and then a spoonful of whatever was going on top of that. They used to refer to a man being "a one bowl man" or "a two bowl man" or "a three bowl man". If he was a big hefty man he could get through three bowls of rice but if he was small and not very strong, he might be doing with only one or two bowls of rice. But they seemed to thrive on it and work hard on it and enjoy it.'[18]

Stowaways

Feeding the Passengers

'They nearly all slept on deck but there were some below decks. We did carry a few first class passengers but only about a dozen or more. They were mostly what they call steerage passengers. And there were bunks, which probably cost a dollar or two more than just lying on the deck, but they all had their mats; they did not have comfortable mattresses like we use, they just had a rush mat made of reeds, which ensured that they had something clean to lie on. They could lay it down anywhere and just lie on that. Of course it was more or less tropical weather all the time.'[18]

'There was sometimes a certain amount of competition for the space because of the cargo, particularly during the winter when there was a lot of fresh fruit. These beautiful Swatow oranges – the best oranges I've ever tasted – used to go down to Malaya, and because there was no mechanical ventilation or refrigeration or anything like that they had to be carried on deck, or at least the shippers insisted they were carried on deck, or at the worst in the upper 'tween decks, and so the poor old passengers had rather a rough time. We had to ensure they did get the space but it meant fearful arguments. The consul wouldn't have allowed it to be otherwise.

'But there was one cargo that came out of Swatow that was rather amusing: "hatch eggs", huge baskets of eggs were brought on board in Swatow and chaps travelled with them, in passenger space. They were passengers and this was their luggage you see, these baskets of eggs. When the ship got to sea they would spread out flat bamboo trays and get the eggs out and spread them about. The trick was to get these eggs to hatch just as the ship was entering Singapore harbour and so you either got them down in a hotter place or up in a cooler place if they were coming too quickly, and of course that did cause an awful lot of arguments with the passengers because these chaps were travelling all the time and knew their way around, and they spread their trays all over the place and pushed the passengers out of the way. That was one of the odd little cargos we carried in those days.

'The point of not letting them hatch before they reached Singapore was that if they hatched too soon they would die before they got there. I don't think they carried any food or water for them. I think we could have provided water but they had to be newly hatched. It would have been a problem for them otherwise. They would have died. Just think of thousands and thousands of little chicks all over the ship.'[9]

The solitude of life at sea was not to every British officer's taste and short spells on shore or a night in port were eagerly awaited. In every port there were cabarets which though they might not be as luxurious as those in Shanghai, still offered sailors an opportunity to fall from grace. Some simply drank, not necessarily to excess but often heavily. But then on the China coast alcohol was cheap and plentiful.

'Mostly on the China coast ships it was a couple of gins before lunch and again before dinner. Or maybe at eleven o'clock you would have a drink with the passengers. But I have never ever seen "the bottle of gin a day man" that we have heard about. I have never seen one. Never in my life.

'Most people did not like drinking at sea, but very often when you were sailing first thing the next morning, maybe at five or six o'clock in the morning having not been ashore all the day before, you might have a few drinks that night. However you knew that you had got to be on the top line in the morning to take the ship out. Now sometimes I had been drinking. Perhaps I had one or two. And I had a very good old faithful boy. (He was a white-haired man, although we called him "boy".) I suppose because he liked me he was faithful to me. He was the captain's boy. Anyway I might be well away before I went to bed and I would tell him I was going to bed and he used to come to my room – in those days the iced water used to be in gin bottles – and he would ask me what I would like, and I would say give me a tot of gin and then he would put bitters in it. And he would ask me if it was enough and I would say, "Put a little more gin in there." And he would do it again and then I would begin drinking it and away he would go. Then he would come back again. Well, the next morning I would be sailing and feeling good. No effects at all you see. Then the boy would tell me, "You didn't drink so much last night because when you asked for gin I give you water." Now that was a true servant and someone who cared for you and your job, the ship and everything and I liked it and I thanked him and I said you keep that up. Now I know other types that would be very glad to see the captain or the boss drinking too much.'[19]

'It could be very lonely at sea. Masters of ships in those days didn't really talk to anybody except their Chief Engineer. There's more fraternising now than there ever was before. And then the master of a ship could drink at sea because he had no other duties, but there was this tremendous loneliness, and it was only bachelors now I come to think of it that would commit suicide. There weren't many but they were bachelors. There was no explaining why, but they would gradually get moody, I suppose. There was a tremendous loneliness about the life. There again I was young and didn't notice it. And I had friends I suppose.

'There was a certain amount of drinking. And then somebody would go and shoot himself. Not a great number but enough to echo through the fleet and then somebody sent out this memo typed on Butterfield & Swire memo pad; that the management was gravely concerned about the increasing number of suicides in the fleet and in future would officers contemplating suicide please use their own ammunition.'[17]

Ships' officers carried personal arms and ammunition because of the everpresent danger on the China coast of being pirated. On the islands and in the creeks, particularly north of Hong Kong, gangs of Chinese pirates hid up waiting to seize control of a ship to steal its cargo, or more often to kidnap a wealthy Chinese who could be held for a substantial ransom. Any company running ships on the coast was forced to take stringent precautions against the risk of piracy.

'The working part of the ship was in a block at the centre; that contained the navigation bridge, all entrances to the engine room and the European officers' accommodation. And both ends of this central island were barred with these metal bars usually with revolving spikes at the top. In it were either British personnel, passengers if you had any, and loyal crew members like stewards that you could trust. All of the deck passengers were outside this area, and these partitions, iron bars and revolving spikes and things were patrolled by armed guards, trained anti-piracy guards. And they kept two hours duty, two hours off, something like that, all the time the ship was at sea.

'They were armed Chinese trained by the Hong Kong police and usually under a White Russian sergeant. He might have been an ex-Hong Kong policeman since quite a lot of Russians joined the Hong Kong police. And the ship's officers were all armed, of course, but we did not carry our arms with us, we had them in our cabins at the ready.'[18]

Grilled: Anti-piracy grilles on a coastal ship.

'Officers had a Winchester .44 gun on the rack on the ceiling of their cabin and a .38 Webley revolver. Everytime you left your room to go on watch you put your belt and your revolver on. And the *Fatshan* had steamer hoses to keep people off the bridge if necessary which was a very good system.'[19]

'There were often leakages of information about the movements of pirates. Perhaps there were two lots of pirates around and one was a bit jealous of the other. So if one thought the other was making a move to pirate a ship they would spill the beans so that their rivals would be caught. Then they would move in. But we had quite a good spy system in Hong Kong, and if there was any suspicion of any particular ship being pirated it was broadcast. A message was sent to the ship radio. A favourite method of the pirates was to come aboard as deck passengers. They just brought their baggage with them, big bundles or bags or anything at all, any kind of container. And, of course, things to sell, merchandise like salt, fish, any kind of fish. And they would conceal their weapons in these bags of fish or boxes or wherever, or they might even be in league with one or two naughty members of the Chinese crew who would hide them for them. And then at a given signal they would pass out the arms.'[18]

'We probably had a ship pirated every year or two. It was a fairly fixed sort of drill really, if the piracy was successful the ship was brought down (usually it was on a ship leaving Shanghai going south) to Bias Bay which was not very far from Hong Kong, south of Swatow and north of Hong Kong, and the pirates would take ashore any bullion they found or anything of that kind on board or valuable cargo and sometimes a few Chinese hostages for ransom. They didn't normally interfere with the officers from the point of view of taking hostages. And the general system was that if the piracy was successful you allowed it to proceed, because we had had one or two cases where trying to be brave and recapture the ship had had rather disastrous results. Like setting fire to the ship, which was on balance not a good idea. Usually the success or failure of the attempt was a matter of the moment, because it normally depended on somehow deceiving the guard on the barricade. The crew had to pass through these barriers from time to time, while they were working and so they would call out to have the thing opened, and of course it was just possible for the pirates to pretend to be crew or to put a gun in the back of a crew member and make him go and get the gate opened up. It shouldn't happen, of course, because they were supposed to open the door on the chain and call out the rest of the guard or at least the sergeant before they opened the door, but I think every now and then somebody slipped up, it happened, and the pirates got through and then they would rush the bridge and take control.'[9]

'The pirates were mostly after kidnapping rich Chinese who may have been travelling as passengers on the ship. Or if they knew that there was anything valuable on board in the way of cargo, bullion or anything like that. Once they got control of the ship they just took what they wanted. But it was easiest to take rich Chinese, and sometimes European officers as with the Nanchang pirates who took the ships' officers when the ship was anchored outside Newchwang waiting for a pilot. They took four officers and held them at ransom for six months. And they changed hands several times during that six months.

'Another bunch of bandits got to hear that this particular gang of pirates had four European officers who they were holding for a huge ransom and they said, "Oh why can't we take them, we'll hold them for ransom", you see. So they had a fight with the holding gang and they were successful, so the ship's officers changed hands and the ransom was demanded by somebody else. If any ransom was paid on this occasion it was done secretly by the Japanese, who controlled the area.

'A lot of people wondered whether they should make a fight if there was an alarm. I personally would have put up a fight because the company would not have given me guns otherwise; they would expect me to do it if there was a chance. But there were one or two who doubted the wisdom of always putting up a fight because at one time one of B & S's ships was very badly burnt out, and if no fight had been put up that ship would have been all right. So there was argument for and against, but just because we were expected to fight I would have put up a fight with the others.'[18]

Pirated

There had always been pirates off the China coast ready to seize a wealthy merchant or traveller and to hold them to ransom, or to steal a valuable cargo. And in the years between the wars the pirates continued their lucrative trade despite the certainty of death if they were caught. Indeed it has been estimated that there were over fifty major cases of piracy in this period, mostly involving British ships, and that twenty British Merchant Navy officers lost their lives. And this is to ignore the many piratings of Chinese junks with wealthy passengers kidnapped, cargoes stolen and crews killed. Such cases rarely reached the front pages of the foreign language newspapers.

Shipping companies such as The China Navigation Company were compelled to take precautions against the risk of piracy. Armed guards were put aboard coastal steamers, officers issued with revolvers and Winchester rifles and the central part of the ship, comprising the bridge and the officers' quarters, screened off by metal grilles from the areas occupied by Chinese deck passengers who, it was suspected, might be in league with pirates to the extent of having smuggled arms aboard in their belongings.

The majority of piracies occured in southern China. The area around Bias Bay north of Hong Kong was a particularly favoured place of shelter and retreat for the pirates. The northern coast of the country, however, was free from maritime buccaneers, but then in March 1933 the CNCo's ship *Nanchang* was pirated at Newchwang. Four of her British officers, Clifford Johnson, Archie Blue, William Hargrave and a man called Pears were taken off the ship on March 29th by ex-soldiers of the Manchurian war lord Chang Hsueh Liang, known as the Young Marshal.

Chang's army had been disbanded after the Japanese conquest of Manchuria was complete and it is safe to assume that in accordance with Chinese custom throughout the centuries many of his one-time soldiers took to a life of banditry and piracy. But if the principal motive of the particular band of pirates who attacked the *Nanchang* was private gain, it also seems likely that by their action they hoped to draw the world's attention, and particularly that of the British, to the Japanese conquest of their country, and to the manifest political sham represented by Japan's setting up of the puppet state of Manchukuo in what had hitherto been Chinese Manchuria. It is dangerous to lay too much stress on the political motives behind the piracy, but the Manchukuo – for which one should read Japanese – authorities' frustrated attempts to rescue the British officers scarcely presented the

Caught: Chinese pirates guarded by Sikh policemen after their capture.

Sitting it out: The Navy keeps guard over a band of pirates.

world with an image of a state securely living under the well-regulated rule of law.

Be that as it may, the original pirates' plans went seriously awry as emerges in the following account of the piracy, which to a considerable extent is based on a remarkable diary kept by Johnson on scraps of paper during his captivity and subsequently published* when he returned to England after enduring imprisonment along with Blue and Hargrave for over five months.

On the morning of 29th March, 1933 the steamer *Nanchang* lay at anchor at the mouth of the Liao Ho River nineteen miles from Newchwang. As was usual, the port had been icebound from November until March but now the ice had broken and the *Nanchang* was waiting with seven or eight other ships for a pilot to take her into port. It was eleven in the morning and Johnson, Pears, Hargrave and Blue were whiling away the time until their pilot should return from having taken the first ship into Newchwang.

The Attack

'The four of us were sitting in the mess room chatting, waiting for a pilot when we heard what we thought were firecrackers, so we didn't pay any attention to it. Then these people burst into the room and it was all over in five minutes after they'd fired off a few shots. The captain was up on the boat deck, but they never went up there, and the chief engineer was down below, so they didn't capture either of them.'[22]

'We four jumped up and ran to the forward portholes. A junk was made fast alongside the starboard rail. Men were scrambling aboard. Two were already on the deck, firing up at us. More men aboard the junk were firing wildly at saloon and bridge. We rushed for the door and all got jammed in the doorway. Blue, the second engineer, collided with us, shouting: "There's pirates on board!"'

* *Pirate Junk*: Jonathan Cape 1934

'Our cabins were very inconveniently situated at the four corners of the deck; the captain's room was on the boat deck. He made for his cabin by climbing a boat davit, while each of us rushed to our own rooms to get our guns, which we had to keep unloaded on account of the Chinese servants. I flung open my door; but as I did so, a pirate came up the ladder a couple of yards away. He fired at me as soon as he saw me. I heard the shots strike the steel plating near my head.

'There was no time for me to get my Winchester and load it; so I swung round and ran along the deck to the second engineer's cabin, at the after end of the deck, thinking I might get one of his. Pears was there, too. As Blue got the cartridges from his wardrobe – the guns were already lying on the settee – I popped my head out and had a look round. Hargrave, the second officer, was peering out of his after porthole. A second junk, which had come up alongside opposite his cabin, was keeping up a heavy firing; and he couldn't get out. I was just going to shout to him, when a bullet struck the steel plating just by me, and another struck the glass of Blue's porthole. As I nipped my head back, I saw two pirates climbing the ladder six feet away, those who had chased me along the deck came into sight at the same moment. They fired wildly into the room. God knows how we missed being shot. Blue was loading the first gun – he had got the catch back – when they crowded into the room and jabbed their revolvers into our ribs.

'It was no good; we had to put our hands up. One man, evidently the chief pirate, dressed immaculately in the uniform of a Manchukuo officer, jabbered excitedly at us in Chinese. We couldn't understand. They pushed us out of the cabin and along past Hargrave's room. As they went by, they swung open the door and fired at him. The bullet went through his coat and shirt sleeve but didn't hurt him. They yoicked him out and the four of us were marched down on to the foredeck where one or two of the Chinese crew were standing dazedly talking to the pirates. When we came up, they sent the ship's carpenter to fetch a rope-ladder, which they hung over the ship's side. Then we were made to climb down into the junk.'[23]

The pirates ransacked as much of the ship as they had time for and set sail in two junks for the extensive mudflats in the north-west corner of the Gulf of Liao Tung into which the Liao River flowed. For most of the journey the four British officers were imprisoned below.

'About 3 p.m. the hatch was thrown back and a bowl of rice with chopsticks was passed to each of us, followed by a small bowl of shrimps and three of boiling water. But we had no appetite and they were returned almost untouched.

'Some time later the hatch was opened again and two of the pirates dropped down and sat on our legs, as there was no floor-space left for them. One of them, like a grinning monkey, was wearing my thick brown overcoat and wrist-watch. I pointed out that they were mine. But as he couldn't understand a word that we said, we smiled at him and in a gentle voice repeated every swear-word that we knew. He was very pleased and smiled back. Then he rubbed his first finger and thumb together, to show that it was money they required. He pulled out his revolver and held it at each of our heads in turn, and so that we should understand what would happen if the money was not forthcoming, he ended by falling backwards as if dead. A pleasant man!'[23]

It was generally accepted on the China coast that only in the rarest of circumstances were prisoners ever ransomed for money by British companies or by the British authorities. So the *Nanchang* officers' principal hopes of freedom rested on being rescued by the Manchukuo government forces or in organising their own escape. The four officers decided upon escape.

April 2nd

An Attempted Escape

'Hargrave crawled on deck, threw a cotton-padded blanket over the stern on to the mud and then dropped down, himself. The blanket muffled the noise and prevented us sinking in too deep. We followed him. It was bitterly cold. The mud came up to and then over our knees. The sky was overcast, not a star to be seen. We climbed the bank slowly and plodded in the mud. It slowly got deeper and deeper. It came up to our thighs. We found it hard to get our feet out to take another step. It was still freezing and there were great chunks of ice lying around. We grew numb from the waist down.

'We plodded on for another half hour. There was still no sign of firm land. We grew desperate. Our first thought now was not to escape but to save our lives. We had to turn back to the junks.

'The mud was so soft that it had flowed back and covered our tracks. The impressions were faint and hard to trace in the darkness. We didn't speak a word, just dragged our numbed legs free only to plunge them as deep again into mud with the next step.'[23]

'And we just made it back, but the pirates never knew we were away. They didn't keep any watches, you see, so it was all perfectly safe.'[22]

In the meantime the pirates had decided that one of their prisoners should be sent to Newchwang with a message demanding a ransom. The four officers played poker with a set of makeshift playing cards made out of empty cigarette packets in order to see who was to be fortunate enough to leave the junk. Blue won, but the pirates decided that Pears should be their messenger. Hargrave and Johnson had been captured in uniform, Blue was wearing a sweater and blue trousers but Pears, who had been in the enginer room just before the piracy, was wearing his boiler suit. Clearly, the pirates thought he was the least important of their captives. So it was Pears who set off for Newchwang.

The three who remained behind spend most of their time below decks in what they came to call their 'glory hole', a compartment which was some four feet high, five feet long and nine feet wide. But because of the upwardly sloping sides of the junk the width varied from six feet at the floor to ten feet at the roof. There was no room to stretch out full length and little protection from the weather. The three men slept on damp dog skins, sacks and a Chinese quilt. They were fed by their captors, but it was a basic diet.

Pears successfully reached Newchwang and contact was established between the pirates and the Manchukuo authorities. The principal gain from this contact for the three men still aboard the junk was the arrival of food parcels.

'In the parcels we got chocolate, big lots of sugar, not cube sugar but coarse sugar, toothpaste, Walls pork sausages and Bovril. And there were socks and those felt shoes. They sent a lot of stuff knowing that the pirates would take some of it. The pirates went over it first and then we got what was left. In the very first parcel we got a Mandarin phrasebook which was a great help. We kept the contents of the parcel in a bag and it was doled out. We used to measure the Bovril with chopsticks.'[22]

The Manchukuo authorities, encouraged by the British consul at Newchwang, were making every effort to find and rescue Johnson, Blue and Hargrave, but they were hampered by the fact that the pirates continually changed their position amongst the mudflats and many creeks of the area where they were holding their prisoners. The gang of pirates who had stormed the *Nanchang* were not the only pirates in the area. There were others who quickly realised that three British officers might be transformed into a sizeable ransom if they could be seized from their original captors. This was the fate that befell Johnson and his two companions on 11th April, a little less than a fortnight after they had first been pirated.

'This area is full of creeks and one night we saw some junks further down the creek where we were anchored. There were about three or four junks and some of the bandits from aboard them came up to talk to our people and they evidently saw us although we'd been hustled down below. So later that night we were attacked by this lot. They came up and fired off their guns and quite a few of the gang who had originally kidnapped us were killed. We were kept down below and bullets went through the wooden sides of the junk. I remember during the fighting somebody lifted up the hatch and looked down to see us and shut it down again. These were bandits pure and simple. They were a real rough lot.'[22]

太古

'The firing stopped as abruptly as it began. The hatch was again pulled roughly off, and two monkey-faced bandits dropped down into the glory hole. Then we knew, what we had feared, that we had been captured by another gang, this time of bandits, not pirates.

'Someone threw down a blanket to them and they took Pears' thick fawn dressing-gown. Then they began to "shoo" us over to one side, taking half the glory hole for themselves. Finding that didn't work, they pushed us until I was lying up the curvature of the junk's side, resting on Blue, while Hargrave lay immediately beneath the hatchway. They chattered incessantly and played with the revolvers which they had just taken from the pirates.

'Suddenly they saw our provisions on the shelf at our feet, and took everything, biscuits, cigarettes and Bovril. We lay there watching, not able to do a thing in protest. The thought came that we had eaten the chocolate, so they couldn't get that; but it wasn't much consolation.'[23]

This second gang of pirates, bandits as Johnson chose to call them, were indeed bandits pure and simple, interested only in the ransom they might extort from the authorities in exchange for their prisoners. Greed, not political protest, was at the heart of their kidnapping of the British officers.

'There are now five junks tied up alongside the bank. At a rough guess there must be about seventy men. One of the bandits in our glory hole seems to be a very old man, his red weather-beaten face like a chunk of raw beef; he has probably been a fisherman. The other is fresh-faced and must be about thirty. We have decided they are the two chief bandits. After every few words, they spit, like real Chinamen. They don't mind where they do it, on the blankets or the ship's side just behind our heads, anywhere in fact.

'They keep fiddling about with the Mauser pistols they seized from the pirates. The young one passed one of them up to a man at the hatchway, and as he did so, it went off. There was a terrific bang. The bullet whizzed past Hargrave's ear, went straight through the bandit's hand, and buried itself in the blanket at Hargrave's feet. This is Hargrave's second lucky escape. It seems to have cured the bandits, for a while at least. They put the guns away and bandaged up the wounded hand with a piece of our white paper.

'Dozens of bandits crowded round the hatch during the morning to see the "foreign devils". Some leant down and tugged at Hargrave's hair, while others went further and dropping down into the hole itself pulled our ears and noses, saying how big they were.

'They were stopped by the young bandit chief, who told us to write a letter to the British consul. While we did so, the men crowded round. They demanded two million dollars. Someone mentioned gold rings (we've nicknamed him the "Ring Bastard"). Everybody agreed; so we had to add eighty gold rings. The three of us signed it and it was snatched from us by the Number One, who handed it over to a messenger. (We called the young one Number One, the old one "Father".)

'Later, it came fluttering down the hatchway, which doesn't look very hopeful for its delivery to the consul. We gave it back to Number One, who took it and went on deck.'[23]

Towards the end of April the weather grew warmer, and with the early summer weather came lice.

'We were quite experts when it came to lice. We used to do de-lousing every morning once it got warmer weather. It was too cold for them at first. But we managed to keep them down. You killed them between your nails. They always seemed to be in the seams of your trousers, so you ran your nail down the seam to get rid of them.'[22]

太古

'Scratched so much during the night that under my sweaty shirt my skin is raw and bleeding. Hargrave's is even worse. We have our clothes off and go hunting. Crack, they go, one by one, between our thumb nails which look like little bloody battlefields. The junkmen eat their dead lice, but we're not that hungry yet.'[23]

'They were always asking us questions about Britain and they were terribly surprised that we had trains. They seemed to think that we were at the same stage as they were, more or less. And they were quite interested in Scotland, where I came from. They were very interested in our noses, because compared to the Chinese we have big noses. They used to point at them and it seemed to amuse them.'[22]

'Red letter day. One of the bandits brought half a pig on board and left it alongside our hatchway, giving us a smile and a nod of his bullet head. The bandits clustered round, pawing it with their filthy hands; the sight of meat was so tempting that our mouths watered and I could not resist having a poke at it myself. Then the old junkman, who is official cook, dragged it away; our eyes never left it a second. In less than half an hour it was chopped into small bits and put into the great stew pan.

'When the meat was done, they served it to the men on deck, each man a bowl of boiling hot pork. The air was so full of its sweet scent that lumps came into our throats and the saliva ran down our chins. We sat and watched them shovel the food into their mouths, their chopsticks working so fast that we felt almost dizzy.

'The meal finished, the remnants were poured into a single bowl, which they gave to us. We gobbled down the tasty bits of rind and fat, finding sometimes even a piece of lean which they had overlooked; and when we had eaten all, we each took a sip at the soup left at the bottom. We left the bowl empty and spotless. We lay back feeling twice as strong.'[23]

The Japanese authorities in Manchukuo were making strenuous efforts to locate the bandits who had captured the British officers from the gang who had originally pirated them, and their aeroplanes flew sorties over the creeks and mudflats at the head of the Gulf of Liao Tung.

'The plane came into view, flying from the south; suddenly it changed its course and headed straight for us. The click of rifle catches and the noise of breach-loading; we lay in wait. The plane swooped, looking as if it was going to crash on top of us. The bandits were filled with panic. Some got up and ran, dragging us along with them; others opened up a wild and rapid fire. As it passed, directly overhead, its roar was deafening and drowned the shouts of the bandits and even the noise of their shots for a moment. Stumbling along, I looked up and plainly saw the faces of the airmen, as they leant over the side. Then she roared up into the sky and the noise of her engine softened as she rose. It's a very remarkable thing they didn't bring her down. We were all rather demoralised. The bandits got up and wiped their foreheads with their jacket sleeves. I was all shaking and had to beg a few puffs from a cigarette to steady my nerves. Then we trooped back to the junk.

'After much argument, Hargrave got Number One's consent to fetch a tub of clean water from the butt and had a good wash with the remaining cake of soap. Blue and I followed his example. We are going to use as much of it as we can before they take it away.

'The youngest bandit – a mere child, the son of Number One – is ship's barber. He shaves them with a penknife, a piece of glass or an old razor. Soon after he arrived about a fortnight ago, he was objectionably cheeky in his attitude towards us and annoyed us very much. The bandits treat him as an equal, and when he holds forth, they listen to him with open mouths. Once I saw him even ordering the men about; everything's topsy turvy in China. He has been better lately and treats us with a mixture of mild pity and friendliness. When Hargrave and Blue suggested that he should shave them, he readily agreed and ran off to tell the mob, so that they could see the fun. The amusement proved so popular that bandits came over from the other junk and crowded on board until there was no room left to stand. Two in their haste to get a place on board slipped from the gangplank down into the water. Hargrave was given the mirror when his toilet was finished and looked with some surprise at his bald white scalp, which looks like a white skull cap above the well-tanned face. Blue's straggly beard then fell to the shears and soon there wasn't a hair left on his head, except for his walrus moustache. Rather unwillingly, I had to yield to pressure and have my head shaved, but I wouldn't let them touch my beard.'[28]

Nearly two months after they had originally been pirated, Johnson, Blue and Hargrave witnessed an event that left them in little doubt as to what their fate might be if they were not ransomed, rescued or successful in escaping.

A Coolie is Beaten and Killed

'A junk has come. A message at last. We are sitting in the glory hole, ears pricked to catch any news, as the junk scrapes alongside. Everybody is talking at once; men rush here and there. We hear laughter and curses.

'Later. We asked Number One for the message. He said there was none and beckoned us to come on deck. In the new junk drawn alongside, was a Chinese prisoner, bound with ropes and propped up against the mast. Number One talked so fast we couldn't understand him. We gathered, however, that they were holding him for ransom. As he refused to pay $10,000, they were going to shoot him. But how could a coolie pay that sum? As the excitement subsided, a bandit pointed to the wretched man and asked us how we'd like to be in his place. They kept repeating he would be shot, because he wouldn't pay. He looked haggard and in pain; his hands were tightly bound behind his back. Every now and again a bandit gave him a cutting smack across his face, and stamped his foot on the deck and, cursing, spat on him. They whipped themselves up with words and grew mad. There's no telling what a Chinese mob will do, once they grow mad. We thought this man was a spy and suddenly one of the bandits ran forward, shouting, "You dirty Japanese spy." He struck him on the shoulder with the butt end of his rifle. Striding along the bank from the next junk, a man with a long black gown and a face almost as black, shouted an order to the excited men. The victim was half-dragged, half-pushed down the gang plank and up the bank. (The man with the black gown is obviously the *real* Number One, as we have long suspected. We shall continue, however, to call him "Black Face". But now we call our Number One by his real name, Li Wen Chi).

'Li Wen Chi told us to follow him ashore, and he guarded us. Bandits ran past us, shouting and waving their guns. They hauled the man to a clearing in the reeds, about a hundred feet in diameter. We had to follow after.

'They stood him in the centre and untied him; he was made to strip. The middle of the rope was tied round his neck and made fast behind, a length running down each arm and fastened above the wrists. A spare fifteen feet of rope hung down on the ground at each end. The bandits stood about in groups; a crowd formed round us, their faces white with passion and excitement as they cursed the Japanese and threatened us with the same torture that this man was going to suffer. The Ring Bastard and another grabbed the lengths of rope hanging from the victim's wrists and ran off in opposite directions, till the man's arms were jerked taut with the rope, in a sort of crucified position.

'Black Face stepped forward, tucking up the wide sleeves of his gown. He had a knotted two-inch rope in his hand, about a yard and a half in length. I looked at the man; he was watching us with beseeching eyes as much as to say, "I'm going through all this for you." I couldn't stand looking at him and turned towards Black Face. He swung the rope above his head and brought it down with a crack on the man's bare back. The man let out a cry. A weal came up where the rope had fallen. All the bandits were shouting and cursing like madmen. Blood began to trickle, then flow, from the wounds upon his back. Then he swayed and fell forward unconscious, his face buried in the soft mud; his back was raw with blood. The Ring Bastard and the other one ran to him and began to kick him, to get him on his feet again: another brought a kerosene tin full of river water and flung it over his head.

'The man spluttered and raised his head. Seeing that he could still feel, Black Face lifted up his rope and beat him where he was, on the mud. The man tried to get up, raising himself on his hands; but he fell back again. Never before have I seen such cruelty, and all for our sake too. He lost consciousness again and they couldn't revive him. The skin of his back was flayed to bits.

'We were taken back to the junk and as we were going up the gang plank we heard a shot. They told us the man had regained consciousness and so they had taken him down the river bank and shot him.'[23]

Throughout May and June Johnson and his companions continued to receive food parcels and messages from Newchwang. Now they knew that the Manchukuo authorities were negotiating with the bandits for their release and were holding twenty-six of the bandits' relatives hostage against the continuing safety of the British officers. But the negotiations seemed to go by fits and starts. Were the Japanese in Manchukuo buying time until they could land a military rescue party? At any event on 5th July the bandits, still in their junks, came under attack.

'Suddenly at breakfast this morning we heard the cry of "Feijin, Feijin!" (aeroplane, aeroplane!) which all the bandits took up. The hum grew louder, louder than we had ever heard before. In our haste we had to leave everything; we did not even have time to put on our shoes. The tide was full, just on the turn. We jumped barefoot on to the bank and through the reeds, cutting our feet on the sharp stubble of last year's crop. Everybody left the

The Junks are Attacked

97

six junks except the old junk men. We all lay among the reeds, which rustled high above us and we heard the bandits round us constantly using the word "soldier". We thought of "on the alert for any eventuality", but showed no sign of having heard them or understanding what they said. The hum, which was the throbbing of many engines, grew nearer, till the air seemed to pulse with the noise. As they passed overhead, we saw six bombing planes, flying in two arrowhead formations. Judging by the volume of the noise, we thought they circled for a few minutes; but, lying where we were, we could only see them when they were directly above us.

'Then they began to bomb the opposite bank of the creek, some little way inland. We were glad we were not on that side.

'So we lay till noon; at noon the planes flew back to Newchwang. Then we were taken back to the band and had to wade knee-deep down the soft mud to the junks, which lay in the centre of the creek. Arrived there, we washed our feet and got our shoes on, in case the aeroplanes should return. The bandits rejoined the junks, irrespective of which was their own, and the junks were poled up stream with difficulty against the ebbing tide.

'After circling round for a short time, they flew off and we returned to the junk. The bandits told us there would be no more trouble that day, and when we got to our compartment we took off our shoes again. The junks shifted back to midstream and anchored. Thankful that the strain was over for the day, we lay down to rest; and when our pings came along, we mixed three cups of Ovaltine and set to. The bandits squatted about the deck, feeding and chatting.

'Suddenly there was a burst of firing from the left bank; and we heard the sharp noise of bullets striking the side of the junk. The bandits dropped their bowls, caught up their rifles and crouching behind the hatch coamings, answered the firing from the shore. We caught all the blankets, skins and chunks of wood that we could find and huddled into the far side of the compartment, hoping that we would be protected against any bullets that penetrated the side. More and more bullets struck the wooden junk and whistled overhead; from the constant clicking of the bandits' rifles it sounded as if in their excitement they were firing so fast that the barrels of their rifles would get red hot.

'A hoarse excited voice shouted down to us to jump on deck immediately. But for us there was no excitement; we could do nothing; we had only fear. So we didn't move; none of us wanted to be propped against the firing in the hope that seeing us the attackers would stop. The voice again demanded we should go on deck and the gun was pointed down at us. I rushed up – I've never moved so fast – and threw myself flat on deck. Blue followed and then Hargrave. The bandits were so crowded on our junk that they lay two deep, one atop of the other; the top and bottom man each firing as fast as their guns could. We were told to jump into the water and we thankfully slid over the edge of the junk away from the firing. Three bandits jumped in afterwards, shouting to us to swim for the bank.

'We swam as fast as we could, trying to out-distance the bandits. As I swam, I noticed that all the other junks were under fire. A dead body floated past me on the incoming tide. We three were separated as we swam and scrambled, stumbling, up the mud bank some yards away from one another. The bandits were there before us, but they all three fixed on me, as I ran up towards the reeds. Blue and Hargrave in the confusion managed to get away. "Each man for himself." One bandit went off cursing to look for them. The other two caught hold of me by the seat of my pants and jabbed their guns into my back.'[23]

'We escaped a second time at the end of the period when we were on the junks. At first we had decided that we wouldn't escape unless we could all go together, but later on we decided that each of us would take our chance if there was an opportunity. This particular time a number of junks belonging to a different gang of pirates were anchored in our creek. There were about seven or eight of them and we were attacked from one side. Our gang decided to abandon their junks after a lot of firing and we half waded, half swam ashore and all three of us disappeared, took the opportunity to escape them.

'I just shot off into the reeds and went about a hundred yards and sat down until the hue and cry died down. Then I carried on and I heard them coming after me. They recaptured me but we pretended that we hadn't escaped but were just trying to get off the junks.'[22]

'Then Blue was brought in escorted by two men. He looked frightful; his feet were grazed and cut. I was glad to get him back, even though I was sorry he hadn't succeeded in escaping. It's better when there are two. We sat on the soft mud, guarded by five bandits with drawn revolvers and he told me what had happened. He and Hargrave were behind me, and, seeing a chance to escape, they had fled, he to left, Hargrave to right. He meant to try to get across the river to the soldiers. He hadn't gone far before he heard the bandits who were abandoning the other junks. So he dropped flat on the ground. At the same time he heard shouts from another quarter. The bandits hoped that hearing them they would come back. Those who were abandoning the junks and were by this time only a few yards away from Blue, turned aside and made for the sound.

'When they had gone, he got up and went on. He had to flop down again there, because a bandit rushed past him – miraculously unobservant – and stopped a few yards away, pulled out his revolver and started to fire at the opposite bank. Blue said the bullets chipped the reeds all round him. He had to lie where he was, hoping the bandits whom he could hear rustling through the reeds, would miss him and that when it was dark he could cross the river unobserved. But by bad luck, a bandit, by name Peiping, tripped over his body a few minutes later and quickly covered him with his revolver. So Blue came back.

'The sun was setting. The firing had grown intermittent. It looked as if Hargrave had got free, when suddenly Blue said, "Here's Hargrave", and I turned round and there he was, between two bandits. He could hardly walk, his feet a running mess of blood. As he came up, there was a murmur of pleasure from the bandits. He slopped down beside us exhausted, smeared the blood from his feet and put his shoes on very carefully.

'We pestered him with questions, but as soon as he was ready, we were told to get up. Our wrists were roped and a bandit took hold of the end of each rope. We marched off in single file downstream under the shelter of the dyke. A few men were left behind to keep up the firing and cover our retreat. The full moon clearly lit our way and we were glad, because the going was hard, splashing through waterfilled holes, and our feet were sore. Often I had to turn back to pick up one of my shoes, which had been wrenched off and left sticking in the mud.

'After about an hour and a half, we were surprised to find the junks, two of them at least, beached high and dry up the mud. The bandits bent to and pushed them down to the water. We all jumped in and sailed away down river.

'It was a big relief to get into the junks again. After cleaning ourselves the best we could, we looked about for something with which to dress our feet, especially Hargrave's. There was nothing; so as a last resort we plastered them with Pepsodent, of which we had received a tube by the last parcel.

'And then we tried to sleep.'[23]

For their part the bandits appear to have been convinced that they were about to be attacked by units of the Japanese army, so they decided to abandon their junks and make their way inland with their three prisoners.

The Bandits Abandon the Junks

'"Zo, Zo, Zo!" (Go, Go!) Roughly pushed, we scrambled to our feet and leapt from our junk into the soft mud. Three bandits stood waiting for us, each with a length of rope; and we had to drop our bundles into the mud while they tied us up. The rope was fastened round our necks and round each arm, leaving a trailing length of some feet which the bandits held, trudging behind us with their revolvers drawn ready for any emergency. Winding in and out of the reeds, sploshing through mud, we reached a small hollow beside the dyke; and here we rested. The bandits followed, in groups of six and seven, each carrying in addition to his belongings some stores or utensils from the junk.

'Finally everyone was present, over a hundred all told. The junks were left deserted; even one of the water butts was brought ashore and filled from the river with water carried in kerosene tins. All day we lay with the muddy hollow as our bed and our small bundles as pillows, the sun pouring down on our heads, till we felt they were splitting.

'They dug a hole for a fireplace but were afraid to light the fire for fear the soldiers should see it. So we had to eat a small portion of yesterday's pings which we had left untouched and had to drink the filthy creek water cold and unsterilised. We dared not take more than an occasional sip of it for fear of contracting dysentery or worse. Even the lowest coolie in Manchuria drinks his water hot.

'The soldiers were still supposed to be all round us but still we did not see them.

'The lice were very bad; spots of blood oozed through our filthy shirts where we scratched. Round our belts it was worst, because it was there we sweated most. Often when the blood dried, our shirts were stuck to us. When we asked them to release us from the ropes so that we might delouse, they just laughed at us and repeated our request to one another and laughed again.

'"Sharmuns," like overgrown horse-flies with thorny heads, swarmed round and bit us in preference to the bandits. It was like being picked with pins all over; we got no rest by day.

'At night, small crabs crept out of myriad holes in search of food. Our arms were always on the go, frantically pushing the damn things off before they could get a firm grip with their large claws. We got no sleep. A swamp may be a paradise for a mosquito but for us it's hell.'[23]

Now began the worst part of the three British officers' captivity as they were force-marched through the countryside.

'When we awakened some time in the afternoon, the sun was blazing down. My head felt splitting; lucky it was no worse. The temperature in the sun must have been 130°F. We had had no food and our bellies were aching pitifully. Hargrave just grunted. Blue said "Another two days of this will finish us off." Our bodies were stiff and ached in every limb from the hours of unaccustomed plodding through the mud. Hargrave showed us his feet. I wanted to vomit. From the wounds, swollen and angry like little vocanoes, yellow pus oozed over his muddy feet.

'"Zo, Zo, Zo!" Again the damned order to march. We struggled to our feet and pushed on again. Only the feeling of pride kept us going; if the Chinese could stand it, we could. I kept saying to myself, "I won't drop, I won't drop." And I didn't.

'The reeds grew fewer; little cultivated patches were dotted about here and there. A farm appeared in sight.

'As soon as we reached the farm we sank down in the courtyard and rested, exhausted. And food was brought us. Hot pings, which seemed a blessing; and the farmer's wife came with a few onions.

'After we had eaten, they gave a letter into my hand; but I passed it to Blue. He tore the envelope open and read it out to us. It was from Clarke, British Consul at Yinkow. He read: "The bandits will not listen to reason, so the authorities are going to launch an attack on them in about a week's time. Wear some conspicuous garment, such as white shorts, so that you can be easily recognised; the likelihood of your being accidentally shot will be lessened." We looked down at our rags, at our shorts once white but now a stiff, foul, brown and grey mass. Blue read on: "P.S. – If the bandits want to know what's in this letter, tell them it's about your relatives." Li Wen Chi stood by and asked what the letter said. I collapsed and lay with my head in my hands and said that my father had died of grief at my capture. They came round and sympathised. One brought me an extra ping, another the stub end of a cigarette. Blue and Hargrave wished that their fathers had died.'[23]

Johnson, Blue and Hargrave had by now been prisoners for over five months, their hopes of rescue or release continually being raised only to be dashed again.

The Prisoners are Force-marched across Country

What they could not know was that the matter of their kidnapping had been raised in the House of Commons on 12th July and intense diplomatic pressure was being brought to bear on the Japanese government in Tokyo to find the three of them and secure their release. Negotiations between the bandits and the Manchukuo authorities were beginning to bear fruit, but first the authorities wanted to be certain that the bandits were actually holding the British officers. On 7th September they were visited by two officials, one of whom they later learned was a Korean called Lee.

'Late in the morning, Li Wen, very excited, came to us and said two men had arrived and wanted to see us. He had scarcely spoken, when the two men came in, followed by a crowd of bandits, farmers and children. One of the men was in officer's uniform, the other wore a grey suit. They stood in front of us and bowed. The man in the grey suit spoke. He was very nervous. I saw he couldn't keep his hands still. He explained in very good English that he had come yesterday to identify us, but as he approached the bandits' headquarters he was fired on and thought it wise to beat a hasty retreat. As a rumour had been circulated that the bandits were going to substitute three Russians in our stead, he had now come with written particulars of us and would be obliged if we would answer his questions. He pulled out the paper, asked our names, addresses, ages, etc., and then quite satisfied, said he would have to go back to Panshan some thirty li away and make his report. He hoped to be back to take us away that evening or early morning. We asked him to get back as soon as he could. We could have hugged him. He said good-bye and then the two of them stepped towards the door. As he reached the door, he swung round and said, "Oh! and here are a few cigarettes." He handed Blue a tin of cigarettes and a box of matches. Blue lit one at once and said, "Cheerio and thanks so much."

'Some hours later we reassembled at a cross-roads and marched forward along a dyke which I had noticed bounded a large creek. Right ahead was a village. We saw men on the flat roofs waving frantically. As we approached, the leading bandits went on and disappeared through the mud wall while the rest of us sat on the dyke top.

'We were jerked to our feet and went in through the village gate. A few soldiers were standing around in groups. As soon as he saw them, Father let out a yell of fright; and back we were rushed again.

'Three times we went through this manoeuvre before we got through the gates, and marched into one of the mud huts. Soldiers stood on guard at the door. As he passed, Husky Voice spat on one. I thought there was going to be a fight. The soldier must have had strict orders; he never turned a hair.

'We had only been a few moments in the farmhouse, when an officer came in. The bandits covered him with their rifles; but he calmly walked over to us and unfastened our ropes.

'Then he led us out again, followed by a few bandits and we went into another house, where there were three Japanese officials, including Captain Obata and Lee. A parcel of clothes was waiting for us and we hastily changed. We learnt that there were only fifteen soldiers, besides the three officials. They had all come on horseback and had brought a farming cart in which to take us back.

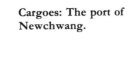
Cargoes: The port of Newchwang.

Newchwang: Where the Nanchang piracy began.

Released: Hargrave, Johnson and Blue in the front row, with a Japanese officer.

Safe?: A Japanese soldier watches as the release of the three hostages is celebrated.

Agent: Ian Grant, the B&S agent in Newchwang at the time of the piracy.

'The bandits had already received the money, but we could not go until each individual had received his share. It is a true saying that there is honour amongst thieves, for what was there to prevent the bandits – one hundred and twenty of them, from taking the money and killing us who were only twenty-two in all. Nothing – except the fear of consequences.

'Finally at 8 p.m. we set out. When they said good-bye, the bandits were charming. They gave us cigarettes and shook hands and said, Why didn't we join them next year and kidnap someone else? and that if they ever attacked a ship and found us on it, they wouldn't molest us. One apologised, saying that this was their first year at kidnapping, but that the gang would be better at it next year with what they'd learnt from us.

'It was a heavenly ride back. It was incredible to be free.

'The lights of Panshan hove into sight. We crossed the railway bridge and wound our way through muddy streets up to the Japanese barracks. It was too late to reach Newchwang that night, so we were to put up at the barracks and leave at five next morning.

'We had had nothing since a couple of tasteless pings early in the morning. Our bellies were empty. We drank and toasted for what seemed hours; "saki", Japanese wine, is strong and we got slightly tight. It was toasts all the time; we couldn't refuse such hospitable friends, especially after what they had done for us.

'I went away and was sick, but came in for the supper, which was marvellous.

'Then we went to bed to lie in peace and comfort, but not to sleep. After a quick wash next morning we walked to the station. The train was ready – a special armoured troop train. We all boarded it; a large Russian guard stood at either end of the carriage.

'At 7.30 a.m. the train pulled in at Newchwang. There was a battery of photographers waiting. Would we pose on the steps of the train? We did.

A crowd of Japanese officials handed us their cards. It was just like collecting tickets at the theatre door. We smiled and bowed to all sides, until we reached the jetty where a powerful launch was waiting for us.

'Would we pose on the launch? We did.

'The launch hummed over the water. Everyone talked to us at once. We did nothing but laugh. Blue tried to tell how his false teeth had fascinated the bandits. How he had to keep opening his mouth to let them fall. But his voice trailed off as he burst out laughing; and with difficulty he stopped his false teeth from falling out.

'At the police station, we sat round a big table and drank tea and smoked cigarettes. I couldn't keep still. I was smiling and trembling all over. I didn't dare look at Blue. I should have laughed and it seemed so silly to laugh. I began to think my smile would be a fixture.

'Then we went into another room, where we were officially handed over to our own consul by the Japanese police. We toasted the success of the negotiation; and there were speeches in Japanese, Chinese and English. It was Thursday. We were going to Shanghai on Saturday.'[23]

A Tale of Three Outports

If Shanghai was the social and commercial hub of western life in China before the Second World War, then revolving round it were the twenty or so outports along the China coast and up the Yangtze River. No one outport was exactly like another – some were large and cosmopolitan like Harbin or Tientsin in the north of the country; others like Hankow, once destined for greater glory as the centre of a huge cotton industry that failed to take root, never developed properly; a third group, Swatow or Amoy or Foochow for example, were small and for some Europeans attractively provincial, though for others they could represent a sentence of exile. But when one writes of the relative size of these outports one is measuring them by the numbers of westerners who lived and traded there. Hankow, for example, effectively three Chinese cities at the conjunction of two rivers, was one of the largest centres of population in the central Yangtze valley.

Butterfield & Swire were represented in most of the outports. In the smaller towns they might have just one man as their agent, in others he would be assisted by one or more other people. The company's business was concerned primarily with the carrying of goods in their fleet of coastal and river ships. They also sold insurance and sugar – they had built their own sugar refinery in Hong Kong in 1884. In some ports they might act for other trading companies.

The agent would live in a comfortably furnished house provided for him by the company in that part of the town reserved for westerners. If he was a bachelor then his junior or juniors might live with him. Though if he were married they would be bound to find their own accommodation. What was certain was that he was some way away from his office. In the case of Amoy, for example, Europeans lived on an island and travelled across the harbour by boat to their offices in the Chinese city.

The agent would have a Chinese staff in that office, the most important of whom would be the compradore. The compradore system had come into being when the west first traded with the Chinese at Canton in the eighteenth century. Unable to speak Chinese, they were compelled to recruit middlemen who spoke some English, compradores, to act for them in their dealings with local merchants. When this interpreting service was no longer required, the compradore remained as a guarantor for the honesty of the Chinese staff, and to secure business from local merchants who preferred to deal in a traditional Chinese way. In the years between the wars Butterfield & Swire began to question the continuing need for compradores and indeed commissioned an extensive report on the whole matter, but the system continued in some form or other until the Second World War.

It can be argued that one side effect of this compradoric system had been to isolate Europeans from the Chinese communities they lived in and traded with, that they were thus thrown back upon each other's often limited company, particularly socially. But to be fair, many Chinese deliberately chose not to deal directly with Europeans. However, in a smaller outport, where a man might be posted for as long as three years before being moved on, agents and juniors could feel very isolated. It could indeed be a lonely life up river away from the diversions of Shanghai or out on the edge of the China coast.

Social Life in the Ouports

'It all depended on the people. If you wanted a lot of varied social life and if you could not live without concerts or the more refined amenities, shall we say, it was not very good, but the ordinary chap tried to make the best of it. You had your work to do, which took most of the day. The community was very friendly, all sorts of people and there was a very cheerful club. You probably had shooting, and certainly tennis; in other words if it did not go on too long it was fine. The trouble was that you could only take life like that for a year or so because it could be very very restricted and very limiting.'[4]

Hankow was one of the larger ports on the lower part of the Yangtze River, some miles up from Shanghai. In the high water season it could be reached by ocean-going liners. It was its damp humid climate which had once seemed to Westerners to make it an ideal centre for a Chinese cotton industry, but the anticipated industry never developed, though the elegant waterfront of the western concessions with their extensive buildings was testimony to these hopes.

European Communities in Hankow

'There was a very large European community in Hankow. One must remember that there was the British concession, the French concession, a Japanese concession, and there had been a German and Russian concession. That was about the lot I think. But the various concessions were simply a strip of river frontage going back a few hundred yards. And the British concession was next to the Chinese city and the customs house. The next I think was the French concession, then came the ex-German concession and then the ex-Russian and Japanese concessions. Now the German concession was taken back after the First War and it was described as a Special Administrative District. They coined that term and it was known as SAD. The Russian concession, of course, had been taken over long before and I think the British one went in 1927 and became SAD I.

The Nationalists take back the British Concession

'I was there when the British concession was taken over, when Chiang Kai Shek's forces, with a good deal of Russian assistance, made their famous march from Canton to the Yangtze River, which they struck at Hankow. And they hadn't been there terribly long before there was trouble. They worked up huge mobs at the end of the British concession demanding its rendition. The Chinese official who is those days was responsible on the civilian side was a man called Eugene Chen. Anyway the thing culminated in fearful mobs at one end of the British concession, which was next to the Chinese city. They had no trouble at the other end, which was a Chinese Special

Administrative District. So in the end it was decided that all the Europeans living in the British concession should assemble in what was known as the Asiatic Petroleum Company building and just live there for the time being. It was too dangerous to leave because one never knew just how far the Chinese might go. So we settled all our staff into the APC building and I was then seconded to the British consulate, two of the staff there having cracked up. I was attached to the consul. He was all right; it was the other two who had failed. The main part of my work was deciphering and ciphering codes. And the doctor of one of the British gunboats there was also lent to the consulate. The drill was we got there at nine o'clock in the morning and we went back just across the street to the building where I was living any time from five o'clock in the evening till midnight, according to what work had to be done before we packed up.

'Eventually a man called O'Malley was sent down from Peking from the embassy there and had a negotiation with this man, Eugene Chen. In the end they came to terms and I had to type out the actual document which was signed. I had to do it because I could type better with one finger than anybody else who was working there. This was duly signed and that was my contribution. Anyway after that was signed things settled down and people returned to their various homes and so on.

'There was a magnificent race club at Hankow, though as far as the British were concerned were really two clubs. There was the town club, which was just a large house, with a bar and a dining room and a billiard room. But it was purely a town club and men only. The real club was the race club which catered for almost everything. To begin with it had a huge area of land and it had a race course. Inside the actual course itself there was quite a lot of land. There was the odd football pitch, cricket ground and so on. In addition the club had an eighteen hole golf course. The club itself had a large club building with all normal facilities; a very nice verandah where when the weather was right you could go and sit at a table and have the odd drink and laze about. It provided meals though not normally dinner, though there were occasions when there were dinners. The club had all nationalities in it, though the Chinese themselves turned up very little. However they came in for the race meetings, but since we only had two or three race meetings a year that was a relatively small side of the club. Apart from all these outdoor facilities we had a curious arrangement inside the club house. There was a swimming bath which in winter was turned into a dance floor. It was bridged over and became the centre for the leisure of the whole community. As I say the club had members from other nationalities as well as the British, but it was predominantly used by the British rather than anybody else. The French had their own club in town and the Japanese kept very much to themselves.'[3]

Clubs

It was in Hankow that one young Butterfield & Swire junior had his first proper taste of China and the Chinese way of doing things.

'I had parked my car on a very wet day on the "Bund" the waterfront, and turned round to see an old Chinese lady, with a paper umbrella down against the gusting rain, crash into the back of my car, break her umbrella, and sit down in a puddle and burst into tears. So I naturally went back and helped

her up. Then a policeman, a Chinese policeman came up. (It was only just the two or three heads in the police force who were British; the rest were Chinese). And he said, "What is all this about?" I did not speak or understand any Chinese then, and a torrent of words from her and he said, "I'm afraid you'll have to come to the police station, she wants to lay a complaint for damage and so on." I said, "This is most unreasonable; I've got an appointment out at the race club and I shall miss it." And he said, "Well, look here how about giving her five dollars and forgetting it?" I said, "No, I don't mind giving her a lift or helping or anything but I am not responsible for it and I don't know where it will end if I offer money so I won't." "Then you'll have to come along to the station. She's made a complaint." So I went along to the police station and sat down and he said, "You know there's an hour before the sergeant is available to look into this case." I turned obstinate and said, "I've missed my appointment, anyway, I'll wait an hour. But I am not going to be put upon." In due course the sergeant appeared, and he was British, and he said, "Yes it's quite obvious, but you know if you'd lived in this country a little bit longer you'd have said not five but two and walked away. And that's precisely what I'm going to say to you now. I'm going to tell her that her claim for five dollars was absolutely outrageous, it was all her fault, and she ought to watch where she's going, but this very nice young man who has not got very much money will give you two dollars to get a new umbrella with." Everybody burst into smiles and the whole thing was settled. I would have settled it myself if I had been longer in the country, because if you are a person of supposed wealth and authority and you become involved with somebody who is wanting, the legal rights and wrongs of the matter are barely a factor. The point is what is the decent way to behave if you are involved in this situation. The answer is you can say what you like, but you must go some of the way: there are no hundred per cents in justice in China. If it is absolutely outrageous you pay a token; if it is cut and dried the wrong way the person to whom you are obligated would never dream of asking a hundred per cent of you. He would expect a lively bargain down to ninety-five per cent, then everybody is happy. You can find the same thing in up-country insurance. The amazement when they have got a proper claim and do claim and are paid in full is extraordinary. The people do not behave like that in China. Nothing is black and white, somewhere close to one end or in the middle is a gentleman's adjustment of almost any problem – financial, legal or whatever it may be, and that is another of the things you had to learn.'[1]

In some respects Hankow was a miniature version of Shanghai. The Bund was dominated as was Shanghai's by the offices of the Hongkong and Shanghai Bank, the principal British bank in China. And there were the usual cabarets with their complement of white Russian taxi dancers.

'They were just like cheap ballrooms really. The girls all sat at one end of the room, and the men went in and sat at a table, and they could invite a girl over. I remember them in Hankow probably better, because they were nearer at hand and you sort of sauntered down there more than in Shanghai. People used to go to the cabarets mostly after they'd packed the womenfolk home, and dropped in there for a drink. But that's all they were. I used to go up to one cabaret in Changsha, up river from Hankow in the evening and buy drinks for a Russian girl called Mila. And there you couldn't just buy what you used to call "business water" in Shanghai, just a little drink or something, in Hankow you had to buy a small bottle of champagne. I remember my chits used to be one bottle of champagne, one bottle of beer; one bottle of champagne and one bottle of beer. And this Mila was a run of the mill girl like they all were, and just making do. And she said, "Excuse me I do ballet." They used to get these poor girls on a little dance floor and they'd go floundering around, because they weren't trained for it; and once I was idly sitting there her glass of champagne already poured out of this gold topped bottle (gold top was more expensive) and without any concern in the world I just happened to sip it. The owner of the place was called Baronoff and he and his wife (Mrs Baronoff was big and fat) were sitting in a corner (the whole place was very small). And I saw Baronoff say something to his wife and she sprang to her feet waddled across the dance floor, sat down opposite me and said, "Vell?" As I hadn't a care in the world, I was left non-plussed about this. In the meantime the girl had stopped doing ballet and was watching us and I said, "That's ginger ale." And she said, "Vell what you want? You want to make the girl drunk?" And do you know to this day I don't know what the right answer is. She then sailed off and left me, and the girl came back and finished her ginger ale. But I can't imagine what was the answer. I didn't want to make the girl drunk. They did have a dignity in their poverty.'[17]

At the head of the part of the Yangtze River navigated by Western ships lay Chungking. It was the last outport on the river from which the Western nations traded and stood at the top of the celebrated Gorges. The European community was small and their life there a good deal more leisurely than in Hankow or down the river.

'My introduction to Chungking before I was married was quite interesting. Blackie, my number one, met me off the ship I had travelled up on, the *Wantung*, and took me to lunch. Lunch consisted of three or four gins plus curry. I had my drinking boots ready by that time. Then we got on to these wonderful Szechwanese ponies and they were only about nine hands high so when I put my feet down I could touch the ground. Chungking is very hilly up the first range and you go up stone steps and then you get into a valley between the first and second range and there are stone steps going round paddy fields. Blackie said, "Now we'll go off to the Grey-Jones." (He was the number two at APC there.) And I saw my number one going at great speed round the corner and slap into the paddy field. I just managed to pull my beast up in time. Anyway he came out very muddy and dirty and I said, "Is this usual?" He said, "Oh yes, sometimes you fall off your pony." Thank God I did not fall off mine. Anyway, we arrived at our destination safely. Riding in Chungking was really quite something because the ponies are miniature horses. I do not know where they came from but they were game little devils. You could ride the whole day and they never seemed to get tired; in fact you were the one who got tired.'[10]

'The foreign community all lived on the right bank, although the left hand side going up is a better way of explaining it. And by some kindness the geography ended up in a whole lot of little hills, like a lot of camels' backs, fairly high, a few hundred feet high, and on the top of each hill various European firms built their own houses, so there you had the Swire house, and the Postmaster's house, and the customs man's house, and of course APC. Shell, who were called APC in China, were the big people, oil was the thing. They had a big hill with a road winding up it, and on the way there were juniors' houses and a mess, and on the top was the manager's house, and underneath the manager's house, the ground floor was the office. If you wanted oil you got a sampan from the city and you crossed over and you walked up this hill to their office and you bought your oil. So they lived in a very grand manner. But everybody had to have a sedan chair. There were no roads to speak of. The ordinary public used a three-man chair. That was two men, one in front and one behind, and a man doing relief. But anybody who was anybody, even I as a ship-wrecked mariner, had a six-man chair, for crossing the river. Everybody had an office in the town across the river except Shell, and it was quite a sight to see the foreigners setting out, going to the office. So many people, like a crocodile, as all these chairs came down.'[17]

Chairmen: A two coolie chair, much used by Westerners in China before the Second World War. Missy rides, but Master walks.

Streetwise: A couple setting off in rickshaws.

Four and two: A woman and child are carried by four chair coolies in livery.

'I remember that to go to the office your sedan chair would appear in front of you with four bearers: two at each end and a spare man because they kept changing places. In front of the chair was an old retainer called the "Laoban", who used to look after the chair coolies and at night would walk in front with a lantern. You got into your chair and you were carried from your house down the wharf where the firm's motor boat was waiting for you – a fairly large one. Your chairs were put on the roof of the motor boat and you went across the river at an angle because of the current. You yawed across it. Once across, your chairs came off, the coolies got out and you were carried up the steps of the native city to your office down a narrow lane. There were no cars there in those days around there. There *were* roads but they were outside the city so your movement was by sedan chair unless you wanted to walk. In wet weather the chairs were completely enclosed with mackintosh sheets and they all had the firm's insignia on them. The chair coolies wore a company uniform, which was usually blue with just the company's insignia on it, the Chinese insignia. In the case of Swires, it was "Taikoo", which meant "Old and honourable" with the two Chinese characters, and each firm tended to use characters like that.'[5]

'I was very glad to have the sedan chair, especially in the heat of the summer, which was jolly hot. But we also did a tremendous amount of walking, but if we were going out to dinner or anything like that, we took our sedan chairs, so we did not arrive in a muck sweat.

'When the coolies' shoulders got tired, because the two coolies in front had the pole on their left shoulder and the coolies at the back on the right shoulder, they put a stick underneath the chair and changed shoulders and on they went. The rate those coolies used to go was quite fantastic, they seemed to go up a hill just as if it were level. It was astonishing and great fun.

'The sedan chairs were supplied by the firm. I think the coolies got at least ten dollars a month but they were very happy with that. The yardstick for the cost of living in town in those days was the cost of a picul of rice – a picul being 133 English pounds. Szechwan being one of the garden provinces of China, they used to get two crops a year, and sometimes three. A picul of rice cost only a dollar so the coolies spent a dollar on rice, kept perhaps a couple of dollars in reserve and the rest went into the bank or whatever it was. Everybody was happy in those days you see. Our number one boy got, I think, at least twenty-two dollars a month and he was the big man. Actually our particular boy was quite a usurer and the rates of interest up in Chungking were quite fantastic. We noticed he was always very well dressed and there used to be quite a string of people coming up to the back door of our house to borrow a bit of money or pay it back!

'Later, when I was married, I came back to Chungking as agent in Taikoo house. It was a fantastic house on the end of the Yangtze some three hundred and fifty feet up and in the high water season you see the reflection of the moon on the water. If you were sitting on the verandah it really was a most romantic sight.

'It had a lovely garden. My wife and I were very keen gardeners, though a Chinese gardener, until you have broken him into the foreign way of gardening, just thinks it is all a lot of damn nonsense. But once you have got your ideas over to them they have got completely green fingers and they produce the most wonderful results and very colourful ones too. Sadly all our photographs got lost during the war. They were only in black and white, but they did give one a very good impression of what a Chinese gardener with instructions from 'missee' or 'master' could produce in the way of flowers. Roses grew beautifully up there because of the very heavy thick soil and funnily enough the heat did not seem to affect them unduly in the summer. My father sent me quite a lot of seeds from Scotland; broom, which of course is the worst thing you could possibly put in as it spreads like wildfire. Anyway my wife and I planted some of this broom in our garden in Chungking and I believe it did very well, though I never saw the result of it because we went on leave.'[10]

'In the summer time many residents moved out up to the second range of hills. There was no road but they had cooler weather. All the mountains were paved with slabs and everything was carried in a sort of basket on the coolies' backs, rather like an Eskimo carries a baby. And on top of that they would put the cargo, and they'd carry cargo for a couple of weeks maybe. Each night they would use the cargo as a pillow, winding their way over the mountains. I remember a cartoon in the Shanghai paper, a picture of these people, called Szechwan elephants because they carried such incredible weights. A priest once told me that going on a journey for quite a number of days he had travelled with his chair. (He said the bearers talked about money the whole time.) They kept the conversation going from back to front, and he said on the road they had to stand to one side for an organ going up.'[17]

In the late 1920s social life in Chungking was still extremely formal.

'You most definitely called on people when you arrived. Blackie said, "Now I'll give you the names of people who you must call on." So I set off walking at the beginning and then getting into my chair, dropping cards, because in those days everybody had their pasteboard visiting card with English on one side and Chinese on the other. I was given a very good Chinese name which was very close to my Scots name, Kinloch. I became Gin meaning Gold, Lo meaning Happy and Ker meaning a guest, which was very close to Kinloch. When I went down to Hong Kong my name became Gun Lock Er or something terrible like that. I am afraid I never could cope with Cantonese chit chat.

'When you went to a house to call, usually one of the chair coolies went ahead and rang the bell and then the boy would come out and you presented your card and waited for a bit. Then the boy of the house came out and said, "Missee will come, be very glad to meet you, master." And that's how one made one's friends. Of course, as we were in an outport, with a comparatively small foreign population, we all got to know each other very well. Most people were very nice but you had the inevitable bastard and the bloody woman troublemaker and so forth. But basically we all got on really well together and had great parties.

*The British
Consul*

'There was a rather eccentric consul in Chungking when I was there – old Stark-Toller; "Stark Naked Toller" as he used to be referred to. He lived in a charming old consulate. The consul general at Chungking was right in the city, but I think the British must have built it years back. It was a charming old house with a lovely garden and old Stark-Toller took the trouble to speak quite good Chinese and the Chinese loved him. He was one of these really impressive looking Britishers and he had a wife, "Old Mummy". She was a strange lady, shall we say, but Blackie and I were very fond of old Stark-Toller and we wanted to get him and his wife over for a weekend because living on the South Bank we had running water which they did not have in the city. But old Stark-Toller always made excuses saying, "Mummy and I have our own bed and we like it." "Well bring the bloody thing over, for God's sake," said Blackie. But we did not get them to stay!

'Why was he called "Stark Naked Toller"? Well, Stark-Toller was his name. It was hyphenated. He was always known as "Stark Naked". He was a very dignified old chap and he did the British community a lot of good because he seemed able to stand up to the Chinese very well. In those days, in Szechwan particularly, you had warring war lords and each had their own territories and it was a matter of sort of "fixing" a local war lord. Some war lords tried to trespass or seize British property and it was up to the British consul general to effect a compromise.

'The basic thing for the British consular staff, was to keep the peace between the Chinese and the Britisher and they did it pretty well on the whole. We had some hopeless British consular failures. They just did not fit and they should have been kicked out. I think when they joined in those days they had to go and do a two year language course up in Peking and they really should have been sized up by then by whoever was in charge. (The minister or ambassador should have sorted them out.) If they were not weeded out they tended to become dead loss cases who drank too much and were incompatible with the Chinese. Generally they were a pretty representative bunch who were more useful than unhelpful.'[10]

For most Europeans in Chungking social life centred on the club.

The Club

'I remember Saturday night was *the* night, club night, so as to get everybody there. The men played poker all night, and the younger men danced around. I doubt if there were but two or three unattached girls at that time.'[17]

It was in an outport like Chungking that one met the missionaries who worked in rural China. Missionaries of all denominations who preached their gospel and built and ran schools and hospitals and universities.

Missionaries

'I saw a lot of them, of course, from Chungking and the smaller ports. In Shasi when I was there there was one married European running a large cotton press packing plant and other than that there was a Jesuit mission. I saw a lot of these Jesuit fathers. They were American Jesuits and I was particularly friendly with the Father Superior would it be? The one in charge

– a man called Father Leo Ferrari. We used to shoot a lot, because there was a lot of very good shooting up the Yangtze River and he would put on his hunting kit and was just an ordinary person. I can remember one night going back to the mission when his younger men were out in different villages and we were dining alone. And he would say to the boy, after a good day's shooting, "Boy, have you got any wine left?" (This was at a time of shortage.) And the boy said, "No, master, only some communion wine." "Is it consecrated?" "No." "Oh, well, bring it in." He was a wonderful man. He had a very strange bunch of people in his mission. One had owned a large American football team and had suddenly seen the light and become a missionary and I remember Ferrari saying he was very worried about one of them because he had got a young Chinese village girl in the family way. What was he to do? I spent a lot of time with him. Other missionaries ran hospitals – very worthy work. And many of them regarded the young commercial type as a bit "off" because he drank and smoked and some of them did not like drinking and smoking. That was a barrier. But on the whole they were good people. I saw a lot of them and they were very kind and hospitable.'[5]

It was the missionaries perhaps more than any other western group in China who really came to know the Chinese. For most people with only a smattering of Chinese it was difficult to make local friends; the nearest one came was in one's daily contact with the office staff and the house servants.

'During the time my wife and I were engaged, the Chinese National Aviation Corporation started an airmail service from Shanghai to Chungking. Well despite this, my fiancée's, as she was then, letters were not arriving and I got terribly upset. I used to wire back in desperation. I thought I had been chucked you see. And she replied, "Oh I can assure you I've been writing regularly." You know once a week or twice a week, whatever it is when one

Servants and Staff

is engaged. Well eventually I discovered that the office boy, a nice little chap, who wore one of these funny little Chinese caps and God knows only earned about fifteen dollars a month, but had three wives who he had to support, was opening up my fiancée's letters to improve his English! However we managed to stop that one.

'There was another occasion when two of the house servants were discovered with their feet in the fridge. The number one coolie and the cook. Blackie and I came back one summer's afternoon (we had decided it was too hot in the office and we had not anything particular to do) and found these two young devils with their feet in the fridge, keeping themselves cool. So we poured a bucket of water over them and we never had any more trouble again. On another occasion after I was married and had been appointed agent in Chungking, the number two insurance clerk who had been off duty for several days wrote a letter in impeccable English saying, "Dear Sir, I regret to say I have been suffering from heat prostitution, therefore I cannot come to the office. I hope I may be excused, your obedient servant." I think that was rather delightful.'[10]

But these same Chinese office clerks were not above testing the integrity of a young British businessman. They saw nothing wrong in 'squeeze' or bribery. As the Europeans discovered it was one of the ways in which they did business.

'The day after I first arrived in Chungking there had been a conflagration in the city. They had awful fires there. In low water season squatters' sheds by the river went up. But this was the high water season. Anyway there had been a terrible conflagration and we would be involved with the insurance claims. Well when I went into the office I opened my desk drawer and discovered there was $10,000 there. So I called two insurance clerks in and I said, "What's the meaning of this? You know we don't do this sort of thing in Swires. Take the damn money away. You're not educating me in your ways because I've just arrived." Anyway after that they knew my approach to business integrity and I think it did me a lot of good being firm. Even though getting $10,000 for nought, especially after just becoming engaged and having had to pay for an engagement ring would have been rather useful! However I managed to resist that temptation and I think I gained quite a lot of face. I never had any more trouble from that time on or in any other port I was in because obviously the word went round that they were not going to be able to buy this foreigner whatever they put in his desk or gave to his wife. The firm insisted that you accept nothing because the Chinese might take advantage of you. However at times like Christmas the most fantastic presents used to come in, rings and gold and silver, but we worked on a very sensible basis, for face purposes and so that we did not offend anybody we could keep anything perishable such as whisky and gin and so forth. And everybody seemed to be happy with that.

'If you had accepted anything more valuable you would have had it. They would have just sort of twiddled you around their finger and got exactly what they wanted out of you. Those foreigners who were stupid enough to accept squeeze must have got themselves into terribly tight spots. The British in those days did not go in for squeeze. In those days they were very strict as to what could be accepted and what should be accepted, mainly so that you did not offend any old client, any old big shipper or something like that. But clients knew exactly how we regarded the whole business. They used to send us, say, a suit length. I suppose that was perishable but if half a dozen lengths came you only accepted one and sent five back with grateful thanks and wished them well. I know it was the proper basis on which to work and the way the firm and London wished us to approach dealing with the Chinese.'10

In the middle years between the two World Wars when China was continually at war with itself Western travellers travelled prepared for trouble.

'Chungking was very cut off, and it was all war lords. I had a revolver and ammunition with which I thought I was going to protect the junks, but I put the ammunition in the bottom of a suitcase and then we found that the local war lord in charge was searching every ship, and when we got ashore they searched all our stuff. The chap ran his hand round the inside of my bag and never touched the ammunition. I don't think we could have done much about it, but he didn't see it anyhow. The war lord there had a nephew in Suifu, one hundred and fifty miles above, and they didn't get on and so the war lord in Chungking stopped any traffic, anything that might help his nephew, which meant that a lot of stuff didn't get in, ordinary legitimate cargo wasn't allowed to come in.'17

'There used to be a story in Chungking that when the city changed hands from one war lord to another, there was a gentleman's agreement that you never fought seriously. (Europeans were asked to walk around with umbrellas up so that they would not get shot deliberately.) You exchanged a few shots and then sent in an emissary and said, "Well I've got 2,000 troops, how many have you got?" And the winner took the city for the next year and milked the population.'5

'General Fan, who was the local fellow, had a terrific house which he had built with the aid of squeeze he had extracted from the Chinese and he had an Australian tennis pro, whose name I think was Gordon Lumb (his sister Ada later on started a very big shop in Hong Kong. But they were Australian-Chinese anyway.) And Blackie and I and Blackie's successor Dick Tippan knew Gordon very well. This meant that if the consular people could not get exactly what we wanted, we could say to Gordon, "Have a word with the general and see if he can do something." Sometimes it worked, but not always. However it could be a help. We never were daggers drawn with Fan; actually he was a nice little chap. I remember one example of this concerning Sir Miles Lampson who was the British minister, because Peking had not been raised to embassy rank then. Sir Miles, who was a terrifically tall man and who had been at Cambridge with my father, arrived with Rob Scott, as his secretary, who later became very well known in the consular service, and old General Fan laid on a terrific dinner. General Fan was about five foot nothing (four foot nothing I would think!) and Sir Miles round about six foot five, and in they marched to what turned out to be very excellent Chinese food, with an awful lot of wine drunk. And old Fan had his own foreign style band, and as they marched in the band played "Drunk last night; drunk the night before", which of course went down well with the British present.

'It was terrific how we managed to keep fairly straight faces but the dinner was a great success. Sir Miles was a wonderful chap with the Chinese and he did a lot of good for British interests in that particular visit.'[10]

Along the Yangtze up to Chungking British interests were protected by a flotilla of gunboats under the command of the Rear Admiral Yangtze.

The Defence of the Yangtze

'The Yangtze Flotilla was very important because when you had these various skirmishes between opposing war lords, a British gunboat might say come to a treaty port or a semi-treaty port and just that presence seemed to cool things down and the Chinese seemed to be very much happier. They did not get scared so much. Of course we lost all those rights after the Pacific war, when extra territoriality was abolished and no British ships or gunboats were allowed on to the Yangtze or the West River where they had a flotilla too. The ships of the Yangtze Flotilla were very impressive, actually, and to see the old White Ensign coming up was really a very encouraging sight and all the matelots looked a good bunch. They were all more or less specially chosen, particularly the officers. The matelots enjoyed themselves, but they behaved themselves too.'[10]

It would be wrong to think of Europeans in a city like Chungking as being confined to their offices, their club and their homes across the Yangtze. They could and many did ride out into the hills and it was perfectly possible to visit the Chinese city, though few of them can have found such a visit congenial.

The Chinese Sector

'The dwellings in certain sections of the city were dreadful and the squalor was dreadful, absolutely dreadful. It is difficult to describe. We had this terrific rise and fall of the Yangtze River. I suppose eighty or ninety feet between low water and high water. And as the water dropped you had all these squatters' huts built out of bamboo and heaven knows what right down to the water's edge and invariably there was a terrific conflagration. Yet before the ground was even cool people had gone back to establish their rights. Then as the water rose they were all pushed back and you had this terrific congestion inside the city proper. Sanitation of course did not exist. You had your running drains in the street and so forth, but the missionaries did a lot of good in supplying basic medicines to the Chinese and they obviously progressed, but to a white man the squalor was awful. And when we came back from the Chungking Club we would often see people lying in the street on a divan smoking opium quite blatantly.

'Of course leprosy was very prevalent and the sight of some of those beggars with their faces eaten away was dreadful. In fact it was so nauseating that one really had to look the other way because of these running sores.

Sadly there seemed to be an awful lot of epilepsy among the coolies working for us and if they had an attack, all they did was get a roll of straw and bung it into their mouths so that they didn't bite their tongues off. There was a certain amount of rabies too which was rather terrifying but I must admit in those days I did not realise what rabies was, thank goodness. But I made damn certain of not being bitten by some foul looking dog.

Opium

'When one went riding up into the hills there were the opium poppies hidden from the sight of the casual observer from the river all growing away, all banned, all strictly controlled and collected by the military and taxed here, taxed there and taxed the other place. You got shot if you attempted to smuggle it, not because the authorities were against opium but because they were against any breach of their monopoly which magnified the price. It was smoked all over the place. A lot of rot is talked about opium: its real evil was that it was so expensive that it could ruin you, if you were not near the source, as you were in Chungking. It was like alcohol and I rated it about the same, as a vice. Several Chinese I knew of had been smoking six pipes of opium every day for years and years. It seemed to be as controllable by will and as harmless or harmful as alcohol. Just as there are some people who start by drinking a couple of shorts a day and end up beggared alcoholics so there are people who ruin themselves with opium but others for whom it seemed almost a social drug. In Chungking in one street there were at least seventeen opium dens. We call them opium dens, it's rather melodramatic. In fact, as you had a tea house so you had an opium house. You would have your favourite pipe just like your mug at the back of the bar hanging up. It was an unwinder. Forget your troubles, have a smoke and go on. You could go on for fifty years as far as I know, I know people who have, but for all sorts of reasons I never tried it myself.'[10]

As an outport Swatow was different from and yet similar to Chungking. It was on the coast some four hundred miles south of Shanghai and had once been the centre of the trade in beancake, agricultural fertiliser made in the north of China from the remains of soyabeans after they had been crushed for their oil. Like Chungking it possessed only a small European community, and as in Chungking that community lived away from the Chinese city across the harbour at a place called Kakchow. Butterfield & Swire had an agent and a junior assistant posted there, and it was just as difficult for them to get to know the Chinese community as it was for their peers in Chungking.

The Chinese in Swatow

'In Swatow at that time it was not possible to get close to the Chinese. There was a little group of young Chinese, sons of well-to-do people like our own compradore Pow Lee and others who'd at least had part of their education abroad in England or in Hong Kong or Australia or somewhere, and between younger foreign members and them there was a perfectly ordinary natural relationship. We used to play tennis together a bit, and went to the odd party. Just that little group. But in general the Chinese, in Swatow particularly, were at that time very Chinese indeed. They were a dour lot. The Swatow Chinese was a very peasant type, like a Normandy peasant of the nineteenth century, you know, not really get-onable with. There were the business dinners and that sort of thing. We'd throw dinners for a group of shippers, but that was very formal. I'm afraid they used to ply you with drink so much that I can probably remember the beginning of a dinner better than I can the end! It was always Johnnie Walker Black Label I know, and there was a lot of "Yum Sing".

'The translation is literally "drink all", emptying the glass. It means swig it right down like vodka or schnapps. It had to go down in one go, and so there was a lot of toast drinking across the table and all that. It was very difficult to keep sober. At least I found it so. You had to be very much in control not to be rather high by the end of the meal anyhow. It's one reason why I never got to know much about Chinese food because they used to love to tell you what it was you were eating, and how much it cost too for that matter, but I'm afraid at these banquets it didn't always sink in. Swatow wasn't famous for food, but they could lay on very good Chinese food. To be quite frank I don't think there were any Swatow local delicacies. If a person wanted to impress you he would produce a Peking dish or a Cantonese dish – I don't think he would say this is a Swatow delicacy. I don't remember them ever saying this.'[9]

Swatow was one of the string of ports along the China coast served by ships of the China Navigation Company (CNCo) fleet carrying cargo up north and down south, sailing between ports by night to unload one parcel of goods by day and picking up another, and occasionally carrying passengers.

Office Duties

'It was my job as the number two in the office to see that the ships got the service that they wanted from the shore and that they got away on time. I also was supposed to check on the accountant, who was a Chinese, that is to say do formal checks on the accounts to make sure they showed a proper picture of what was going on, but mainly it was liaison with the ships. I used quite often to go on board and breakfast on the ships which had come in over night and find out what they needed and what had got to be done and when they could hope to finish discharge and that sort of thing. There was a third European on the staff who was the wharfinger in charge of the godowns and the procedure for cargo, stevedoring and delivery of cargo and claims. He was a former floating staff officer usually, he certainly was at the time I was there, so I wasn't concerned with that side.

'I would go on board the ships first of all; if they were anchored in the harbour I'd go there first, and then come ashore and go on board the ships which were at the berth, at the pontoons, and see the captain and the chief officer, and have breakfast with them probably. Then I'd go ashore to the office, bringing any papers or stuff they wanted dealt with, and find out if everyone was fit, did they want a doctor. What did I do in the office? I'm dashed if I can remember. I sat at a desk and must have done something. Well there was a routine check of the cash-book entries for the previous day. Every day I used to do that just to not let it get too far ahead. And various other accounts. I suppose I wrote some letters although the agent would tend to do most of the correspondence.

'I was responsible for a rather small insurance account and I sometimes used to go and inspect properties which wanted insurance from us and recommend acceptance or otherwise. Or really not so much that as give a description of the property so that the insurance experts in Hong Kong could decide whether they wanted to accept it. We didn't sell any sugar in Swatow, because Swatow was a sugar-producing area of its own.

And towards the end of the day there would be a certain amount of panic as to whether the ship was going to get away. But there wasn't much that had to be done; the captains used to clear their ships themselves as I remember. I didn't have to do very much with the customs house, and they didn't require pilots, they did their own pilotage. I don't remember what I did, to be quite honest, but I was busy I can assure you. I was very busy. There was always something to do.

'One of the good things about Swatow was that it covered a lot of nationalities. And excluding the two missions, both of which were quite large, I should think there were a couple of hundred people. Somewhere between a hundred and two hundred, I should think. And there was a British and an American mission which must have accounted for another sixty or so people. The British mission was very much concentrated on medical services and they had a large hospital and quite a lot of medical staff. The Americans I think concentrated mainly on teaching. They were a little more remote and I'm not quite sure what they were up to most of the time. Except I do remember there were one or two red-haired Chinese kids in the village outside their compound!

The Multiracial Community

'One of the nicest things about this mixture of nationalities was you got an awful lot of New Years – Russian New Year and Chinese New Year and Greek New Year and so on – and national holidays. But we had to make our own amusements really. There were no clubs, I mean there was *a* club which was just a place with a bar and a billiard table; it was a rather a poor club and there were no night clubs or cinemas or anything of that kind, so it was largely a question of entertaining each other in our houses, either a proper formal thing or nice long Sundays. Or what often happened was that after drinking, after being in the club, at say about nine o'clock we'd all decide to go to one house or the other for dinner, and the club boy by a sort of bamboo wireless would go and tell the house-boys that there were going to be an extra six people coming along, and your boy would then find out which six people they were and if he was short of food he'd get something in from their houses, because the whole Kakchow side was a stretch of less than half a mile along the waterfront, so it was all very compact.

'There was the British navy and some American naval ships; French naval ships used to come in occasionally and there'd be a certain amount of entertaining, and being entertained on board. We used to play the crew at games of hockey, football. We played the Americans at softball on condition they played us at cricket. I must say we played softball better than they played cricket. So that was another group. There was a little island at the end of the harbour called Masu, with a little beach on it, and it was nice to go down there, and there was a certain amount of nice hilly country to walk around in at weekends. But the best thing about Swatow was wild fowling. There was a little season from about late November until the end of February when all the lagoons and the groundnut fields round the edges of these big lagoons at the back of the harbour were absolutely alive with geese and wild

Sporting Activities

duck and that sort of thing. There were a couple of up-country travelling boats. ICI had an up-country travelling boat still, and BAT did too. And they were marvellous weekends.

'We would push off on Friday evening. (I may say it was rather difficult for me because I had to work the weekend. The ships were in and out and it was rather difficult, but I usually managed to get away two or three times during that little season.) We would push off, go about ten miles across this huge lagoon, up stream from the harbour to these rather desolate mud flats, and we'd anchor in some creek. There was a crew and a boy with us, and lots of food and drink, and we'd have a nice fusty sort of evening in the cabin, because it was quite cold at that time of the year. (Although we were in the tropics it could be quite cold after sundown.) I remember we'd get up about half past three or four o'clock in the morning and get on to the dykes round the paddy fields in this beautiful spot and wait for the flight at very first light which was in off the sea early in the morning. Then there was also an evening flight back on to the sea, or was it the other way round? I've forgotten. I think it was that way. It was enormous fun, enormous fun. I wasn't a very good shot but good enough to bag the odd duck and they were very good eating too. There was great variety, mallard, widgeon, teal and geese.

'We'd probably have to come back Sunday night. At Chinese New Year, you could probably extend it a bit. The Chinese New Year weekend was a very good time. Then we occasionally had visitors up from Hong Kong to do a bit of shooting with us.

But there wasn't anything much else of that kind. I know somebody did organise a miniature golf course on land belonging, I think, to the British consulate. No sailing, strangely enough, but I think that was because the harbour was really dangerous. The speed of the tides and the currents were so fast that it was extremely difficult to sail in the harbour. No ponies either for some reason. No horses. Difficult to keep them through that long hot summer.'[9]

Social life in Swatow seems to have been less formal than it was in Chungking, but then during the interwar years there was a general unbending of the social rules.

'I don't think we were so fussy about "dropping cards" in Swatow. The community was so small that you met each other in the club on the first night there and then you were in their houses the following evening, so there was no need to stand on ceremony especially on the Kakchow side.

'You see the numbers on the Kakchow side were really quite small. On the Swatow side there was quite a large customs staff and the Syrians who traded there. They made up quite a fair sized community. And there were a lot of smaller, one-off people, people who didn't belong to the big firms but just had a little business, including some Germans, who incidentally didn't have extra-territorial rights. I suppose the poor chaps had it pinched from them after World War I. They managed to get by. I think in a curious way our extra-territorial rights seemed to rub off on them. You hardly ever heard of them being in trouble.'[9]

It is hardly surprising that in so small a western community made up of so many individual national groups there could be social tension.

'Social feuds were apt to occur; people's sensibilities get rather amplified in small communities. There was one representative of a certain firm who when he had more than one or two drinks, was extremely rude to the British consul, who came from a Jamaican strain. And he was referred to in a full dinner party as a Sikh policeman, which did not improve relations. Well some people took one side and some another, but you had to be careful who you asked to dinner together.'[10]

As in Chungking the club had been designed to be the focus of social life in Swatow.

'It was a bungalow type place with a verandah which was the usual type of thing there. It had a good billiard table, a piano, but it didn't have a bar as such that you could stand up at but drinks were served by the boys. I don't know whether there was any reason for that – perhaps they didn't want anyone to drink too much and thought they wouldn't if there wasn't a bar. It may have been a deliberate decision, but I don't know. But there was no limitation on drinks, you could get anything you wanted. You shouted from the verandah for the boy. There was a tennis court outside and a very large piece of ground, a garden, which was in fact a sort of perk for the boy because he was a very hard-working bloke and he cultivated all this large piece of ground with vegetables and flowers, and a certain amount of fruit. I remember the ships were quite glad to get fresh vegetables off him from time to time. That was really his perk, he made a little living out of that. But I think it was his spontaneous idea to make use of it. No Chinese will let a bit of ground go begging.

'In clubs there were the most elaborate dicing games played for drinks when you were in a group. The most popular drink, in my circle anyhow, was the gimlet. I remember it was a frightful drink, lime juice and gin, supposed to be a cool version of an alcoholic drink. The serious drinkers used to drink a lot of whisky of course. In those days very little wine was drunk, but if it was drunk it was at posh dinner parties no doubt, but not a great deal by young people like me anyhow. The only other thing was that the late hour at which dinner parties started, or when one dined, meant rather a lot of drinking beforehand. And that tended to mean that one rarely seemed to dine much before ten o'clock. It was rather awful.'[9]

'There was a club there run by the Chinese maritime customs and they had a very big staff there. I went over to it one night and shaking liar dice was the great thing. Anyway an awfully nice young Hongkong Bank man was there and I achieved the great thing of having lost eleven bottles of gin to him in one night's dicing! So that night I was obviously not very good at liar dice. I still have that brought up against me.

'There were certain men who obviously drank too much. And a noggin of whisky is very much higher proof out in the Far East than at home. Some of the drinking was quite ridiculous. I suppose I realised this and I probably absorbed too much at times, but if I had absorbed it at the rate some people did I would have had the DT's in no time. I think that drinking in pre-war days was pretty terrific. I suppose there was nothing else to do and a lot of people had a fairly easy job, whereas in Swires we worked damned hard and we did not have time to do too much drinking. We had a blinder every now and then but to try and do a day's work after absorbing too much alcohol was damn silly. Do not think I am trying to make myself out to be one of these wonderful chaps. I was not; I took my noggin just like everybody else but I do not think I took them to excess like one or two people might have.

'The Jardine agent then was a charming fellow but I am afraid he used to drink quite a lot of White Horse whisky for which Jardines were agent. I was quite a young man and my wife did not come down with me from Shanghai. Anyway I needed to talk to him, but he was not in his office and since it was a matter of some concern I went to his house. I think the Japanese were trying to grab Jardines' godown and our godown. So I arrived at his house and was met by a very large nice old fashioned "boy". I said, "Can see master?" And he said, "No very sorry, no see master." I said, "How fashion?" He said, "Very sorry; master today got very bad whisky and he no can walk!" That is a relic of the outport days when Jardines had some fantastic characters, but I do not think they would have survived very long in Swires, I think they would have been let out.'[10]

Riding the River I- The Yangtze Kiang from the coast to Ichang

The Yangtze Kiang is one of the world's great rivers and the spinal chord of central China flowing from west to east, rising in the mountains of Tibet and running over three thousand miles before it flows out in the China Sea beyond Shanghai. To command the Yangtze River is in effect to command central China.

But the Yangtze is not one but three rivers, albeit joined into one great length of water. It rises on the borders of Tibet and flows on through the great elevated plain of the province of Szechwan, gathering water from its tributaries on the plain until it reaches the Gorges beyond Chungking. Through countless millennia the river has cut its way through the mountain ranges which separate Szechwan from the rest of China, and over the centuries it has cut deep, producing a series of narrow spectacular gorges which vastly lessen the river's spread.

For three hundred and sixty miles, from below Chungking to just above Ichang, the waters of the Yangtze are concentrated into a series of defiles, and the resulting speed of the river can be as great as twelve knots at certain times of the year, particularly in the spring when the Himalayan snows melt into the river's beginnings. This is the Upper River, impossible to predict, difficult to navigate, unique to China.

Above Ichang the river bursts out into the plains of central China. The Upper River becomes the Middle River. This second Yangtze runs from Ichang to Hankow. As it begins it's devious and exceedingly twisty. Indeed so tortuous is the river's path that you can steam away from Ichang with its famous pagoda and you can steam for a day and still see the pagoda at nightfall. But at Hankow the river begins to settle itself and to broaden its girth.

The Lower River, the third Yangtze, runs from Hankow to the sea. In the years between the two world wars, ocean going liners ran up the river as far as Hankow when in the summer the water was high. For as the Yangtze approaches its estuary it stretches itself. The impetuous youth of the Gorges, the seemingly middle-aged calm of the Middle River give way to a generally serene and stately old age. At the point where the Whampu, the river on which Shanghai lies, joins the Yangtze its estuary is some fifty miles wide and its waters made quite yellow by the alluvial material they have gathered on their journey.

And the yellowness can be seen fifty miles out to sea. If you had travelled by passenger steamer from Hong Kong to Shanghai it would be announced over the ship's public address system that if passengers were to look over the side they could see where the China Sea ended and the Yangtze River began, for quite suddenly blue water became yellow.

In the years before the Second World War the Yangtze was the great thoroughfare of central China, the principal – indeed only – way of reaching the interior of this part of the country with any ease. The railways were underdeveloped and a network of serviceable roads unthought of. It was the river which carried men and materials; and the British in common with the Europeans had established themselves in the trading ports which ran the whole length of the Yangtze: Chinkiang, Wuhu, Nanking, Kiukiang, Hankow, Shasi, Ichang, Chungking and others too. And it was British ships in the main which carried most of the passengers and cargo up and down the Yangtze. True there was one Chinese owned shipping company, but generally the river belonged to the ships of the British companies B & S and Jardine Matheson.

Butterfield & Swire's shipping interests were run by a subsidiary company, The China Navigation Company; and CNCo as it was known had fleets on the China coast as well as the Yangtze River, and expected its ships' officers to sail both coast and river.

Working 'On the River'

'One day you would arrive in Shanghai and the superintendent would say that there was a chit for you. It was what we called the "shifting chit". They used to come very regularly, especially to the deck officers. We knew the man who brought the chits from the superintendent's office. "Shifting chit," we would say. And he would reply, "Yes." "For whom?" "For you." "My goodness, where am I going now?" "You're appointed chief officer on so and so on the river." Well I liked it because it was a change.

'One thing you noticed though is you often heard a man saying, "When did that happen?" "When I was on the river." And a man who had been on the river a long time would say that quite naturally, "When I was on the river." Now the other day I was talking to a man here and he said to me, "When I was on the road." He was a commercial traveller you see. And I recall our B & S river men would say, "When I was on the river" as opposed to "When I was on the coast."

There is another thing you notice when you have been on the river a long time and by and by you get a shifting chit, and are appointed to the coast again, it is amazing how blue the sea looks after months and months on the muddy river. You would think it would become natural to you, but no, you kept on looking at the very blue sea. And the Yangtze River at the high water season is very, very muddy; thick with mud.'[19]

太古

Navigational Problems

'I didn't really enjoy the river because it was not possible for people like ourselves who were really deep sea navigators to get to know all the intricacies of the river. All the river ships carried two qualified pilots, a day pilot and a night pilot, and very often an apprentice pilot, a young man who was just there learning the job. Although there was an officer on the bridge with him all the time, the officer, if he were truthful would say, "Really I left that river after perhaps a year not knowing one more thing about it, apart from knowing we are coming up to Hankow now I can see so and so." Some people took more interest in it than others but I think most of us who were on the river would have hated to have been told, "The pilots have gone on strike, you take this ship from Hankow." I don't think there would have been many volunteers.'[18]

 The principal hazard in navigating the Yangtze was water level, for the river has one of the highest rises and falls of any river in the world.

In the spring the melted ice and snows from the Himalayas could produce rises in the level of the water of over thirty feet in a night, bringing with it danger and destruction. For when the water was low the Chinese would move down the river bank and begin cultivating the rich alluvial mud that the shrinking river had bequeathed them. Then they were often caught unawares by a sudden spate as the river in flood now reached back for its old banks. Mass drownings were not uncommon. One British sailor recalls that it was nothing to push off twenty or thirty bodies that came down and got wedged between a ship's bows and its anchor chain.

And with the rising water came yet more silt. Silt that changed the geography of the river bed, closing off existing navigation channels and scouring out new ones.

'The ever-changing level of the water in the different seasons meant you took different channels almost every voyage. Because in the winter time when everything was frozen up, in the Himalayas and Tibet, there was no water running and the water gradually fell lower and lower in the Yangtze and ships had to find the deepest channels to get up and down. But when summertime came and all the snow melted, then there were floods. I remember just after I had gone out to China first in 1931, there were terrific floods. I think there were literally millions of Chinese drowned in these flooded areas. And during the high water season with all this surplus water you could almost make a bee-line from one place to another, go over the tops of the islands. There was a picture of the ship *Nanking* sitting on top of an island high and dry. She went on in falling water and the water did not rise again until the next high water season and there she stayed until eventually she was broken up there for scrap.'[18]

'In the summer you went straight up to the river without too much trouble. In winter you had to go around the sand banks which formed all the time. They used to vary a little bit. There was a customs river patrol which used to keep you informed as to how the water was.

'I have known ships to run ashore when the water fell quickly and the ships would be high and dry. In one particular place, the ship had to pay ground rent to a farmer for using his field, and she had to be launched into the river again.'[20]

The British had been trading along the Yangtze since the middle of the nineteenth century and by the 1920s had developed particular types of boats for the river, for no one particular design of boat was suitable for work on all three of the rivers which make up the Yangtze. Many of these ships were built in Scotland on the Clyde, shipped East and reassembled in Hong Kong or Shanghai.

'Boats on the Yangtze last a long time. They run in fresh water and therefore their hulls last. So it is economical to run the boats into old age. In fact I think the *Nanking* spent her fiftieth birthday ashore where she'd run aground, otherwise she'd have run for longer. And eventually they had to break her up because she'd run ashore at high water, run into a paddy field and they couldn't get her off. The age was quite significant in some of the old ones I was in. In fact, on the *Poyang* the old skipper had been there for twenty years himself, which is quite a period. But they're not the originals, they'd come from America. Those boats hadn't, but the prototypes had come from America, when America was the big noise on the river. Butterfield & Swire came relatively late.

'However, there were one or two American style stern-wheelers for use on the Middle River, for the very shallow bits on the very unpopular, very unused Middle River. Yes, there were some paddle-wheelers when I was around but not in Swires, they'd gone by then.'[17]

If many of the river boats were Scottish, so were the officers who ran them. The majority of officers in the China Navigation Company were from Scotland. And there might be three of them to each river boat: a captain, a chief officer and another in charge of the engines.

The crew, however, were Chinese who had been recruited locally. But as one CNCo officer recalls the European presence on the river had bitten its way into the Chinese who worked on the ship, providing Britons with more than passable imitations of home comforts while abroad.

'The name of the ship was the *Wanliu* and there was this Chinese on it who had worked with a German butcher. The Germans were very influential and there were many of them in North China. This particular cook used to make beautiful sausages. I was chief officer then and I did not believe that they were made aboard the ship. They were absolutely delicious and I asked who made them and was told it was this cook. Then I found out that when he had been a young lad he had worked with a German pork butcher. We were regular on the river and people living in Ichang and Chungking knew when the *Wanliu* was in and they used to send their cook down to get some sausages from our cook, a lot of it without the officers knowing. It was a private transaction between their cook and our cook. They were delicious and I wish now that I had had that recipe.'[19]

Throughout China the Europeans had traditionally carried out their business through the Chinese intermediary known as a compradore. The compradoric system continued to flourish in the first three decades of the twentieth century, with compradores, who were company employees interpreting between Europeans and Chinese, and more especially undertaking business arrangements which the Europeans were reluctant to involve themselves in.

For example it would be a compradore on the Shanghai wharves who would supervise the loading and unloading of river boats by coolies, and who would employ the 'tallymen' who monitored the coolies' work.

'If they were carrying bags of stuff, rice or whatever it was, up and down the gangplanks on their shoulders they would sing all night long. And each time they passed a tallyman they would be given a bamboo stick. It was the same in the daytime. And they would count their bamboo sticks and maybe a fellow would say, "I have got about ten there; I've got enough for 'the flutter'. There was a fellow on the quay who would maybe make him a little gamble. Then he would look at his pile and say, "If I win I could knock off now." But very often he would lose and come back working again. But they were good workers. Very often a B & S ship would pull in at say four or five o'clock to the Bund from the other side. They would load all night singing songs and in the morning, seven or eight o'clock the ship would sail.

'A lot of the coolies used to sleep on the Bund but that would only be a sort of temporary sleep, a snooze. They did not live on the Bund. I think they lived in some shacks round the corner, out of sight somewhere.

'I used to see them sleeping alongside the coffins because we carried a lot of coffins. Many Chinese like to be buried in their native little villages or towns and it was common to carry quite a large number of huge Chinese coffins on our ships. Because of that, when the ship pulled alongside you might see half a dozen coffins; one here, one there, one a bit further along. And if it was very cold and windy you would see a fellow lying down alongside it and having a sleep; just like a wind break.'[19]

The principal pattern of trade with China was similar to that with other underdeveloped parts of the world between the two world wars, whether they were part of an imperial system or not. Raw materials were shipped out in exchange for the manufactured products of an industrial society. And it's the raw materials that most river men recall in detail.

'When I first went up the river, which was during the Depression years, the main cargo downstream (though we were rather short on cargo) was salt for one thing, salt and wood oil particularly. The big Chinese junks, had been carrying wood oil for many many years, carrying it in oiled paper baskets, but the steamers started to build tanks and the junks couldn't compete and there was a lot of heartbreak about it because the junks then became unemployed. There were three small ships built by Swires for the Upper River and they only carried a hundred tons, and when that hundred tons was on board in wood oil they had no more dead weight for anything else. There were also medicines. The soil in the Szechwan province is very productive of Chinese medicines, herbs and God knows what. And, of course, opium. There was lots of opium grown up there. There are forty million people there, so their products were very popular. And there was what was one of the biggest exports from China, what they politely called casings. Pigs' intestines. Miles and miles, millions of miles of casings, because before plastic or whatever is used now you had casings. And many of the casings came from China. There were also barrels of egg yolk for the bakery business. Millions and millions of eggs came from all over China, and much of it from the province of Szechwan, and the Yangtze Valley. Surprisingly enough the only thing that seemed to come from the Middle River was cotton. And there were no cotton fields. Cotton was grown round the hundreds of villages as a sort of staple crop, so that hundreds of villages gathering cotton made a huge quantity and raw cotton was a very big export. So much so that one of the

Cargo

Down to the sea:
Chinese junks on the
Middle Yangtze.

big foreign firms built a cotton-pressing, cotton-packing plant there. And then the cotton was taken to Shanghai for the big cotton mills.

'It was surprising to find that in that part of the world there was also wildlife, though how game could exist when there were so many people to eat it I just don't know. The whole countryside teemed with quail, snipe and pheasant, golden pheasant. But that's the sort of cargoes that we got. The big refrigerating companies had plants on the Lower River where they froze all sorts of game. Eggs were exported by the million, but mainly I can remember the products of the pig. Casing and bristles. I'm sure that China was supplying the world with bristles for hairbrushes and toothbrushes because there was just so many people raising so many pigs.

'Human hair too was a very big export. In those days ladies wore hairnets. And hairnets then had to be made by hand. They're really like tiny little fishing nets, all knotted. Now they'd be made of nylon but at one time there was no way of making a hairnet except with human hair. Millions of women had little paper cups that they put their little bits of hair in when they combed them out (just in the same way as little bits of cotton would be gathered together) and so they ended up as bales of hair which from there went down towards Shanghai to be made into hairnets in nice little paper packets and sent to England and elsewhere'.[17]

'Coming down the river, the main thing I can think of was tung wood oil which was oil they get from a nut. If I remember rightly it is crushed and the resulting oil is just like varnish. It was used in the manufacture of the best varnishes in those days. A lot of people just used it on wood and did not bother with varnish on top of it.

'Going up there would be general cargo for the needs of the country, piece goods and the things that the Chinese wanted to buy from the Westernised coastal area. There was always a certain amount of food; rice mainly.'[18]

But perhaps the principal cargo on the Lower and Middle River was human. *Passengers* The China Navigation Company's ships carried passengers from port to port. European travellers had quite a comfortable time of it, particularly on the larger ships: shared cabins, perhaps a saloon and by general agreement particularly good food.

For the Chinese on the other hand a river journey was a more rough and ready business. For one thing the company mostly leased out the Chinese passenger business to a compradore, who was allowed to make his own arrangements for booking passengers on to a ship and ensuring their comfort while travelling.

'Chinese passengers travelled in great numbers and they tended to get rooked by their own people fairly thoroughly. We had three classes, first, second and third Chinese and then first class Foreign, and the foreigners lived the good life. The Chinese passengers could travel Foreign but there were not so many wishing to do so because there really wasn't the mixing. (Before my time they stopped the missionaries from travelling Chinese class in the Chinese section which they sometimes wished to do, because it upset the

Chinese. They were all crowded together as it was and they hated to have a European practising his art on them in their confined areas.) Eventually things improved, and the first class Chinese was as good as the first class Foreign but in a different style, with Chinese food and so on.

'The ships were under the compradore system and he was responsible for the Chinese passengers and the company sold the job of looking after passengers to the highest bidder so the poor old passengers had, I'd say, a fairly thin time of it. But they tended to accept what was there and hope for the best, that the voyage would come to an end. They're philosophical in that way. But their conditions were such that you wouldn't have liked it, nor would I.

'Each passenger's berth would be six feet of deck sleeping space, that would be along the coast as well. A deck passenger was entitled to thirty-six square feet, which would include recreation spaces. But normally a deck passenger or a steerage or third class passenger had a space to lie down on the deck. Second class passengers would have tiers of bunks, and the first class passengers would have a miniature cabin. But Chinese passengers were basically quite happy. As long as they were moving they didn't seem to object to being crowded in if they'd got a bit of security. I think they felt more secure in a crowd, but it's not the sort of thing that anybody not used to it would like. Basically I would imagine that's one of the things where we differ. We're used to spreading out and they're used to closing ranks.'[17]

The well-being of hundreds of Chinese passengers that might be travelling on a river steamer was in theory also the responsibility of the compradore, but it was beyond the capacity of a single compradore to supervise every aspect of his travellers' journey, particularly when it came to feeding them. So just as he had leased the right to sell passenger space from the shipping company so in his turn he leased out the catering arrangements to 'teaboys'.

'The teaboy was the man, as his name implied, who brought the passengers cups of Chinese tea for so much a cup, and served the meals. The meals would be laid out on the deck and then the people would sit round and he was the one who cleared away. But his main object was to try and make a living himself, having paid for his job.

'He paid the compradore for his job. So if there was a change of compradore, there might be sort of friction.'[17]

'The teaboys were like leeches. They would see the passengers coming on board and they would go up to a man and say, "All right I'll look after you. Where are you going? I'm your steward." Whether the passenger liked it or not, the teaboy would tell him how much he had got to pay, and he would bring him cups of tea or anything else he wanted or needed, but he had to be paid for it. This is on top of the poor passenger having bought his passenger ticket. And B & S could see that a lot of these passengers were being rooked, and they did not like this at all. They thought they would get more passengers if they could do away with this robbery, banditry whatever you would like to call it. So they tried to stop it. So the teaboys went on strike, and I rather think some of the crew went on strike in sympathy with them but I know at one time the ships just did not carry passengers because the teaboys would not allow them to do it. Teaboys had a very strong union. There might be fifty teaboys on one small ship three hundred feet long, one teaboy per passenger, they would just claim him and rook him. And the poor passenger had no option but to pay up. After having paid his fare. We all knew it went on, in fact we did try to get the police to put these teaboys off the ship. They weren't signed on ship's articles or anything but we had no control over them whatever, they just made themselves at home and cornered one little part of the deck, and said, "This is mine." Nobody dared touch it. And if he got a passenger, he would see that he was nicely laid out there and he would bring everything to him and charge sweetly for it.'[18]

'The teaboys had got out of hand, and there were so many that the company decided to clear them off and put on paid staff. (I suppose the compradore was going to have to pay.) So they took a ship, the *Woosung*, which was their best river steamer and a very handsome ship too, off the river and put it up at what they called the Arsenal, up above the shipping. They anchored her and then had a "wait and see" policy to get the teaboys off. And the teaboys wouldn't go. There was the ship and there was an impasse. Eventually they decided to throw them off. We always had plenty of big tugs in those days and they got the tugs alongside the teaboys were ejected. There was no fighting, they were just pushed off. In Canton the Seamen's Union was very communistic and they got hold of this and they started the *Woosung* Tragedy Support Committee, and it started a boycott in Canton where all our southern trade was centred; because in Hong Kong there was very little trade. It ended up eventually after a tremendous loss, with the teaboys all going back to the ship with the gongs beating and bands playing. The shipping manager later told me that they'd had to pay a big sum in Canton. On the other hand the teaboys were a race of people that were pretty hard put to it to make ends meet for their families, because every Chinese has got a family to support. You hardly ever get a man, as in Europe, who is a freelance and can spend his salary as he gets it. Every Chinese that I've ever known has responsibilities. I suppose a beggar has got a family somewhere. So the teaboys had to make their money, and the best way to make money was to either hold the passengers up for a bit for ransom or smuggle. Smuggling was not the same in Chinese eyes. To carry a bundle of shoes from one place to another for example was not smuggling to a Chinese, even though there was a customs duty at one end. It was good business.'[17]

Smuggling and Customs Dues

On the river smuggling was not confined to the 'teaboys'. To most Chinese the evasion of freight charges – it cost as much to carry a cargo three hundred and eighty miles through the Gorges from Chungking to Ichang as it did from Ichang across to the Pacific Coast of America – and customs dues seemed a perfectly legitimate extension of their normal business.

However, while freight charges were the concern of the shipping companies, customs dues were a principal source of revenue to the Chinese government.

Chiang Kai Shek, the effective leader of China from the middle of the 1920s, had pledged himself and his movement – the New Life Movement – to restoring China and the Chinese to full moral health. There was to be an end to corruption. And in particular the growing and manufacture of and the traffic in opium was to be outlawed. But the corruption continued, and opium still found its way down the Yangtze from the poppy fields of Szechwan, despite the efforts of the Anti-Opium Bureau, who to some observers seemed less anti-opium than anti other people trafficking in opium.

The problem for Chiang was that he was never completely the master of his own house. His civil war with the Communists diverted his attention, his resources and his energies away from disorder and law breaking elsewhere. Local bandits, gangsters perhaps, continued to thrive.

'The opium smugglers had, fortunately, except for the Lower River, ceased to worry foreign shipping. You'd think where the opium was growing it would be a problem for us but it was not, and I never encountered opium smuggling on the Gorges. By that time the "New Life Movement" had come in and Chiang Kai Shek and Madame Chiang Kai Shek were hot on the subject of "New Life".

'The New Life Movement of the newly established Chiang Kai Shek regime was to stamp out all bad influences, and it was certainly very laudable to stamp out the carriage of narcotics, it was mostly opium in those days. The whole of Szechwan seemed to revolve round opium. Whether local opium was there before the foreign opium, which was supposed to be an added attraction to improve the quality of the local stuff, I'm not sure. I've often wondered which came first, the opium from India say, or the local stuff. The foreign opium, especially the Persian stuff, was very high grade, it was rather like bringing in whisky to people who had been drinking rotgut.

'Anyway the Chiang Kai Shek regime instituted an Anti-Opium Bureau which was supposed to be in full charge of opium suppression. And we must thank the Anti-Opium Bureau, because it took all the weight from us. Any opium that was carried was carried under their auspices so we mustn't be too critical, but opium still continued its merry way because it had to be grown for the people to make a living. The whole province of Szechwan grew opium.

'The Anti-Opium Bureau didn't actually carry opium on the river because they didn't need to, but they could direct where it was going. The customs (the Maritime Customs, which originally had been under foreign supervisors but by then had been returned to the Chinese) weren't allowed to touch opium. It was the Anti-Opium Bureau that had the authority to find out and to stop it and to do everything else with it, and they were not allowed on British ships and the customs were. This meant that the Anti-Opium Bureau were able to dictate and bring down safely chests of opium loaded in a Chinese ship. And that fortunately relieved foreign ships.

'I had a brush with the Anti-Opium Bureau. I remember waking one morning and hearing rifle shots (everybody had rifles in those days) and I went on the bridge – I was the chief officer – and I was astonished to see the captain firing through the rails at a launch. He said that this launch had tried to board us. It was just becoming dawn so we carried on and got clear of it. There was fire coming from its funnel as it tried to keep up with us, but we out-distanced it. Later on we stopped at a boat station and a whole lot of people came on board and we had to anchor. They had guns. And they said there was opium on board and they were determined to find it. They said it was in the engine room, and they tortured some of the crew, but they couldn't find it, so we were released.

'On the Lower River the opium smuggling was gangster controlled; like in Hong Kong where you had local triad gangs. To the ordinary Chinese, and that includes the crew, opium was a dirty word. It's "foreign mud". If members of the crew were smuggling opium they would be very few and far between, unless they were put in by the smugglers. I know from my own experience that the Chinese crews would not as a body have anything to do with opium. Carrying vegetables, potatoes and stuff they were in far more than anybody could dream of, but they would not touch opium.

'However, sometimes the gangsters would get their man on board and he'd be accepted as a crew member, and everyone else would keep quiet, and he'd be the man taking the opium down.

'That's the way it was done. But on the Upper River it was not necessary because the stuff was shipped down in Chinese ships in bulk, in big boxes. There was no need to hide it around the ship and put it here and put it there and hope that nobody found it. Once I went up to the Scotch mission in Ichang for tea and Dr Tocher, the missionary in charge, was due in from up the Gorges, but because he didn't arrive there was a lot of agitation. When he finally arrived he said quite brusquely – he was a good Scot – that he had been delayed in the Ichang Gorge. He'd come down in one of the Ming Company ships (which was a new shipping company, a very good Chinese company) and been held while it discharged opium. These poor ladies, good Scotswomen, were terribly upset about this because at that time there was this tremendous amount of drum-beating by Chiang Kai Shek and his wife about how they were stamping out this sort of thing. He said, "Look don't be silly about this; you've got to be worldly in these matters. This is the way it's done and that's the way it is. It goes into a lighter, and it goes ashore and then it by-passes Ichang, because the military in Ichang would want their cut, but by-passing the town it avoids local duties."

'In the early days when they had customs on the job they would get a tip-off that it was on board. If they had a tip-off they would search very thoroughly because they would get quite a large proportion of the value although the opium was eventually burnt, but certainly the finders would get quite a large sum. I think it was in Hankow that a Lower River ship was supposed to have some opium in the hold and they couldn't find it, but they were determined to find it. I went down as a youngster to see what was going on. They brought a smeller. The smeller was seldom sent for because it meant that they had been unable to find the stuff, and they had to share the profit with an expert, who demanded quite a cut. He wouldn't be a customs man, he'd be a smeller. I watched this man as he went round. We've all played the game "You're getting warmer". He went round, and I'm quite sure he was leading them a dance. The customs officers were following him around with long faces, thinking about what this bloke was going to cost, and I suppose he costed it by the amount of time he took. So it was like a little play. With these glum chaps following the eager beaver until eventually he found it. But I think he knew where it was all the time; he'd got a good sense of smell. He was just getting his money's worth. He got it and then they were all on to it. Great fun. It always remained in my mind as a picture of the hunt.

'But I do know that no British ship in my time on the Middle or on the Upper River, where you sailed through miles of growing poppy, was ever in trouble. The crew may have had some for themselves, but then our crew were mostly Shanghai and were not addicts. Our teaboys may have done so, the passengers certainly would want their opium because some used to give it to their children for stomach ache. It was really a universal remedy for everything.'[17]

'The officials were successful in finding opium hauls, but I think it was possible mostly on information. Someone was not getting his, or what he thought was his, proper share, so he might inform the officials where to look. But the Chinese were very ingenious at finding new hiding places for opium or cocaine or anything at all.

'I remember one search on the river in particular, which discovered one hiding place that I thought was a most original and ingenious one. All the ships had double bottoms. If they had no cargo to keep them down in the water they filled these double bottoms with water to give the propeller a good hold and they carried fresh water in them for domestic use. When empty they were ideal places for smuggling. Access to the tanks was gained by manholes held tight by bolts which were removed to put anything other than liquid into the tanks. Then the bolts were screwed up again until the ship reached its destination. I remember on one occasion, over a ton of copper coins, because copper is particularly valuable, were found in these double tanks, I forget the tonnage, but sacks and sacks of copper coins came out of one of these double tanks.'[18]

'I can remember passengers smoking opium, but not crews. A lot of these things are for the people who haven't got enough to do. Where crews are working hard, it's rather like drinking.'[17]

If some Chinese had their opium most Europeans, and certainly ships' officers on the river, had their alcohol.

'The drink before lunch from eleven o'clock on was gin, mostly pink gin. Then no one drank in the afternoon unless he was an alcoholic and there were not many of those. They were always emptied out at the first opportunity. Then funnily enough in the evening it was whisky rather than gin. I don't know why. In the evening it might not matter if you had one over the eight, you could just go to your bed and forget about it. But I would not want to give the impression that this happened every day to everyone and there was no work done. The work continued just the same.

'Drinking on the river was different from being at sea. You see you were anchored; you were in port when you were drinking. When you were on a sea-going ship safely tied up in harbour, you would have your drinks then too. It was only when a ship was under way that you did not drink. It was an unwritten law at the time. A man who drank at sea before the war was looked on as being on the downward grade.

'Sometimes people drank because of boredom, sometimes worry, sometimes because they enjoyed it, sometimes to give them a bit of a shine before going ashore to make whoopee for the night. All sorts of normal reasons for having a drink. But mostly social. One officer would decide, "It's time for a drink now," and he would press his bell and the boy would come along and he would order and say, "Talkee second officer. Askee he what he want." Or the third officer or whoever it happened to be. And the boy would go and say, "Chief officer askee what you wantee drink." And that was the signal for them all to go back to the chief officer's room, and they would have a couple of drinks and depending on the circumstances they might even have three. There was a fair amount of drinking but I have never known of a ship put ashore because of drunkenness. I think there was maybe a sort of camaraderie between the junior officers and the captain. One would not let the others down. Several captains I came across drank far too much for their own good and everyone else's. And had the powers that be known the amount they were drinking, they would have been asked to resign, but their loyal officers saw to it that that did not happen. There were occasions when the ship was run by the junior officers and the captain did not know whether he was in Timbuctoo or anywhere else. But that could happen in business ashore in offices where the boss was an alcoholic or that way inclined. The business carries on and he is sitting at his desk, but half the time he has not got a clue. So I suppose there is nothing unusual about it. I would not say that ships' crews drink more than shore-based people.

'The drink was very cheap. When I went out to China I think gin was one dollar eighty a bottle, and the dollar was about one and threepence, so it was about two shillings odd for a bottle of gin. Whisky was slightly dearer, but still under three shillings a bottle. It was all duty free of course. So possibly the cheapness of it was the reason for more drinking than there would be ashore. Right up until the war, you could go to a hotel in Shanghai and the boys would be just waiting to jump to your table whenever you required any attention, and you would order your drink say whisky soda, whisky water, whisky anything or maybe gin, and the boy would bring the bottle to the table and the glass and pour it out. He would continue pouring until you said "when" and when you did he would just turn the bottle up and leave it there. There was nothing to stop you drinking that down and pouring another quick one if you were unscrupulous. But nobody seemed to bother to do that, drink was so easy to get and so comparatively cheap. But the drunks would let the boy pour until it was right up to the rim whereas good people like myself, perhaps a thimble full would do just to be sociable.'[18]

Few of the men who sailed the Lower and Middle Yangtze have forgotten the sights and sounds of the river. Nor the smells. For the Chinese who farmed the fertile land on either side of the river with admirable if malodorous thrift, fertilised their fields with night soil which in the humid heat of high summer must have been particularly pungent, though less offensive in the bitter cold of the winter. The Chinese seen on their sailing junks in the river and on the banks seemed unaware of the extremes of the climate in the Yangtze valley, to take for granted the plagues of rice flies which could extinguish a ship's light in summer by clinging to it in clouds, or simply add another layer of quilted clothes to the five or six they were already wearing as the thermometer fell below zero. And there is a quality of timelessness about some of the memories of sights remembered on the river.

The Sights of the River

'We were at anchor in the Tung Ting lake. It's a very shallow sort of lake and full of game, full of birds and things. This chap had a sampan, covered with matting, a fore and aft pole with the matting over it, and along the top was a row of cormorants. He had a long thin bamboo in the stern and he tipped off the first one and it dived in the water and eventually up it came, its head with a little fish sticking in its throat. It had a ring round its neck and so the fisherman kind of gathered it in his bamboo pole in the water, picked it up, took the fish out and gave it a little something and put it on top of the bamboo matting. And then all the others moved along, just shuffled along. It's quite a common sight to see cormorants fishing, everybody's got them, but the Chinese have got the art of getting little animals and things like that down to a fine art. And fishing with otters – they've been doing that for years. How, in the muddy water, they can pull an otter down at the end of a line and not get mixed up with a fishing net I don't know.

'I remember watching a man fishing, throwing in his circular net, he was by himself in his boat and he pulled the net up, and after he had got the net more or less up he leaned behind him and he gave his hand to what looked like a little old man I thought, but it was an otter with his little whiskers looking about. He brought him on board. That otter had no restraining line or anything. And it was rather like a dog or a cat, it ran to where he was emptying the net, hopefully, to see if there was any fish.'[17]

The Yangtze Flotilla

British interests on the Yangtze were protected by British gunboats, what was called the Yangtze Flotilla. There were fourteen ships in the flotilla, twelve of which were divided into two classes, the so-called 'insect' class – craft with names such as HMS *Bee* or *Cockchafer* or *Ladybird* – and a second class named after birds. *Petrel*, *Teal* or *Widgeon*. There were six ships in each of these categories and two additional flat-bottomed craft for operating in a particular tributary of the Yangtze by Changsha. Every boat was armed with six inch or four inch guns, some had a mounted Lewis Gun and they carried small arms for issue to their crews in the event of trouble.

'They used to come aboard and have a gin with us and we would maybe have a gin with them. The Navy commanders there had a dickens of a job to keep their crew from getting bored. It must have been a big problem. They

Senior service: *HMS Gannet,* one of the gunboats of the Yangtze Flotilla on the river.

were all the time organising walks or hikes, something for the crew because they were only small ships, these gunboats, though the accommodation would be super. They were small ships and only drew a few feet some of them. I was sorry for the commanders and for their crews, having to deal with boredom.

'The men were all in immaculate uniforms. They had their certain patrols to do, and if there was any trouble with anything British, like a British merchant kidnapped or held for ransom, they would dash up and show the flag and nine times out of ten the man would be released. The officers were quite sociable. They had their parties and liked their gin like a lot of sailors do. The recognised time for gin was eleven o'clock in the forenoon, and just to show that it was gin time, a special pennant was put up to the masthead to let people know, "All right we are starting our gins, would you care to come and join us?" How they worked it out, whether they took turns or not I do not know but I always seemed to be kept too busy on my own ship to think of visiting their gin times. But the gin pennant was a bit of a joke really.'[18]

But the boredom could be relieved by 'policing' operations, and in particular in the 1930s by the rescuing of hostages, often missionaries taken by the Communists who were particularly in evidence on the Middle River. They hoped to exchange their hostages for cash and military hardware to continue their struggle against Chiang Kai Shek and the Nationalists. But the authorities generally refused to pay ransoms with arms, preferring to offer medical supplies. Ordinary shipping in the river was continually aware of the presence of Communist troops in the villages on the banks of the river.

Communist Activity

'They did penetrate down to the Lower River to a certain extent, but the Middle River was their hunting ground. After the floods in '31 I got my first promotion as skipper of a small ship. And I was two years as the sole European on the little ship, most of the time on the Middle River, so we knew about the Communists. There was a general there called Ho Lung who was in charge of the Communists in that part of the world and you would call them roving bands really, but they were very well organised.

'They were on the move the whole time, and they took missionaries as hostages, they had Catholic priests, and of course the Catholic church was very strongly anti-Communist. These priests were chained because they were "enemies". The Communists were very well organised. There were, I think, several hundred miles under Communist control. They had their own post office. Foreign shipping was anathema to them, carrying our Red Ensign on their own waters. They used to fire on ships, they put up huge placards and sometimes they'd have a publicity man banging away with a stick as you went by to get the passengers to take notice. But they knew nothing about ships at all. They used to fire at the funnel. We carried guards but our job was more to discourage the guards from indiscriminate firing than to protect the ship. The Reds used to move around a lot and would get into a village and fire from the village. It was no good firing back indiscriminately. The villagers had done nothing wrong.

'If we didn't have guards we'd fire back ourselves. I used to have a Winchester rifle and I don't know whether you've ever seen a Winchester rifle, but unless you put the sights up you've not got a hope of hitting anything because the barrel's got to be way up in the air, there's a big lead bullet in them. So I always left my sights down and then I was quite sure of not hitting these poor souls.

'I remember one time watching the Reds as we were steaming along. They were in the town and the Nationalists were attacking one end and the Communists were running out the other end, and there was one chap left behind and he had evidently got a pair of shoes from somewhere and this was the reason he was left behind because he was running with shoes which he didn't know how to run with. Eventually in sheer desperation he took them off and flung them in the river. There was this capturing and recapturing of towns all the time. Even the town of Changsha, the big city, would fall to the Communists and then would be re-taken, there would be a slaughter of a lot of innocent people.

'They started to try and run us aground by shifting the beacons. In the Middle River there were no lights on the beacons, they were just bamboo poles, but they hit upon a wonderful way of doing us in; they realised that the beacons were for crossing the river so if they shifted the beacon instead of destroying it, then we would be led across the wrong part, and this added to our trouble.

'One time we did have trouble. One of the Upper River steamers was going to take up her duty after her overhaul in Shanghai and going up for the winter. She ran aground in the Middle River. It was a lonely part of the world, and there was nobody there, no protection, nor any guards and the Communists evidently just happened to be massed around the place. It was quite ugly for a time. There were four Europeans and they had I remember thirty-seven rounds of ammunition each and until the gunboat eventually came and towed them off it was quite a shooting match between them. But then again I don't think anybody really got hurt.

'There was no doubt that Communism was well and truly in control over a vast area. They would attack a village and open up the rice stores to the people which provided a very welcome addition to the local pot. People could stand a lot of that. And then they would go into the country and destroy the boundary marks. The country people were bound to the landlord and the money-lender, so their crops would be in pawn. What they'd get for their crops would only buy the seed for the next season, and so they went from generation to generation in poverty and naturally the Communists were as welcome as the flowers in May. And also the Nationalists were a dispirited bunch really.

'I remember once a column of Communists were marching along a hillside and I measured the length of the column on the chart and it was two miles of carriers. It was single file of course and they were carrying all sorts of stuff.

'From each village they got the people to carry their stuff to the next village so they got the labour. I was watching these chaps through my glasses, and they had their banners and they stood back and I saw a puff of smoke and then bang, and a whole lot of rubbish, nails or whatever fell into the water close to us. They had a little mortar or something and they fired it off at this foreign ship, just for the fun of it. But there again it didn't do any real harm to anybody.'[17]

Riding the River II-
The Gorges

By far the most spectacular section of the Yangtze River was that part of it called the Upper River, the 380 miles of water between Chungking and Ichang where it ran through a series of deep gorges and across potentially treacherous rapids. This was the most difficult and dangerous part of the Yangtze to navigate and for many years since the river had first been opened to foreign traders by the Chinese it had defeated the Western trading nations in their endeavours to reach into the interior of China. For the Gorges formed a natural bottle-neck between the fertile province of Szechwan beyond Chungking and the broad plain below Ichang through which the river wandered to the sea.

As the British Admiralty Sailing Directions made clear the Upper River was a very distant cousin to the placid Middle and Lower Rivers:

'Its character above Ichang is quite different from that below. No longer does it meander through a vast alluvial plain, from which isolated hills rise abruptly like steep islands out of the sea, but its course is confined to a valley, sometimes almost a ravine, little wider than the river itself, with mountainous land on each side. The river is tortuous and passes through several narrow gorges, where vertical cliffs rise on each side to heights of some hundreds of feet above the level of the river. The summits of the cliffs rise again to the mountains behind them, and are intersected by narrow ravines, which occasionally produce waterfalls.'

The Character of the Upper River

The China Navigation Company were not involved in trading through the Gorges until the years immediately after the First World War, when they acquired interests in Chungking. It was in the 1920s that their officers first saw, and navigated the company's ships through, the three great Gorges.

'The Ichang Gorge is thirteen miles long. The Wuchang Gorge is twenty-five miles long. And then there is the Windbox, four and a half miles long. The breadth of the river in these gorges would be about two hundred and fifty to three hundred yards in some places and as narrow as one hundred and fifty yards in others. It is these narrows that form the bottle-necks.

The Gorges

'The cliffs on each side were very very steep. The Windbox Gorge is like a mountain three thousand feet high, split down the centre. It is like a vast corridor one hundred and fifty yards wide but it looks very narrow when you have got these high cliffs on each side. If you want to see the sky then you

Windbox: The
Windbox Gorge, one
of the most
spectacular of the
Yangtze Gorges
between Ichang and
Chungking.

have got to put your head over the rail and look up, it is so steep. But it is very awe-inspiring.'[19]

Spectacular though they may have been the Gorges posed great navigational problems for the sailor and what made them so difficult to navigate was the fluctuating water level. The river was as difficult for the Chinese junks which had sailed it for thousands of years as it was for the specially built highly powered ships with their flat bottoms which Western trading companies like the China Navigation Company ran between Ichang and Chungking. A sudden 'freshet', a rapid rise in the water level caused perhaps by melting snows at the Yangtze's source in Tibet, did more than simply speed the river up, it altered its very character as this rising water was quite literally shot through the Gorges. The river bed changed; sudden and potentially fatal whirlpools were thrown up. 'Know thy water level' was the first commandment obeyed by every sailor on the Upper River.

*Water Levels and
Navigational
Problems*

'Most people don't know that water levels rise and fall, and though it may only rise and fall eight feet there's a maximum and a minimum. Say the maximum is eight feet and the minimum is zero, in between there's a middle period of four or five feet which is the norm. That might be the base line, a bench mark, a datum that everything is measured from. You don't measure it from the very bottom of the ocean or the river or anything but from a base line, and on the Gorges like everywhere else, when they want to make their charts they fix a base line and call it zero. They fix the zero for one spot and they fix a base line further along and that's a zero there, and so on all the way up the Yangtze. There's a big slope in the river between Chungking and Ichang naturally because it's a very fast flowing river, but there is the base line zero at selected spots all the way. And when the river rises above that, they've got all these marks ready painted along the various places and you know what the watermark is: it's so many feet above the zero mark. That's terribly important because if Chungking's watermark is falling, then the river is easier to navigate, and if it's rising it's harder to get along. The customs give the watermark for various towns and you can judge what the river is doing. If the river is rising rapidly and the watermark is going up and up, then it's serious, there's a freshnet. If it's serious then nobody moves, especially the junks because the junks have it all calculated. But they can only calculate on what they see, they didn't have the telegraphic information that we had; but the watermark is the be-all and end-all of the Gorges. Everybody knows the watermarks, and little children ask their mothers (which is a compliment to the mothers, because the mothers know the watermark too), it's so important. It's life and death to a junk to watch the watermark and see how it's going. Sometimes you can see it rising in the Windbox Gorge two hundred feet from high to low in a season.'[17]

'I believe there is a record rise in one place, twenty miles above Wuchang Gorge. There there is a two hundred and seventy foot rise between low and high water, two hundred and seventy feet – that is a big rise between low and, a few months later, high water, isn't it?'[19]

Every spring the trading ships which had wintered in Ichang would be waiting and watching for the water level to rise to a point where they could navigate through the Gorges up to Chungking. At last the water would briefly reach the minimum level necessary to get through safely. It was what was called the 'false rise' and not until the water level was ten feet above the base line was it considered safe for the ships to weigh anchor.

In the beginning there were two classes of ship in the Gorges. Winter ships and summer ships built to take account of the different conditions in the Gorges at these two seasons of the year. Later the distinction was blurred. Whatever their craft, few sailors have ever forgotten their first sight of the entrance to the first Gorge, the Ichang Gorge up river from the port of Ichang.

'As you were leaving Ichang you saw a blank wall, a rocky mountain, and then as the ship turned the corner you left the flat part of the river altogether,

On the rocks: Aground in the Gorges after the water level has fallen.

145

it was just a complete change; as though somebody had changed a slide in a magic lantern. There was an opening and you went in and that was the Ichang Gorge. It was a very spectacular and dramatic entrance to the Gorges.'[17]

The responsibility for taking the powerful little Western ships through the three great Gorges and over the rapids at Hsintan and Futan lay with Chinese pilots. And since the pilots spoke no English it was by the simplest of hand gestures that they gave their instructions.

Pilots

'The pilot didn't do anything while the ship was in port, or within the port limits or was anchoring, all that was done by the master. But as soon as you cleared a port or cleared off an anchorage then you handed over to the pilot. They used to serve an apprenticeship of fourteen years, seven years in a junk and seven years in a steamer. And they all came from one village. They would never speak, which was traditional as much as anything. It was all done with the forefinger, and they would be watching the water the whole time, watching and moving the forefinger. You had your own quartermasters, but in some cases, say in gunboats, the pilots would carry their own steersmen. You also carried boatmen. The three pilots would come on board with six boatmen. They were for running a wire ashore and handling the sampan, and sounding from the ship with a bamboo. The pilots were very much a local product with long costumes, long moustaches, and little hats. They were very proud old gentlemen, and of course we had our own pilot so we knew them quite well. But they worked in silence moving only one finger, although as you got near to a rapid he'd pull his long sleeve up and increase his watchfulness, and then perhaps in the rapid he would move his arm, but that was about the only time you would see him agitated.

'You had three rudders and powerful engines, so the slightest touch on your helm would swing the ship. It was like steering a motor car.

'The pilots and people knew the river so well that they knew where to go. You see Chinese have very good memories. It's because of the way they learn

Watching the water:
A Yangtze pilot
(left) guides a
British gunboat
through the Gorges.

everything by rote. They do have far better memories than Europeans. So your pilot on the Upper River knew every rock, how high it was and how low it was and as he'd never get to Chungking if he stayed in the middle, he had to do a little bit of inshore work, and he'd got to know what was there. Actually he was reading the water, he knew that certain slithers on the water meant that the rock was so far down and so on like that, but it was all from memory.'[17]

At least one British naval officer who served with the Yangtze Flotilla on the Upper River between the two world wars recalls that one of his pilots was the only man on board the gunboat who was allowed his opium. Crews were well aware that their safety lay in the accuracy of the smallest gesture of a pilot's index finger as he guided a ship up river. Contented pilots one might suppose were less prone to mistakes which caused accidents. Progress up the river when the spring water was high was painfully slow, a matter of a few miles in a day and when night fell every ship tied up. No one would risk night steaming through Gorges or over rapids. It was the rapids which offered the greatest challenge to navigation in the Upper River. When foreign ships first began to make the journey between Ichang and Chungking they had insufficient power to be certain of crossing these great stretches of troubled waters with their swirling currents, shallow submerged rocks, and shifting sand banks.

'In the old days the steamers themselves could not go up. There were some gorges, some rapids where a ship would try hard to make a run and then maybe she just could not rise that extra few feet and she'd slip back down stream, get full steam up again and make another zigzag run at it. Very often there might be two hundred coolies on the bank, hoping the steamer could not do it. The pilot and the captain would still try, but when the coolies started clapping hands – slow clap – they knew it was a job for them. Then

the ship had to pull into the bank and throw a rope ashore to the coolies who were going to track the ship over the rapid. It was a light rope first and then a very very long wire was handed to the coolies and they took it up to the top of the gorge and made it fast on one of the big rocks up there or a big boulder. Then the ship made it fast on the windlass and with her own engine speed and propeller and the windlass pulling they could make her get over. But I never experienced that, that was in the days when the steamers did not quite have the power.'[19]

'*Trackers*'

In the 1920s and '30s there were still communities of 'trackers' living on the river banks. But it was rare for powered ships to have to call upon their services. These trackers earned their living physically hauling Chinese junks over the rapids.

'There was a camp for trackers. It was almost a compound. You've got to remember that trackers were considered the lowest form of human life. It was a dreadful business. They wake them in the morning and they have a pipe of opium and they're ready to work. A junk would set out from Ichang and it would employ twenty or thirty trackers, and off it would go up the Ichang Gorge. They'd be tracking either along the shore, or if there was a fair wind they'd be on board. There were paths cut in some of the cliff sides and they'd be tracking along them. It wouldn't be too difficult, until you came to a rapid! Now those rapids have been in existence for a thousand years, and so villages have sprung up which were dependent entirely on that rapid. They had their own pilots and augmented the trackers. So we'll say that it's a bad rapid. The pilot and the number two pilot come on board the junk. The pilot will go to the big oar, a long oar over the front holding the ship steady. It's a huge thing, almost as big the junk. Weighed with stones to balance it. Big stones. There would be four or five men with the number one pilot on this oar. The number two pilot goes to the tiller. Then there's a drum on the junk. It's there all the time because the actual trackers may be up on the cliff face a long long way away. With the beat of the drum they know what to do if the rope gets caught or something. A poor swimmer's got to get in and

clear it! Then they pay out bamboo rope, below the rapid. They pay out a lot of line and it's carried above the rapid to the best place for where the trackers can spread out. Let's say it's a very bad rapid and they've got two hundred men. The rope is led from the midships section up through a block which can be raised or lowered a bit just to get it right. Then the men spread out. They each have a bandolier made of white cloth and a bit of a line attached, a yard-long line with a circular stone on the end with a hold in it, and the line goes through that, so it's rather like a toggle, but it's usually a bit of stone. Now to the main bamboo rope they will attach smaller ropes so that they form a fan – I'm speaking about a bad rapid now. They will form this fan and then each man will attach his toggle with a quick half turn and it will hold on the bamboo rope as long as he keeps the weight on, and then they will spreadeagle down and take the weight. Those left on board will then start to push off with their boat-hooks and she'll clear the bank. Meanwhile the rope has been dragged along the shore and it will be fouled by the boulders and the rocks. This is where the swimmers come in, and they have these young swimmers who must have been even lower than the trackers, and they had to clear this rope on the edge of the rapid. They do so quite simply by jumping in the water and dog-paddling around and they are swept down and then presto! They're standing on the rock, they just get swept into the backwater and up on the rock they go. So then they clear the line and then stand on their little rocks to see that the line remains clear. So then those on board signal on the drum and the trackers advance until they've got the rope taut and they're in a position where they've got their best holding. They don't have to go far; the head of the rapid, that's the difficult part, is only the width of a road or less. They've pulled quite a long way but the head is where they're going to have their problem. And so the drum signals "hold" and then they all hold. Then the pilot in the front works his big oar and slowly the bow of the junk comes out a bit. You lever it out at an angle, and then the drummer signals on the drum and the second pilot brings the helm over and she comes in, but comes in quickly, the trackers quickly advance a foot, two feet, three feet and so on to the very head of the rapid. They've

149

done a lot of "holding" and "pulling" before that but finally it is the last few
feet, and of course the water's rushing around but the junk is over and then
off they go quite happily, everybody's jaunty.

'Now it has been said that the sort of ganger on the side with his long thin
bamboo will thrash the men, but he doesn't. He's testing the pull to see that
their toggle and line is taut, that nobody's hanging back, because it's life and
death for them, if the junk breaks away. And I did see one break away on a
small rapid, away went the junk broadside on, it was only a single line, not a
big fan, and those that didn't slip their toggle quickly enough – they've
usually got their hand on it ready to slip – bounced on rocks like tennis balls.
But in that case none was thrown into the water. The rope dragged clear. But
it was a terrible life, terrible.

'And as the trackers pull they chant or sing a very plaintive song. They always sing except when they are really hard pressed: usually when they were on the march they sang, or when the pull was reasonable and they were moving. When they had what they called a "belly to the ground" rapid they didn't sing.'[17]

Despite their huge horse power and their sophisticated steering system with the three rudders, negotiating the rapids was still no easy affair for CNCo ships, or those of the other Western fleets.

'In fact you followed what a junk did, you went up the backwater. And then as you met the tongue (rapids are just a tongue – a 'V') you forced your way across it. The 'V' is the head of the rapid, and it comes down and it may be that the 'V' gets a bit crooked at the bottom, but normally it's a straight 'V'. There's backwaters each side, and the backwater can be very, very strong. The 'V' is smooth and generally straight, and it is raised above the backwater, so you're scooting along the backwater at a fine speed and quite close to the shore, and that's where the pilot has to know where the rocks below you are because you are in this backwater and you're going along fast. And then as you approach the 'V' coming down, the water is diagonal across your bow. Some ships have very low fo'c'sles for working the big low-geared capstan for 'heaving', and the tendency was to build the fo'c'sle low. Then you hit that descending water while you're going up fast in the backwater. I don't know what happens to the backwater, it just disappears, but you hit the descending water and the pilot swings all the three rudders over and you're in the middle of the top of the 'V'. But in the meantime all the water's come over your little fo'c'sle which disappears for a second or two just as though the bridge has become the front of the ship. That's in the small ships.

'So it's a question of quite literally getting up full steam and almost jumping once you get into the main tongue of the rapid, of using the speed you've got in the backwater to give you a flying start.

'On a hard rapid the ship becomes stationary immediately. Then the pilot starts to bring her slowly from one side of the rapid to the other (moving his finger gently because the slightest touch and she moves a bit) to get ahead and when he gets in close to the bank he can gain a bit more. The top of the 'V' is not at right angles to the bank, it may be quite a long angle, so if he can get the stern over it it's not such a drag to get the stern over.'[17]

For the Chinese who travelled as crew or passengers between Ichang and Chungking the Gorges and the rapids were not just geological obstacles in their journey's path, but possessed a spiritual dimension. And it was important to acknowledge this before setting out and to enlist the help of jossmen, or priests.

'They're a very practical people, and if there is some way that you can guard against anything they take it. They don't just pray for the fun of it, so at the start of the season, when you went up for the "false rise", the amount of firecrackers, and the jossmen on board doing their stuff, was always quite exciting. But that's purely practical. It's insurance. It's, I suppose, Buddhism. And so there are plenty of temples there that supply the people.

'It was important to make the right observance. For instance take a Jardine ship. They had the *Chang Wo*, a winter ship, and she was always in trouble. She really had misfortune after misfortune. She always managed to beach herself, and so they decided after one more repair, because the ship was going down to Shanghai each time and being taken off the run, to give her a new name and tart her up. They painted two eyes on the bow, they put a big porcelain Buddha on the mast, and more important they changed her name to *Hsin Chang Wo*, Hsin means new, because they had a *Chang Wo* which was fifty years old, on the Middle River with no problems at all. They had fire crackers, and off she set and immediately, or almost immediately, had another smash. They sent her down to Shanghai but this time they altered the run of the water to her propellers and rudders, they altered the shape of the stern and she was all right after that. So there you are, they had the willingness to change her name, to put a big porcelain Buddha on the mast and to paint eyes on the bow, all to appease the gods.

'One time before the first departure of the season from Ichang, we had a whole crowd of priests in the saloon, all chanting and praying, and it was always their custom to have their parade of gongs literally to clear the ship of devils. They marched round and you could always tell there were leading monks and lesser monks, the leading monks set off in a dignified manner around the deck, and along came the others scampering after them. The last man of this great tail going round was having the devil of a job to catch up and bang his gong at the same time, and down he fell, and the old Shanghai bo'sun picked him up and sent him on his way; and he said to me, "Joss man all time look topside." And it was literally true. He wasn't looking down where he was going.

'*Silt in Channel*'

'Another time we were coming down in the *Wantung* approaching the Windbox Gorge. It was at the time when the river was falling, and the river was full of silt. At Kweifu there's a huge area above the gorge which in winter has a great shingle bank on which they boil the brine for sale, there's lots and lots of fires all over the place, it's a most peculiar sight, but in summer it's flooded and then after the summer the water starts to fall. If it goes down too quickly the silt settles quicker than a channel can be gouged out through it as it's very soft silt. A signal is then hoisted up on the signal station above the gorge indicating "Silt In Channel". The Chinese call it "Sha fu" or some name like that, meaning "quicksand" because it's so soft and slimy. When we came down that time there was the "Silt In Channel" signal, and you could see the pilot (they always read the water, or they did then, and there were few signs on the shore) looking all over the place to see a channel. I thought, 'My God he's lost it." But there was no channel.

'Strangely enough, when it's like that, it's like a sheepskin rug with the water swirling round because, having been slowed up by the wide channel, it just doesn't know what to do with itself, and it goes on dropping all this silt. Anyway we ran into it. There was not enough water for us. We turned broadside on and then started to list to the downstream side, then a bank started to come downstream from us around the bow quite quickly. You might say dry land started to appear.

'We had on board a couple of hundred volunteers. The Japanese war was on and the Chinese authorities rounded up these people in Chungking to send down as volunteers. They were holding their hats in their hands, which was all they had for uniform. So as we had these people we decided to use them as a balancing weight, and started to drive them aft. A junk had come alongside and we were going to try and carry out a wire to the shore, just to try and pull us around to start us again, and the sailors were all busy on this wire, and in the middle of the fo'c'sle there was a big heaving capstan. I was the chief officer and I was standing on top of the capstan, watching everybody, because there was wire all over the place. Then out comes the sailors' cook with a washbasin of uncooked rice. They all stood still, stood back, everybody was quiet, and he went slowly round the boat scattering rice into the water, as though he was throwing seed into the fields, and the ship moved, came upright (she was listing further all the time with this build-up of the silt) and we went round and round and round, gyrating down through the Windbox Gorge and anchored at the bottom. The Chinese knew what had happened. It was the dragon. He had got us in his jaws. Up in the Gorges especially it is very well known that dragons sleep in the bottom of the river, and if they're disturbed they will grasp the ship. It's not just make-believe or anything, it's a truism. And the only way to overcome this is to give them rice, because rice in China, at least in those days, was more than just a foodstuff, it was the whole backbone of the country. So there you are, you give something irresistible to the dragon, and he, holding the ship in his sleeping jaws, opens his mouth for the rice and releases the ship. And that's what he did with us. There was no joking about it, it was a serious business. As the cook finished his scattering the ship came upright and off we went.'[17]

Dragons and Divinities

Nonetheless there were other times when the dragons on the river bed and the divinities above withheld their blessing, when the river's mercurial character conspired with human error, or simple lack of judgement, to provoke disaster.

Avoiding the Rocks

'The rocks you had seen on a journey up would not be there the next time you went up the river in maybe two weeks' time. You could not see those rocks at all and it was hard to know every rock visible at certain states of the tides. Even the experienced pilots used to touch them now and again or even touch a shingle bank. And very often if you touched a shingle bank you would leak. But in those ships the crews got to be experts at using cement boxes and plugging the leaks. There was not much could be done if it was a big gap, though. We always carried a collision mat that you could put over the side – it is like a big carpet of double canvas with ropes all around the edges and if there was a collision you would put it over the side so that the collision mat was up against the damaged plating to reduce the leak, so that the pumps could cope with it.

'There was one Jardine master who acted somewhat recklessly. He reckoned he could take the ship up and down without a break and he did know the Gorges because he had been up there most of his time. B & S used to give the masters a bit of a break because it was quite a strenuous job, but this fellow seemed to be happy and he liked the Gorges and I believe the company kept him there because he did know them. He had a group of passengers once, when the Chinese pilots went on strike, and he said, "You know for a man as experienced as myself there is not much in it." And just as he said that, "Bump, bump, bump" and the ship touched, so it does not do to boast does it?

'You did see wrecks of ships in the Gorges. You would be looking up at
some ships that were on the rocks. If a ship went on a boulder say at very
high water and if she failed to get off in that high water season you would be
looking up at that ship up there. Amazing.'[19]

Coming down the Gorges from Chungking to Ichang on a full flood could be
just as daunting an experience as the journey up. For one thing, as one sailor
recalls, you were moving across the river beds at speeds of thirty knots or more.
And as with the journey up river the level of the water in the Gorges was crucial.
You had to wait in Chungking until the water rose to a certain level to permit safe
passage to make for Ichang. How safe depended again upon the Chinese pilot and
his index finger, and how the ship's quartermaster interpreted its movements.

'We were all waiting in Chungking and it was pouring rain, and there was
no rise. The customs' recommended level was twelve foot six to leave
Chungking but our captain was anxious to be off. (It was my first trip.) He
was a very experienced man and a very sound man, and we'd had a visit from
one of the Shell captains, saying, "Let's all stick to the twelve foot six mark."
We had the company's shipping manager on board, and he was anxious that
the ship go down again. Eventually the captain, without I suppose saying
anything to anybody, although he'd just been listening to all this hoo-ha,
suddenly said, "Right. We'll go." It was ten feet something, but off we set.
Thirty miles below Chungking the river divides around a big shingle bank in
the middle. On the left hand side, there's the winter channel where the little
ships go round, an in-curving thing which is quite exciting because it's very
narrow. It's like a street and very fast moving. It's not a rapid but a race, a
small race, and of course a big ship is too long. That is what was the limiting
factor, why the big ships waited for the water to get to twelve foot six so
that they could go down the other channel on the right bank which would
then have enough water in it. This was more of a lazy channel. But when we
got there the watermark painted on the big rock just above the Chaipanza
Wanchitan was nine foot six, and the old pilot was undecided. He had these
long moustaches, just like Fu Manchu you see in pictures, and he stroked
them in perplexity. Now to enter the Wanchitan on the right you had to go

Men not machines: Bamboo cables being rowed on to a junk in the Yangtze Gorges to assist coolies on shore to pull a boat over the rapids.

Lifelines: Bamboo cables used to haul steamships or junks over the rapids in the Yangtze Gorges coiled up on the deck of a Gorge junk.

slow at the entrance, go in slowly, turn in slowly. That was the traditional way of doing it. The captain slowed the engines (a pilot never touched the engines), and the old pilot stroked his long moustache and I could see the number two pilot, a youngster, or relatively young, looking up from below in front of the bridge, sensing there was something wrong. We were going down at a great lick, you see, and the area is quite small. Suddenly the pilot went to the left, the quartermaster put the wheel over, the second pilot down below burst into tears (the only time I've ever seen a Chinese cry) and struck his hands together. The captain put her on full speed to try and bring her round. In the middle of the channel there was a little area called the false channel, in other words here was the shingle bank, then there was what looked like a little channel but wasn't, and some rocks; the narrow channel I was telling you about, the sweep on the left, was beyond that.

An Accident on the River

'We hit the rocks on the top of the false channel. We hadn't got time to get into this left side channel and anyhow we were pretty big to go into this winter channel, you need absolute dead entry at the top. So there we were. We tore the whole bottom of the ship out. We lay broadside on and we had to get passengers off. Anyway two junks came along and it was a marvellous feat, these two empty junks bypassing us quickly and getting into the backwater we'd formed. They swept up back to us, very cleverly and we hurriedly got the passengers off.

'It's strange how people react under strain. The little pantry boy rushed into my bathroom and took one of those red rubber sponges, like a brick, which were new in those days. (I'd bought it in Hankow.) He was sitting in the junk with my red sponge clutched to his chest (he was only a little chap) and nothing else, and I thought, "Well that's the way it is, you know. He's been admiring it all the way up the river and in his mind that's all he wants."

'So then the thing was to try and salvage the ship; we sent messages back with the crew going off to the nearest post office and a Jardine ship came down and anchored above because the water was still below ten feet. And the American gunboat *Oahu* came down, and she anchored above also because she couldn't get near. (The bottom is all rock, as it is everywhere up there.) They couldn't get within a mile of us. And then we started to get the cargo out.

'There wasn't much cargo because of the depression, mostly human hair, and strangely enough salt, and coal, I remember. And we were also carrying silver. I don't know how many cases of sycee, those little 'shoes' of silver, we had. And Chinese medicines. Szechwan is the place where all the best herbal medicines come from. There's something about the local soil that grows good medicines. So we got out as much of the more valuable cargo as we could and got it on to junks and sent it up to the Jardine ship. Then down came a salvage crew from Chungking, but no pumps. They were marvellous people and very experienced. The bottom was torn out from under one of the engines so the thing was to get the engine room dry, and they worked under water, naked, trying to fill the hole with a special type of cement and with sandbags and pukais, those quilted cloths. And they had one man who sat with a bit of string and a bolt on the end, and he just sat and looked at it as though he were looking at nothing, but that was an indicator: if the ship moved he'd suddenly give a shout and fly for his life, and all the others would come out of the water, and they'd all go and sit in the junk. They'd sit patiently and wait a bit, and then they'd come back. Because with the rising water she was bound (at least we thought she was bound) to give trouble. Anyhow we were getting the cargo out and the Americans were very good. They really were. They lent us small pumps, and their men worked on board, and everybody was lending a hand.

'I'd been very cautious. We had no safe or anything to put the silver in, and we had the salt we were carrying in baskets, just ordinary salt, and so under the top layer of baskets in the hold I put the cases of silver, and then covered them over. But like all the other holds the space was full of water and naturally the salt had turned into brine. First of all a man went down, one of the salvage people, and he came up all red like a lobster, so nobody knew what to do about this until the Americans said they'd got these small pumps, foot-pumps I think they called them, and they would get them and we would circulate the water until it was clean. Amongst other things in the hold were bales of human hair destined to be made into hairnets. (Months later when I got down to Shanghai, Lumsden, who was the Marine Superintendent, said, "You made a fine mistake there. You put down human hair damaged by salt water a thousand miles from the sea. Fortunately the cargo adjuster noticed it and we were able to alter it in time." Of course in those days we all stood in fear and trembling before a marine superintendent, but I thought, "Well I won't get another chance, I'll have to tell him he's wrong.")

A Cargo of Human Hair

'One night while we were still up in the Gorges on the rocks we got this hail from the left bank. The shore was close, just across the race. They were obviously troops and they said they wanted to come on board. We said they couldn't come on board a British ship, and they said, "We've come to guard the treasure." In other words to get the silver. They said that we must send a boat, and we said we hadn't got a boat, which was true, we were using the gunboat's boat. And then they opened fire on us, quite rapid fire, and of course between us and them was the junk alongside with these poor salvage chaps in, and they started to howl like hell about it. They were brave under water but they weren't so brave exposed to fire. We sent up a rocket or some signal that was agreed to alert the gunboat. The *Oahu* came down with an armed guard, which was an incredibly kind thing to do, and brave also because the sailors were armed. If they'd fallen in the water they would have gone. They had to cross a small little semi-rapid on the way in this one mile, and it was dark; a pilot brought them down, of course, but it was a very very brave thing to do. We then told the people on the shore what they could do because we were then also brave.

A Boat Comes Under Attack

'They were purporting to be Nationalist troops. The local war lord, who was allied to the Nationalists was supposed to be raising troops for the Nationalist Government. I think the knowledge that there was so much sycee, as they called it, in silver on board was a big temptation to have a "show". But the Nationalist troops were so poorly equipped in those days and with such poor material that they were probably looking for their wages.

'We didn't fire back at them although we had our Winchesters and revolvers but there was no call. If they'd made any attempt we would probably have fired back but we didn't want to start a row because we were few against many. So it was decided we would put the silver on the junk and send it to the *Kiawo*, the Jardine Matheson ship. And then the troops all massed themselves together and marched along the bank following this junk. These troops dotted the hillside, which was very very steep, with shrubs growing on it, and rocks and boulders, and they spread out over it in quite a formation. And then we could hear the gunfire when they opened fire on the *Kiawo*. Of course the two ships were together, so several of the shots probably hit the *Oahu*. But the *Oahu* had little poms-poms and a couple of three inch guns. They just sorted the whole lot out, and hit a tree. The troops were all behind trees and boulders, they would hit a tree and lift the whole tree out. So we thought, "There's really going to be a battle now." From then on all the Americans were armed they carried their side guns all the time. Anyway the silver was got away on the *Kiawo*. It was never ashore, it was afloat the whole time.

'Eventually there was a court of inquiry about the shipwreck in Ichang. Poor captain. When we say he was a silent man, he was silent to the point of strangeness. Even with the consumption of a bottle of Jossman gin he still didn't get garrulous, or even talk. The river inspector held the court. It was a court of inquiry on the pilot, really, because they don't have authority to deal with Europeans because even that far away I think we had London on the stern, and certainly the *Wanliu* was London registered.

'At the river inspector's inquiry, the captain said nothing, nothing at all, and they found that the pilot said that he waited for the captain to tell him which channel to take, that must have been while he was stroking his long moustache. The captain said nothing in his own defence. He just stood there and watched the pilot. In fact he had slowed the ship down ready to take the right hand one, so they slightly blamed the pilot but more or less exonerated him because of his saying he was waiting for the captain to give him an order, so he got away with it.

'Did I explain that I once also sat on one of these courts of inquiry? By that time I had become a senior master as they call them, and you had three senior masters and three senior Chinese pilots on the inquiry. It was into the ability of the pilot, and the case was over a Jardine ship where the ship had gone head-on into a rock coming up in a backwater. It had come flying along, hadn't hauled out quick enough and hit the rock. So the pilot was being interrogated and a dreadful shipping master (no he really wasn't dreadful, but he had no ability to understand Chinese and he was arrogant) was trying to find out how long the interval was between the pilot seeing she was going to hit and her hitting the rock. I don't suppose that the man who was translating was able to translate into the language of the pilot very well, because a lot of these people lived in villages away some distance, so this thing went on to and fro and we were fed to the teeth with it. Eventually this ferocious man said, "Go outside the door and then come in again when you think the interval has expired." So he went out and then the river inspector thought about something else, until he remembered it and he said to the interpreter, "Where's that man?" So he went out and he looked out of the door and he came back and he said, "He's gone home." And that was the time when he said to a witness (I think we must have had the captain there as a witness), "What did the pilot do when the ship struck?" The captain said, "He got down on his knees and banged his head three times on the deck." Those were the sort of inquiries you had in those days.

'However on the *Wanliu* they more or less blamed the captain for not telling the pilot, and they only did that because he just wouldn't speak. He just sat there and took no notice at all. The *Wanliu* was eventually salvaged by the Ming Company and they cut her in two to get her off. It shows how she ground herself on to those rocks. They cut her in two, and took the two halves up and then built a bit for the middle in Chungking and she was then the *Ming Chuen*. I suppose she might even be running now, but that was the end of the *Wanliu* for us.'[17]

China at War

On 18th September 1931 the Japanese army began their conquest of Manchuria. The opening shots of the Second World War had been fired. At Geneva the League of Nations deliberated. Meanwhile on 2nd January 1932 a victorious Japan established the puppet state of Manchukuo under the nominal rule of P'u Yi, the last Manchu Emperor of China, whose abdication from the throne of China twenty years before had paved the way for the founding of the Chinese republic. Then in October 1932 Japan formally withdrew from the League of Nations. She was ready to embark upon her conquest of all China south of the Great Wall, a country still racked by the civil war between the Nationalists, led by Chiang Kai Shek, and the Communists.

The Western nations whose citizens lived in China were of course neutral, and as such there was no reason why their nationals should involve themselves in the conflict, but their declared neutrality did not prevent them witnessing and very often finding themselves caught up in the fighting. How could it be otherwise, when the war both threatened and impeded their trading acitivies, the very reason that most of them had gone or stayed East in the first place?

This was pre-eminently the case with an enterprise such as Butterfield & Swire with agents in almost every major town and city open to Western trade and with their shipping fleets along the coast and up the Yangtze River. Indeed in the very month that they had proclaimed the puppet state of Manchukuo, the Japanese arrived on the very front door step of the West in China when they occupied the Chinese city of Shanghai. But China signed an armistice with Japan. There was a lull in the fighting, until four years later, on 7th July 1937 when Japan manufactured an excuse to continue her aggression. Peking itself was seized on 8th August and Shanghai almost exactly three months later, despite a great deal of talk in Geneva at the League of Nations. For their part the Chinese Nationalist armies gathered to resist and at Shanghai, with only the most rudimentary of air forces, decided to launch an attack on the Japanese warships anchored off the Bund.

'For the previous few days we had known that the Chinese armies were gathering in the country round Shanghai, and seemed to be looking for trouble, and then on this Saturday morning the Chinese air force planes came up the river and tried to bomb Japanese cruisers which were in the river. They missed them completely and bombed the Palace Hotel, the Bund and

Bombing at Shanghai

one or two other places. I think there were about five thousand Chinese casualties as a result of that raid.

'In fact I did go down there and look at the remains of the hotel, but it was pretty well gutted actually. They were quite big heavy bombs which had hit it fair and square. The Japanese cruiser was more or less off the hotel, in the stream not more than about a hundred and fifty to two hundred yards away from the hotel, so that was, by any standards, quite a near miss. The other terrible thing which happened was that they bombed inland, at least a mile from the cruisers. I don't know why they dropped bombs there when they were aiming at these Japanese ships, but they hit a refugee encampment. Thousands of Chinese had been coming into Shanghai from the country as the Chinese troops began to gather outside there, and they planted some bombs right in the middle of an assembly point where there were five or six thousand of them assembled and the casualties were frightful.

'Of course this was accidental but pretty poor bombing really, because I saw them come in. I went on the roof of the office in the afternoon, I remember, and they had another raid. They were coming in very low, about a thousand feet or so up, so they should have really scored a hit at that height that they were coming in, but they didn't score a hit on any of the cruisers. I don't know how they managed to miss them.

'Then the Japanese rushed troops into the settlement, and pretty well took over the downtown part of the foreign settlement, called Hongkew. They didn't occupy the Bund proper, and that part of the settlement and the French concession remained much as they were before, but the volunteers, of which I wasn't a member, and British regulars (Seaforth Highlanders I think) were manning a sort of frontier between the Japanese in Hongkew. And the French were, of course, manning their perimeter, too. The volunteers were manning our perimeter on the west and north, and the result was that you couldn't get out of the centre of Shanghai at all. I lived out in the French Concession, almost on the boundary of it actually, and we were shot up one day, by a Japanese plane while we were walking along a road. The planes came down the road and did a bit of machine-gunning up the road.'[9]

It scarcely required a moment's thought on the part of the Japanese military to realise that the key to their conquest of central China was the Yangtze River, the principal, indeed only means of communication westwards into the interior. To frustrate the Japanese advance along the river the Chinese had sunk ships at certain strategic points on the Yangtze to create a series of impossible 'booms'. But in doing so they had also frustrated the Western trading companies, like Butterfield & Swire, who used the river. It became imperative for them to seek other routes to get the goods they carried up and down the river.

'The Chinese sank a lot of old ships across the river near a place called Chinkiang. It must have been a day's journey or something from Shanghai. Fortunately, whether it was deliberate or not I do not know, but the Grand Canal came in from Peking on the left bank and went out from the right bank down to Shanghai. So we stationed a ship there and Jardines stationed another and a gunboat came and anchored there. And ships came and brought cargo down from the upper stretches of the river and we trans-

Fire power: A
Japanese bomb
lands in Shanghai
Harbour, 1932.

The sky falls in: The
Japanese bomb
Shanghai in 1932.

shipped it into junks that went off down the Grand Canal. I remember I had to send a telegram every night to Hankow by the ship's wireless saying how much they could send the next day and we kept it moving in that way. I do not know who received it in Shanghai, probably the compradore. He had his own methods, but we used to trans-ship it, tally it in and send a telegram to Shanghai saying what had been sent off. But one junk looks very much like another so I imagine there was a lot of pilferage.

'The Japanese were bombing all the way along the river. I remember I had hoped to use our Chinkiang office as a base for trans-shipping, but very shortly after I went ashore there the town was bombed by the Japanese. We had wind of this coming and had moved out to the APC installation, which was outside the town with one or two others. We went back after the bombing and the office had gone completely for a burton. I remember there was a bell on the front door of the office and I pushed it and it rang but the place was in ruins. They were bombing everywhere. Not every day but very often. The Chinese had sirens and the European firms painted large Union Jacks on their ships and on their buildings but that did not always work. I do not think the Japanese took any notice of the flags. You used just to hope for the best. The Japanese were responsible for an awful lot of carnage.'[5]

Despite the boom on the river the Japanese advanced along the Yangtze. And before their armies went the bombers. Hankow, the principal city on the Lower River was a regular target.

'The alarm would go and traffic would cease. The guards would stop all traffic on the roads, and whether you were in the office or possibly out on the river with the ships you couldn't get any work done because they cleared the streets off and the ships were supposed to be in a certain anchorage which was some way up the river. We carried on as best we could, working very hard during the daytime when we could.

'All the Chinese inhabitants were trying to get out. The ships were absolutely packed like sardines so you couldn't have squeezed another one in. And there was an occasion when I had to push the new Rear Admiral Yangtze up a plank in order to get him aboard. The only way he could travel was up on the bridge and this was the only way he could get on because by that time the ship was absolutely jam-packed with refugees, you couldn't get in normally. He simply had to climb over the heads of people on a plank. We took this tug alongside and erected the plank from the bridge of the tug up to the bridge of the steamer, like that, and he had to climb up. He had to climb up and so did the flags. He was hauled and pushed up, most undignified!'[6]

太
古

'The air raids were slightly disconcerting, although no bomb was ever dropped near me. But I remember one in particular when I was awakened in the middle of the night by our wharfinger, who lived in the city property – I was in the agent's house further down – with a somewhat excited telephone message as follows, "Mr Dean, Mr Dean, come at once, the river is on fire!"

And I looked out of the bedroom window and there, sure enough, blazing sheets were pouring down the river. What had happened was that a lighter load of aviation spirit, which quite contrary to harbour regulations had been moored above our city property, had been hit by a bomb, and it was on fire and, of course, as the gasoline poured into the river blazing, most of it went down the main current in the centre. But also a lot of cases of blazing gasoline were drifting down with the current on the shore connections of our upper property berths. So I went upstairs and got dressed and went along to see what was going on and found the whole staff, from the office boy upwards, the wharfinger, foreign staff, Chinese staff, clerks, cashiers, everybody, with boat hooks, lining the shore connections with pontoons and fending off these blazing cases of gasoline where they drifted down to the next customer.'[4]

It was inevitable that sooner rather than later a British ship would be the accidental target of Japanese bombs. And so it was at the port of Wuhu up river from Shanghai on the Lower Yangtze.

'We only had a Chinese agent in Wuhu at the time our ship *Tatung* was there and we had two or three tugs, and a whole series of lighters full of wood oil, which were waiting up at Wuhu and hadn't come down to Nanking, so I suggested that perhaps it would be a good idea if I went up there, because the Chinese tend to disappear into the interior when hostilities get near, as they were doing round Nanking. So I went up there and I'd only just arrived when this formation of Japanese planes came over, flying up the river. And there was a Jardines boat, the *Tuck Wo*, and the *Tatung* alongside our respective hulks, and below us the river gunboat HMS *Ladybird*. And we all had large Union Jacks painted on our hold covers and everything, and on top of our bridge. Suddenly down came the bombs and it all happened. Until they started coming down we hadn't realised what was happening, then suddenly a whistling sound came and down they came, and there was a lot of noise. In fact I was living in a cabin on the *Tatung* at the time because there was nothing ashore for me to live on. I was on the hulk side of the ship and I went flat on the deck just beside the cabin and the bridge just in front of me, and everything went up in smoke. I picked myself up fishing little bits of glass off me, and I looked around, and then the ship started to go down. A bomb had gone clean through one of the holds, and she just started to go down, but the bulkheads on either side held. (I didn't know that of course.) Also there was a fire on the hulk and several corpses around the place. The *Tuck Wo* had also been hit and was going up in smoke, and it was all rather confused.

'I spent the next quarter of an hour putting out fires and jumping over corpses together with the officers, engineers and other crew members. By that time the planes had gone on and so then I went back to the *Ladybird* to see if the *Ladybird* could give us a tow up as it looked as if the *Tuck Wo* was going to drift down on us and set us on fire as she was lying out at an angle and going up in smoke. Anyway the *Ladybird* was not in a position to do very much because it took her several hours to get up steam and she hadn't got steam up. Then this fellow Hurst, who had been at one time a chief officer

A British Ship is Attacked

with the Chinese Maritime Customs and then became a naval river pilot on the gunboats discovered one of our tugs was still afloat. He collected a crew from the CMC lighters and went up and I went up with him to try and get what people we could off the *Tuck Wo*. We went right up ahead of her and drifted down with the force of the current with our stern resting on her bow and our bow resting on the hulk. Hurst manoeuvred it with a very frightened crew. Actually he did extraordinarily good work. He sort of put heart into the Chinese.

'Then we had to try and get the European and Chinese crew off the *Tuck Wo*, and they eventually came down the anchor cable, and so I hauled them on to the tug. Then came the question of getting away because we were being pressed by the river current on to the burning *Tuck Wo* and the Jardine hulk, which had also started to burn by then. Hurst was doing the manoeuvring, being a skilled man in that connection, and I was really sort of supernumerary but we got the tug off. I'm afraid several of the Chinese crew who were badly wounded were burnt alive but there was just nothing we could do about it. We couldn't get them on to the *Tuck Wo*, only those who could move could come down and they came down the cable on to the tug. Eventually we got away and we came round alongside and got the *Tatung* manoeuvred over to the other side of the river towed by the tug. I can't remember whether by that time the *Ladybird* had got up steam or whether it was the tug, but we got her over and beached on the far side of the river where it was shallower. It was all fairly hectic. We had quite a number of wounded crew up in the Wuhu General Hospital which was run by missionaries, very nice people who had taken them in, and I know I went off up to see them.'[6]

'I was on my way up the river to take command of one of our ships and on the way up we had passed through Wuhu, which was only forty miles from Nanking. Japanese bombers, sort of dive bombers, had been enjoying themselves. They'd bombed a Swire ship, the *Tatung*, at least she'd been beached after she was bombed. A Jardine ship had been set on fire, she was alongside her pontoon and both burnt out. So when we got to Hankow we found an uproar about what to do about Wuhu. They'd got a tug and two salvage lighters ready to send down, but the crew wouldn't go. Of course I was younger then and I said, "I know them and I'll go with them."

'And I managed to persuade the crew to come with me. They knew that I'd been around the place quite a while. I think it was just a question of if somebody who was not of their own clan would be a leader then it wasn't their responsibility. On the way down everything was flying away from Nanking that could move, and other parts also. It's a very lonely feeling when you're passing a whole lot of people going the other way. Eventually we met another of our tugs from Wuhu. She was loaded with people, and they were screaming and shouting at us, so our crew got frightened. So eventually we decided to go back to Kiukiang.

'In Kiukiang there was a French gunboat and she'd borrowed the pilot,

Hurst, from the British gunboat in Wuhu to take her up to Kiukiang. And when Hurst got to Kiukiang, everything was going up river, nothing was going down. I knew him quite well (we'd been second mates together in the early days, but he was a strange chap. He was as brave as a lion but he detested authority.) So I agreed to take him and give him a passage back to his gunboat in Wuhu. And that helped us a lot because, as I say, he was as brave as a lion and the crew of the tugs and lighters could see that they had this tough egg. Well, we got to Wuhu where I was to take over the salvage of the *Tatung*.

'In the meantime the Japanese took Nanking, and that was really a terrible business. Ten years before, Chiang Kai Shek's Nationalist troops had come up from Canton and taken the city. They went berserk and amongst those foreigners that they slaughtered and raped were Japanese. The Japanese never forgot it. And I think when the Japanese got back to Nanking in 1937 they just had orders to go stark, staring, raving mad. Orders I mean. No doubt about it. And so it was a dreadful thing. They slaughtered them by the hundreds of thousands I think. And then they sank the *Panay*, the American gunboat, and we were just up river, in Wuhu.'

'Eventually the Japanese arrived in Wuhu under Colonel Hashimoto and by that time the Jardine ship which had come down from Hankow and all the remaining British shipping – tugs – had moved, except the *Tatung* which was beached on the far side of the river. They had all moved down below Wuhu in a collection and presumably the Japanese had been notified that we were there. We were anchored out in the middle of the river, and I was living on board the Jardine ship for the moment. And the first thing we knew was that shells started whistling. The Japanese arrived in Wuhu and lined up their guns on the Bund and started bombarding us. There was nothing we could do. I, together with other odd people including, I seem to remember, a lot of nuns who had been evacuated, were all on the Jardine ship, and we all went over to the far side away from the Bund and were lying down on the deck, wondering when the next shell was coming. We were told that the best thing to do was to go as far as possible, though I don't think with a thing like this it would have done at all. The shell would have gone straight through. Still there we were and there we simply stayed. We were shelled for twenty minutes I suppose. They were dropping round us into the river.

'Hashimoto was the chap in charge, but then another man had come in later and it was he who opened fire on the ships in the harbour, including the British gunboat *Ladybird*. I was alongside the *Ladybird* in a little launch, and the commander saw the Jardine ship under fire, and they also saw another little ship which seemed to have caused all the trouble, under fire, so they started to heave up the anchor and I can remember quite distinctly the commanding officer of the *Ladybird* saying, "What's going on? I'm going to find out." And just at that time two shells hit his ship, one actually hit the breech of his big six-inch gun (they were only little gunboats but they had big six-inch guns like in the siege of Sebastopol or something) and put it right out of action. Another one went through the afterdeck into the sick bay and killed one of the seamen.

'The thing was that nobody could understand what this nonsense was all about. We'd all been to see Hashimoto, the Japanese who'd come the day before and I'd got my pass to work on the wreck of the *Tatung*.

'And then down comes the gunboat HMS *Bee* of all things, she was the admiral's ship, and she signalled. And I can remember that very distinctly, because it was like those old cigarette cards you used to get with semaphore pictures on them. She signalled that she was going to pick up the survivors from *Ladybird* and that left everybody in a terrible state because she was just down below us. I went up in my little launch to find out what was happening and I went alongside the *Ladybird*. They told me about one or two people who had been killed, the captain was ashore protesting, I remember, and the quartermaster on board said, "What do you think of these people? We've got two dead (or whatever it was) and these Japanese are standing on the wharf asking us for cigarettes." They were a ferocious lot. They really were a ferocious lot.

'Later we discovered that the incident with *Ladybird* was because of that little ship, which had come up the river and which belonged to a lumber company. She was picking up passengers and I learned not so long ago that she was going to transfer these passengers to the gunboat. And this military man, who had taken over from Hashimoto, was in charge, with orders to shoot anything moving, and here was this little ship not only moving but putting passengers in a sampan, so he opened fire on her and she went down the river with these shells dropping behind her. And *Ladybird* went to find out what the firing was about. Everybody else ran away, but she went to meet this little ship. It was a very courageous thing to do.

'Anyway I was left behind to salvage the *Tatung* and I had to make a trip to Nanking to get a tugboat, because we had to lay out anchors and things with this salvage. And I went down in a passing ship not long after the town had fallen and it was alarming, fires were everywhere. I didn't actually go ashore, I went on board another British gunboat and there was our tug nearby. It was a very lonely position there, everybody had gone. Wherever you went there was nobody. And the commander actually showed me a wireless message he'd got from Hato, who was the Japanese General I think who was hanged for the Nanking massacre. And it read something like "Will endeavour to stop bombing British ships but cannot hold myself responsible for the irresponsible attitude of young officers." And that's the way it was.

'Anyhow I picked up this tug. I'd taken a couple of men with me and we found the old Chinese chief engineer on board, poor little soul. She had been bombed, this tug and she was listing over on one side but was not sunk and the damage was only superficial. And this little black face came out of the coal bunker.

'When the ship had been bombed, he'd set out with the rest of the crew to walk back the four hundred miles to Hankow. (They were Hankow men and it was a Hankow tug.) At that time the Chinese were all rushing home. But this engineer had a club foot and he'd walked, I think, one day and then he was holding the others up and he told me that he'd turned back. I suppose what he meant was they'd walked on and he found that he could only see them in the distance and he turned back, or lost them completely. So we had an engineer who knew the ship and we went back to Wuhu in that tug. And we managed to salvage the *Tatung* there. Another ship came and towed us down to Shanghai. The Japanese paid, I believe.'[17]

In the wake of their rape of Nanking in December 1937 the Japanese continued their conquest of the river, driving huge numbers of Chinese refugees before them, including the Nationalist government which had been forced to move its capital from Nanking to the comparative safety of Chungking at the head of the Yangtze Gorges. Somehow companies like Butterfield & Swire continued their own business, but with the added difficulty that with the Japanese occupying the whole of the Lower River and much of the Middle River by 1938 replacing river port staff involved the most tortuous of overland journeys.

'The only way to get in to Changsha in 1938 was to go down to Haiphong in French Indo-China and then go in overland. I remember asking how I was going to get from Hanoi through to Changsha as I had some idea of what conditions were, having experienced it up the river. I asked whether I could buy a car and a truck and load the truck up with gasoline because you couldn't purchase any, and drive the car and truck up to Changsha and sell them at the far end. And they looked at me with a bit of a quizzical look and said, "Yes, well, yes, if you can't manage any other way." Things were all a bit chaotic under war conditions. I then went down to Haiphong and then up to Hanoi. When I got to Haiphong where our office was I was told that I should report to the Shell office there, and they would sort of see what they could arrange. It turned out eventually that they had a lad they wanted to get up to Chungking and we waited around in Hanoi I think for about a month, and then eventually we went in on a convoy of American Red Cross ambulances, plus trucks. We were actually not in one of the ambulances, we were in one of the trucks. On the side of the ambulances was painted "A Present from the City of Los Angeles", or "A Present from the City of Chicago" or something of that nature. The Americans had sent over a huge fleet of ambulances and we had various trucks filled with gasoline and other supplies to go to the headquarters of the Chinese Red Cross. We went through Lang Son which was the border post, then we went through Lung Chow and on to Nanking and then to Liuchow.

'Fairly early on one of the lorries toppled over. I think it was practically the first day after we'd got over the border into China. The roads were single track roads but due to the enormous amount of supplies the Chinese military had built up roads on either side with earth, which unfortunately was not very stable at all, and military lorries came thundering along these roads and of course any of the ordinary civilian traffic like ambulances or trucks like ours had to get over to the side. They didn't stop, or slow down, they just came thundering along and you just got to the side or else. When we tried to come out of this the wheels simply churned into it and then toppled over. Of course the villagers just stood around until they got the right price for hauling the lorry up on to the road and then loading it up with the drums of gasoline which had all spilled out into the surrounding countryside. The bargaining took some time.

'The bridges over the rivers too were slightly unnerving because they were openwork bridges with just sort of two or three planks which were just about the right width for the wheels. If you didn't drive straight there could be a disaster.

'The only time really that we met up with foreigners, apart from when we got to the Chinese Red Cross Headquarters and except for the odd missionary occasionally was when we met some Americans from the American University in Changsha, "Yale – in China". It was a very brief passing. And any accommodation that was available had been taken over so we stayed in this Chinese hut. It was only really a single storey but it had bamboos up high with a further bamboo platform resting across it and we climbed up a small ladder and slept on this sort of second storey up above. And I must say I was a little worried because they had strips of meat, pork or whatever it is, hanging on a string between two sticks, and then these things were drying in the sun and covered in flies and that's what we had our breakfast off, with rice. Of course it was all cooked so it wasn't too insanitary. That was our breakfast, rice and they cut a section of this and fried it up and that was our breakfast.

'Eventually we arrived at the Chinese Red Cross with the ambulances and they greeted us and entertained us to dinner that night. We were all seated at a long table and there were French people who spoke French and Austrians and German Jews who spoke German, and the Chinese spoke Mandarin, I think one or two spoke Cantonese, we spoke English and Dr Eva Ho the daughter of the famous Hongkong Bank compradore Sir Robert Ho Tung, was there and she was able to translate all the languages. A brilliant performance.

'Everyone there was a member of the Chinese Red Cross. I think many were Jewish refugees. We only met them really for that one occasion. And then there was the question, as all the ambulances and all the supplies stopped there, of how we'd get on. We were there for I think a couple of days and then we went on with a large German called Fritz Roth who had gone out to China as a forester under the Chinese forestry thing, which had collapsed owing to the war and he had then been taken on to run supplies of dyes and drugs into China on behalf of the big German chemical company Defag, which was roughly the equivalent of ICI, and he had a car plus a couple of lorries, one of which was filled with his supplies, the stuff which he was selling to the Chinese, and the other one was filled with gasoline, to get around. And he gave us a lift on to Changsha where we eventually arrived.

'A Chinese minefield was laid while I was there. I saw junks go into it. The wind was coming from the north and we suddenly saw this large fleet of junks with all sails set coming like an armada up the river and we didn't know what it was, there must have been a considerable number of them, surging up, being blown before this quite stiff breeze from the north. For all we knew it might have been the Japanese arriving in boats, and as we gazed upon them suddenly one went up like that, and another went up, and the others came surging on and passed us. I think about two or three went up, but the others seemed to come through. And all that was left of one which blew up was the bowsprits sticking straight up in the air.

'The important thing from the business point of view was whether we could find a way into Ichang at the foot of the Gorges through this minefield. We scouted round and found that if we went close inshore, some of the mines having been blown up, we could work our way down the river until we got off into the creeks. The first thing was to discover whether we could get through to Ichang by the back creeks. And when I discovered that you could get down river by keeping inshore I sent one of our flat-bottomed tugs through before sending any lighters at all. After about a week or ten days the tug came back and reported that he could get through, but there again it depended on the height of the water because these things are very seasonal. You can only get through at certain times, and then we established this route, because there was an enormous amount of stuff which was trying to get through. The Chinese will trade whatever the circumstances and of course there was an enormous amount of iron particularly. All kinds of iron, steel girders, steel things, which was wanted for the war effort.

'Social life in Changsha was non-existent to all intents and purposes. One got around. I was probably the only one who was really busy apart of course from the customs people. Presumably they were still collecting duties on anything that passed through. I also had a lot of Chinese crews under me and staff and everything. You see they'd all moved down there on to the hulk, two miles down river from the city. It was rather raw conditions but they wanted safety, they considered themselves much more safe. And I lived down there at the Shell oil installation hoping we'd be safe because all these big tanks at the Shell installation had huge union jacks painted on top of them. Many was the occasion when fleets of Japanese planes would come over and circle round and we wondered when they were going to drop them, but they circled round and round and buzzed off. They never bombed us. You always wondered which time they were going to.

Life in Changsha during the War

'We ran out of any drink of course quite early on, and the only drink we had was what we used to call the Changsha Cocktail which was Chinese wine, samshu, and orange juice. If anybody ever arrived or came through with a bottle of drink, it was shared out generously amongst everybody, but it was rare. The last six months I was there we really hadn't got anything except this Chinese cocktail. Luckily the American University (Yale in China) had a sort of experimental dairy farm and we could still get butter, thank goodness, not buffalo stuff because that tasted very rancid indeed on the few occasions I had it. It was completely white and it looked perfectly ghastly. It looked like the sort of grease you use for greasing your car or something like that, and so we used to colour it with carrot juice and make it a nice yellow. It looked like butter then. It tasted all right.

'Generally one lived on the land. I had good servants. I was living on the hulk in the sort of top floor and the boy just produced food. I mean you can live on the land in China exceptionally well wherever you are. The food was coming in all from the country and in fact they were only too eager to let you have it. The only thing was you couldn't get any luxuries of any kind. No alcohol, and as I say no butter. There were lots of things you couldn't get but if you were prepared to live on the land which was perfectly reasonable in China, you could get enough.

'On one occasion I called on Nils Sopp, the commissioner of customs. He was a Norwegian and a nice fellow. He was living in the customs house up in

Changsha itself and I discovered he was in bed with fever or something and not well. And while I was there talking to him, because to a certain extent I had to keep in touch with him since I was still shipping and it came under his aegis which meant I had more to do with him than most people, a rather dishevelled body came in and it was Nils Sopp's relief who had come to take over from him. He was afterwards up in London as secretary of the Carlton Club. He's dead now, poor chap. Anyway he arrived. He'd finished up his journey floating down the Siang River in a Chinese junk with all his gear and he arrived and walked into the house. I was introduced and Nils Sopp asked me if I'd take him round the next day and sort of introduce him to the community that was there because he couldn't do it himself as he had a very high temperature. So I said yes and went back down to my hulk, and next morning I arrived dressed in my usual garb of white sort of Aertex shirt and white shorts and stockings, looking reasonably smart, and arrived and went to the house, rang at the door and the boy opened it and I was greeted by this replacement dressed in a sort of business suiting and looking very smart indeed. And then he took a bowler hat and an umbrella off the stand in the hall and I then took him round and introduced him to what of the community was there. I was a bit taken aback, I must admit, because we'd rather given up those niceties, although the Navy could have put on a bit of a show in smart uniforms. Anyway I took him around and introduced him to the people who were there.

'Eventually the time came to leave Changsha and there were really only two ways you could do it. When I went in there was a fairly regular plane flying between Chungking, Kweilin and Hong Kong. It stopped at Kweilin partly for military reasons and also partly to carry gold out. It picked it up there and carried it out to Hong Kong, but while I was up there the regular call at Kweilin was dropped. So the plane was flying from Chungking straight through to Hong Kong but it did occasionally stop at Kweilin, but it was one of these uncertain things. The alternative route out would have been for me to go on one of my tug routes through to Ichang then up the Gorges and out through the Burma Road. And never having been up through the Gorges and suffering slightly from itchy feet, I though that if I went to Kweilin I might have to wait for two or three months for the plane. So I suggested that I might go out the other way through Ichang, Chungking and so on, but the reply came back that I was to proceed to Kweilin and wait.

'So I proceeded to Kweilin and waited. I suppose I was there about a month during which there was an air raid alarm almost every day. Right alongside the city of Kweilin there was one of these huge pillars of rock – it was almost in the city really – which had been hollowed out. And it was just a gigantic air raid shelter, which the population used to troop into. Anyway if you were on the streets the military were inclined to be extremely rude to you. They might even let off a shot at you. I was staying in a Chinese hotel wrapped in a pukai because there were no bed clothes proper, and all the windows had been blown out and it was quite chilly. All you had was this pukai, which is rather like the duvet they use for the modern bed. But you had to sort of wrap it round yourself and it was quite all right if you didn't roll over too much in the night when it unrolled and you got very cold.

'Every other day or pretty well every day for a month I used to go down to the China Travel Service office which was about a mile away and ask whether there was any sign of a plane or any news of a plane and the answer was "No". I used to go and call on the Jesuit priests who were Italian-American and nice chaps and they manufactured a bit of their own wine there and we used to have a drink. I remember walking up and down the main street of Kweilin arguing religion with a Jesuit American priest – an Italian-American priest. It was really a complete hiatus. There was nothing one could do. I had proceeded to Kweilin and was just waiting for something to happen. I couldn't really get back or anything. By that time actually the whole of the main street of Kweilin had been bombed out.

'Then after about a month I was down at the China Travel Service office and said, "Well, what about the plane?" And they said, "Oh, one came in last night. It's taking off this morning. You'll have to get out to the airfield." Just at that moment an air raid warning went and so I rushed outside and got a rickshaw which was the only means of travel and started off up the street with various odd guards shouting at me, telling me to get under cover. And I was saying very sorry I was very busy, because I had to get back to the hotel to get my belongings, you see. Anyway I think they had a truck or lorry which was going out to the airfield at a certain time so I rushed back to the hotel, chucked my stuff – I hadn't got very much because one travelled pretty light – into my bag, and hared back in another rickshaw, shouting at the odd guard, to the office where they bundled me into a jeep and I was shot through the streets, still shouting at the guards. You weren't supposed to wander around, you might be spying or signalling to the Japs where to drop the bombs. However a white face usually got you through.

'I got out to the airfield and the wretched little plane was sitting there and as far as I remember there was a Chinese man and a Chinese girl waiting at the side. It was miserable, it was wet, it was perfectly horrid. The Chinese man spoke very good English and I heard, though I can't remember whether it was from him, that that plane had come in the previous day and due to the wetness of this grass airfield, it had sort of tipped up. They got it repaired and we were now going to take off in the midst of this air raid, never knowing when the bombs might drop, because of course the one place which the Japs would bomb was the airfield, particularly if they saw a plane there.

'After about ten minutes or a quarter of an hour, we were bundled into the plane and it went down sloshing along through the pools of water because it had been raining pretty steadily, and then we had to take off. I often wondered whether we were going to tip up again but we didn't, we got off. Then we flew to Hong Kong, dodging from one cloud to another over the last period because the Japanese at that time had Canton and we had to avoid and go round. I noticed that you couldn't see anything at all during the last period, and it was only later that I learnt that we'd been deliberately cloud dodging. We'd come out of a cloud and see another one over there and dive straight for it. But we arrived safely in Hong Kong.'[6]

Meanwhile there were still British ships on the Yangtze. But the strain on crews and officers, particularly in the Gorges between Ichang and Chungking, was immense.

'I was sent up to relieve a captain called De Freitas when all this trouble was on, getting people up to unoccupied China, getting the whole of China up through the Gorges. The Gorges was just like that picture of the Klondike. Those men toiling up. Well that was us trying to get the whole of China up through the Gorges. Anyway, De Freitas was a very very fine chap who was a friend of mine, and I was sent up to relieve him because he was going on leave. So I eventually got as far as Ichang and the chief engineer, who was a very fine sort of dour Scot, came on board and his face was like a turkey-cock. He'd been out walking. He was a very lonely, quiet sort of man of about forty-something, and I went along to see him and he said something. It was the funniest thing to me. He called me into his room and said did I object to the top button of his uniform not being fastened. Now I knew that he was a man who very rarely wore uniform if he could avoid it. Then he called me in and said, "Look at those pencils." There were two pencils. And I said, "They're all right." And he said, "Look at the way they're pointing" or "Look at the colour." I remember there was a red pencil. So off I went to see old Dr Brown in the Scotch mission who was a great friend of this chap, and he said that on the next trip he would have a look at him but that there was nothing to do now. And the next trip we came back and little incidents like this went on happening. And I discovered that this engineer had joined the Rosicrucian Society, and he kept himself in his cabin with his curtains drawn. Well, the next time we were down old Dr Brown invited him up, but afterwards he said, "There's absolutely nothing wrong with him."

'So in a while off we went again. One day my number two came on to the bridge and said, "There's a gun gone off somewhere." So we sent for the steward, being sort of brave men, and said, "Knock on whoosit's door and ask him if he wants a cup of tea." So of course all hell then broke loose, because there was the chap sitting in an armchair with a revolver. A forty-five bullet had gone through his head. It was a case of suicide. Old Tocher, the head of the mission, put it down to this taking up with the Rosicrucian cult which aims at perfection, and this fellow had decided he wasn't perfect or something like that. But it was absolute loneliness. After we'd been running for some time there were several chaps, senior skippers, who had nervous break-downs.

'Conditions were almost indescribable. We couldn't get things repaired. Junks which had long been laid up because the steamers had put them out of commission were brought back into use again. The ropes which they used were plaited bamboo. At one time on every trip every junk ordered new ropes to get from Ichang to Chungking, then they would discard them. People used to burn them. But now of course there weren't enough bamboo ropes to go round. So on the rapids not only were they overloaded – because previously when they went up they carried lighter stuff, textiles and things like that, whereas now they were carrying machinery and people and God knows what, and so they were deeper in the water with their decks all open – but they also had these rotten ropes. They were often in deep trouble. I remember I counted ninety visible wrecks in the Gorges between Ichang and Wanshien, over a hundred and eighty miles. Ninety visible wrecks; it was incredible. That doesn't include the number that had broken up, or been holed and fixed again, there were ninety complete wrecks visible in that short space. And so you lived a life of stress. You couldn't sleep at night. It was a terrible life. And then we couldn't get coal. Our ship was a coal burner and Chungking once had coal as good as any Welsh coal but the Chinese military took it, and we used to have to try and find it here and try and find it there. People and their belongings were coming in by the gallon and we were little pints trying to take them out. There was nothing for them so they camped all over the place and the rackets were terrific.

Overcrowding and Navigational Problems

'The main one was to tell these people that they could get them on the next ship. And so you'd have all the sampans full of people with a strong current running and all their worldly goods, and they'd be rowing them out to the ship and they'd be round the ship like cockroaches, and in some cases you didn't have any passenger accommodation. And all the time ships were coming up bringing people from down river including Chinese government people. We did about forty-six round trips in a year, which means to say that we never stopped. We anchored at night, but at night with all the problems we mightn't get into a good anchorage, so as the captain I was on the go the whole time.

It was really incredible. For instance we were going up the Wushan Gorge once overloaded and the freshet was on. We shouldn't have been moving because there was all sorts of regulations forbidding it but they had all gone by the board. We had left Ichang because you couldn't stay there, because you'd be flooded with people, and more people. So I left even though the freshet warning was out. When there's a freshet on it's like a forest fire, everybody gets out of the way, but in this case the conditions were so bad that we couldn't take too much notice of freshet and high water marks and things like that. The Wushan Gorge comes soon after you leave Ichang. Anyway when we got near the top of the gorge we passed wrecks of junks and there were odd little groups of soldiers firing their guns. They were not firing at us, they were firing in our direction and they did us no harm. We had had a long day and were all tired by this time, dusk was coming on, but we had to get through the gorge in order to anchor at Wushan just above. And there was this whirlpool at the top of the gorge which was a stationary whirlpool and covered the whole of the width of the gorge. It seemed to stand above the river. And as we had come up to it we had passed some wreckage with people clinging to it so we knew that there was trouble. Anyway through the cliff we could see some junks under oars trying to get them out of the current away from the entrance to the gorge, they having seen that there was this whirlpool there. It was like a dragon sitting there waiting for them, and they were all rowing like the Belgians do, standing facing forward and stamping, and they were all stamping in a frenzy to get their junk back to the shore. The leader didn't get ashore, I think the others did. The military had *made them* cast off from Wushan and then almost immediately they had seen the trouble, so they were all fighting to get back again.

Coping with Whirlpools

We held back and I do remember we were there like a sort of pony that's had plenty of oats. We were dancing about below the whirlpool, literally dancing because the water was in such a tumult. And then there was this great smooth whirlpool, not moving, and down comes the junk. The crew dropped their oars, they took off the boards above the cargo which I think was wood oil in wooden tubs with bamboo or straw rope round to hold them, and they each got hold of one of these tubs and then the junk went sailing round and round, and got nearer and nearer the centre, and then down. Gone. . Now all junks when they come down the Gorges take down their mast and lash it alongside because the wind nearly always blows up the gorge so they use a sail only for going up. And after a little while out from the whirlpool comes this great mast straight up and right out of the water. And it fell down and went out through the eddies. I don't think it came up through the centre. It came up through the side. I think this tragedy was the most impressive sight I've ever seen, sort of man's inhumanity to man. It was getting dark, and whether any of them would ever be saved was very doubtful. Then we went through the whirlpool on one side of it, as far as we could get over, but even then we had a list on the side towards the vortex, and the old pilot didn't seem to worry about that at all.'[17]

Japan was not only fighting a war against China in the Yangtze Valley. In January 1938 her armies had conquered Tsingtao in the north and three months later substantial forces were landed near British Hong Kong in the south and Canton was seized. Control of the China coast was just as important for the Japanese as dominating the river. Once again aerial bombardment preluded military conquest on the ground, as at Swatow in 1937.

The Japanese on the China Coast

'They came regularly after that around eight o'clock in the morning, at noon and about three in the afternoon. We could see the bombs sliding over the top at an office. After they'd dropped their bombs they went up and down machine-gunning the Bund, and any sampans that were in the harbour, quite recklessly – the wretches. And this went on until 1939. We'd have a regular few days of bombing and then they'd go away for a month or so and then come back again. On one of the early raids they hit the English Presbyterian mission hospital. The superintendent was a very fine man, a Yorkshireman, and he had to get his patients moved out. There was a little isolation hospital over on our side of the harbour at Kakchow, and a little chapel. We had a conference about it all and we arranged to move all those patients from the hospital that night by our lighters. They were towed over by our tug *Taikoo Hang* to the Kakchow jetty and then moved from the jetty. A lot of them were bed patients. Some had typhoid, cholera and all sorts of things and we put those into the little isolation hospital and the other cases went into the chapel, not far away from our house. This went on from six in the evening till midnight – getting all that lot moved, but it was a good job done and in the meantime a lot of European residents at Kialal came across to Kakchow for safety. I got back after midnight and went to bed, and the next morning I came down to breakfast and there were 21 women and children in the house as refugees. And under the house were about 150 Chinese. (We had a house built up about five feet above the ground level on a concrete base with grilled doors all the way round. It was quite clean and open for the Chinese to live in and we had them there for quite a long time.)

'Then later when we got advice that the Japs were planning a raid on us from their ships anchored off, the women and children came across and spent the day at Kakchow with us or with other friends. The Chinese too, mobs of them, used to come across to our side of the harbour.

'Then finally, in June 1939, they started bombing the town indiscriminately during the night and at mid-morning their fleet came into the harbour and shelled us for all they were worth. My wife was on her own then at Kakchow as I had gone across to the office to see what was happening there. And soon after I got there somebody said they'd seen one of our ships coming up the river, which turned out to be the *Tsinan*. We got her alongside and I went on board to see the captain. He was shivering with anger so we each had a glass of whisky, which settled us down a bit. Apparently he'd arrived outside Swatow port and the Japanese sent up signals to him to push off, but not in such polite language! However he was about to be pushing off when HMS *Scout* arrived on the scene with all her guns manned. We'd never seen *Scout* before, though we'd often had the "D" class destroyers in the port. This was a new one. He asked what the trouble was, we told him. The captain of the destroyer hoisted a signal telling him to disregard those Japanese signals and follow him and so he brought her into the port. While I was on the ship the Japanese military had come down and put a machine gun party on the pontoon and refused to allow anybody to go on or off the ship, so our captain got a Jacob's ladder on the seaward side of the *Tsinan* and I went off in my motorboat to see the *Scout* captain (he was anchored off) and told him the tale. He told me he'd be sailing very shortly. So I said, "You brought our *Tsinan* in, don't you think the only thing you can do is to see her out again?" And he said, "What time will she be ready?" I said, "Well the trouble is the *Tsinan* can't get a landing party on the pontoon to release the ship's mooring wires." He said, "I'll see to that. What time will she be ready; three o'clock?" I said I thought that would be all right. So he waited till three o'clock and I told our captain what had been arranged. I forgot how I got back on shore again, though we did have another ship in the port too. So perhaps I came through her. At three o'clock the *Scout* put a landing party on to the pontoon and the Japanese were absolutely furious, but *Scout's* sailors released the wires and off they went.

'Quite soon I was sent for by the Japanese police commissioner and he was in a rage and asking about my bringing the *Tsinan* into the port. There was nothing I could say to him except it was damn silly as I couldn't stop her. In the meantime just before the Japanese fleet arrived our consul was put under examination by an embassy officer and had been suspended from duty. (He'd been neglecting his duties I suppose.) So he wasn't available to give me any help. A few days later I was again sent for by this police commissioner. I went across to see the consul, but he couldn't help so I went to the RN destroyer in port. I knew the captain, and I explained matters to him. He said, "Right, I'll come over." And he put on his best uniform, with medals, sword and cocked hat. Not cocked hat quite, but he came over in full regalia. And we went to see this wretched man and he started blowing me up for allowing Chinese troops on to our properties to fire on HIJM ships and landing parties. (Actually I'd seen a lot of Chinese soldiers in our properties.)

In the end he got rather nasty, so the navy captain slapped the table hard and told him to shut up and said that we were going; he ordered me out, as it were. And after that the Japanese fenced in all their property. It was all very unpleasant. Very nasty too. Bombing going on and the ships bombarding us. I was on the Bund one day and they chased me with machine gun bullets. I don't think they were trying to hit me but they were following me along hitting the wall of the godowns, which made me jump a bit! We finally left Swatow at the end of July 1939. In the meantime a letter was being carried up and down the China coast advising me of my transfer to Hong Kong and eventually it came to me. But we couldn't get out other than by one of the destroyers, which happened to be HMS *Dainty*. The captain got the C-in-C's permission and took us down to Hong Kong. Later on a few of our things came down from the house at Swatow.'[2]

'There was no work to do after the Japanese had marched in because the port had actually been closed. The Japanese had only just marched in so there was a very tight sort of police control over the place. There were sentries everywhere and it was difficult to move around, but they didn't interfere with us. They didn't march into our houses very much but nothing could be moved really and our shippers if they had cargo in our godowns couldn't get it out. Well they could get it out providing they got permits, and it was permits for everything. Even to leave the place, or to come in you needed a permit from the military police. Somehow or other our wharfinger, Lillie his name was, got very thick with the Japanese head of security, a Major Watanabe and was able to swing a few things for us. He was quite a character actually because he was very proud of the fact that he could talk English. We gave him a meal I remember one time and he spouted great lumps of Shakespeare, and he sang *Bluebells of Scotland*. He really was a curious fellow. I mean he can't have survived the war, he must have been shot somewhere along the line. He was very pro-British actually. He was very proud of his British contacts and all that sort of thing. Funny fellow.

'As far as the godowns were concerned Lillie was able, without too much difficulty, to get things in and out of them. There was quite a lot of cargo in these godowns left over from before and he could get it out, but also make sure they didn't interfere. They didn't, for instance, use our pontoons for discharging, for bringing their ships alongside. They never did that. I can't understand why, because we had practically the whole waterfront in Swatow. There was only one Chinese wharf – the old China Merchants Steam Navigation Company wharf – and the Japs used to use that and didn't use ours.

'Theoretically no restrictions were imposed on *us* at all, but in practice as I say you couldn't move. You couldn't get out of the town for instance. I don't know that one would have wanted to, and it was more difficult to go for a walk into the country on Sundays, because of course there were sentries everywhere, and if you got too far away, although things had probably been arranged in Swatow as regards foreigners, they might not know about that and they would all be awkward and there would be a lot of shouting and screaming at you. One unpleasant thing was that the Jap police or security people had a sort of little torture headquarters in a small house that was on a vacant lot right next door to my house. There they dealt with Chinese alleged infiltrators, saboteurs and that sort of thing. And they had black marketeers. But there were some very harrowing sounds coming out of that place I remember.

'We passed our time dining in each other's houses and playing around. I said there was no sailing at Swatow but during this time the godowns were more or less empty and I remember that I and an ICI man there roughly designed and had built for us by Chinese carpenters, a little boat, a little sixteen foot centreboard boat. We went sailing. It was pretty hairy. We didn't keep it up for long. Partly because of the conditions in the harbour which were very, very tricky for sailing, really quite dangerous. Two or three times we found ourselves about five miles out, carried by enormous currents. It was quite a distance up there, and one of the launches had to come and tow us back, there was just no way of sailing back against this awful tide. However it was building the boat and for a time it was quite fun sailing it.

'As far as work at the office was concerned it was a caretaker situation really. One went through the motions. I went to the office every day, but there was really very little to do. There might be a permit or so to apply for, for example. We tried to bring in a ship once a month, simply bringing in supplies for the foreign community. At that stage the Japanese weren't permitting any commercial trading at all into the port, but we were allowed to bring a ship in which would land supplies, so I had to organise that and find out what supplies were necessary not only for ourselves but for the other foreigners. And we were doing a certain amount of repair and maintenance around our godowns. I may as well admit I spent a good deal of time writing comic songs about our predicament with a boozy chorus which went down quite well with the rather rugger club sort of community we were at that time.'[9]

Working During the War

In Europe however the time for comic songs had long since gone. Britain had been at war with Germany since September 3rd 1939.

'I remember hearing the radio broadcast that we were at war with Germany with my heart sinking. We had quite a few Germans in Swatow in those days, one or two of whom were quite Nazi people. And it was a little tiresome because they came into the club the same as everyone else, though they had a perfect right to do so really, but one did feel one had to cold shoulder some people one had rather liked. I remember there was a nice old German merchant, Mr Thun, a very old chap who died I think shortly after the war broke out, in the early winter of that year and I went to his funeral because I'd known him for years and was very fond of the old boy. But it was rather spoilt by these bloody young Germans with their bloody Nazi salutes, and I realised I shouldn't have gone to it really, it was a mistake. But the main feeling was one of depression that in fact there was a war in Europe, that it couldn't be long before we, the British, were involved in the war with Japan. And I'd say very probably lose Hong Kong. I mean I hadn't

War with Germany

any clear idea of what might happen but we all felt that we were obviously moving to a crisis, and I couldn't really see how, even if we eventually won the war in Europe, we could win the war in Asia. Quite frankly I felt very pessimistic about the whole thing at that time. This is before the thing developed properly. And then with the Americans in, that made rather a difference to the situation.'[9]

And the Americans came in after the Japanese surprise attack on Pearl Harbour in December 1941, ten years after they had embarked upon their conquest of Manchuria.

Britain at War with Japan

'The coming of war with Japan was not unexpected. I mean the amber light had been showing for some time and most, but not all of our ships, let us say the coastal ships and some of the river ships, had already been sent down to Hong Kong and they did not all get away but most of them did. The actual outbreak was again delivered to me in a midnight telephone call from the wharfinger in Shanghai, who rang up to me in the manager's house to say, "Mr Dean, the Japanese are shooting at the *Petrel*." Well, the *Petrel* was the relic of the Yangtze Flotilla, one of the British gunboats of the Yangtze squadron, which had been left behind when all the others had gone. She had been left behind as a communications ship for the consulate. On the outbreak of war she had been summoned to surrender and had refused, though the American equivalent had surrendered, which gave us a certain amount of face with the Japanese, at the time. Anyway I got into my car and drove down, and after explaining to the French police, who tried to cordon me off the Bund, who I was, I was there just in time to see the *Petrel* go. They say that the radio operator from *Petrel* managed to swim ashore and remained underground in Shanghai throughout the war during the Japanese occupation. I believe that it is true, though I have never actually verified it. Anyway that is how I heard of the war and then we heard on the radio about Pearl Harbour and so on.'[4]

Britain was not long in declaring war on Japan. Then the British in China were no longer neutral. British banks were liquidated, British businesses seized by the Japanese and British men, women and children eventually locked away in internment camps. This was the beginning of the end of one period of British life on the China coast, an end which came not when Japanese forces surrendered to General MacArthur in Tokyo Bay, but when Mao Tse Tung's armies finally defeated Chiang Kai Shek's Nationalists in 1948.

1 **Eric Price** Joined Butterfield & Swire in January 1925. Served in Shanghai, Hankow, Tientsin and Harbin in 1925–28, mostly sugar travelling. Subsequently Agent in Chungking (1928–30), No. 2 in Hankow (1932–35) and Agent in Amoy (1935–36).

2 **Gordon Campbell** Joined Butterfield & Swire in 1924. Served in Shanghai, Tsingtao and Tientsin, mostly sugar travelling before first leave home and marriage in 1929. Subsequently Agent in Wuhu, Nanking, Chefoo and Swatow (1930–39). Married to Mary Campbell (q.v.).

3 **C.C. Roberts** Joined Butterfield & Swire in October 1922. Sugar travelling from Shanghai (1925–26). Shore management for China Navigation Company in Hankow (1926–28), and responsible for Chinese Staff Shanghai (1932–34). Married to Mary Roberts (q.v.).

4 **Arthur Dean** Joined Butterfield & Swire in June 1923. Sugar travelling from Hankow and Nanking (1924–26). Subsequently China Navigation Company management Shanghai and Agent in Chungking (1927–28), Tientsin (1932–33), Swatow (1935–36) and Hankow (1936–38).

5 **John Wilson** Joined Butterfield & Swire May 1936. Between 1936 and 1939 served on the Yangtze at Chungking, Kiukiang, Hankow, Chingkiang, Ichang and Shasi during the Japanese advance along the river valley.

6 **Robin Blake** Joined Butterfield & Swire March 1925. China Navigation Company shore management Canton, Tientsin, Shanghai. Hankow (1927–38). Subsequently served in Tientsin and was Agent in Changsha (1939–44). Married to Phyllis Blake (q.v.).

7 **Jack Carter** Joined Butterfield & Swire December 1930. Served B & S's interests in insurance in Shanghai, Hankow and Tientsin (1930–38). Agent in Harbin (1938–39). Insurance Assistant in Shanghai (1939–40).

8 **Frank Robinson** Joined Butterfield & Swire December 1924. Served B & S's interests in insurance in Shanghai, Tientsin, Hankow (1924–38), and again in Shanghai (1939–41). Married to Jean Robinson (q.v.).

9 **James Tandy** Joined Butterfield & Swire April 1932. China Navigation Company shipping management Swatow (1934–36) and Shanghai (1937–38). Agent in Chungking (1939), Swatow (1939–40) and Canton (1940–41).

10 **John Kinloch** Joined Butterfield & Swire January 1931. Served B & S's insurance interests in Shanghai (1931–32), then assistant and Agent in Chungking (1932–36), Agent in Changsha (1937–38), River Shipping Desk, Shanghai (1938), temporary Agent in Amoy (1938–39), and Agent in Nanking (1939–41) and Canton (1941). Married to Doris Kinloch (q.v.).

11 **Mary Campbell** Married Gordon Campbell 1929.

12 **Mary Roberts** Married to C.C. Roberts.

13 **Phyllis Blake** Married to Robin Blake after a childhood in Hong Kong and Shanghai.

14 **Jean Robinson** Married to Frank Robinson in Shanghai.

15 **Doris Kinloch** Married to John Kinloch. Grew up in China.

16 Betty Wellbelove Joined Butterfield & Swire in April 1940 in Shanghai as a stenographer after growing up in the city as a 'Shanghai Girl'.

17 Captain Graham Torrible Joined the China Navigation Company in the 1920s. Some sailing experience on the coast but principal service was on the Yangtze River, and in the Gorges in particular.

18 Captain Ernest Bruce Joined the China Navigation Company in the 1920s. Principal sailing experience was on the coast.

19 Captain R.E. Selwyn-Jones Joined the China Navigation Company in 1931 and served on both the coast and the Yangtze River.

20 Captain J. McKinlay Joined the China Navigation Company in 1924 and served on both the coast and the Yangtze River.

21 Marian Arnold Married to Arthur Arnold who joined Butterfield & Swire in May 1925 and served in Shanghai, Canton and Hankow in the China Navigation Company and the Insurance Department.

22 Captain A.D. Blue Joined the China Navigation Company as an Engineer Officer in 1928. Served on the coast and the Yangtze River. Captured by pirates from the *Nanchang* in 1933.

23 Clifford Johnson See Chapter 5: 'Pirated'.

Glossary

Amah A Chinese female servant who usually looked after children

Blood Alley A street in Shanghai noted for its less reputable cabarets (q.v.)

B & S The abbreviated form by which Butterfield & Swire were known on the China Coast

Bund The waterfront of a port

Cabaret A generic term used to describe night clubs and bars, often with 'taxi-girls' (q.v.) in attendance

Cumshaw A tip, often used perjoratively to mean a bribe

Ewo The transliteration of the characters of the Chinese name by which Jardine Matheson were known in China

Godown A warehouse

Hong The general name given to trading companies in China

Hulk An elderly steamship no longer in active service, now moored alongside and used as offices or living quarters

Joss Superstition; pertaining to religion; luck

Kang A raised brick platform in Chinese homes and inns for sleeping on, heated from underneath

Mafu a groom

Pidgin English A usual means of communication between non-English speaking Chinese and the British; a simplified form of English

Pukai A Chinese quilted bedspread

Schroff An office clerk, sometimes responsible for collecting debts

Squeeze Financial corruption; bribery

Taikoo The transliteration of the characters of the Chinese name by which Butterfield & Swire were known in China

Taipan The senior local manager of a Western business in China

Taxi-girls Girls who, for a small price, would dance with customers in a cabaret (q.v.)

Trackers Coolies who 'heaved' junks and ships over the rapids in the Yangtze Gorges

Tuchun A Chinese provincial governor, latterly a war lord

Yamen The Chinese equivalent of a local town hall; the seat of provincial administration

Index

MAP OF CHINA
1919-1939

SZ